Tell It Slant

A CONVERSATION

ON THE LANGUAGE OF JESUS

IN HIS STORIES AND PRAYERS

Eugene H. Peterson

WILLIAM B. EERDMANS PUBLISHING COMPANY

GRAND RAPIDS, MICHIGAN / CAMBRIDGE, U.K.

Published 2008 by

Wm. B. Eerdmans Publishing Co.

2140 Oak Industrial Drive N.E., Grand Rapids, Michigan 49505 /

P.O. Box 163, Cambridge CB3 9PU U.K.

www.eerdmans.com

Published in association with the literary agency of
Alive Communications, Inc.,
7680 Goddard #200, Colorado Springs, CO 80920

Paperback edition 2012

Printed in the United States of America

18 17 16 15 14 13 12   9 8 7 6 5 4 3 2

Library of Congress Cataloging-in-Publication Data

Peterson, Eugene H., 1932-

Tell it slant: a conversation on the language of Jesus in his stories and prayers /
Eugene H. Peterson.

p.   cm.

Includes bibliographical references and index.

ISBN 978-0-8028-6886-2 (pbk.: alk. paper)

1. Jesus Christ — Parables.   2. Jesus Christ — Prayers.
3. Bible. N.T. Gospels — Language, style.   I. Title.

BT375.3.P47   2008

226'.06 — dc22

2008019791

TELL IT SLANT

For my grandchildren

Andrew Eugene
Lindsay Hope
Sadie Lynn
Hans Hoiland
Anna Grace
Mary Crates

One after one, every couple of years,
succeeding one another in turn as babes and infants,
you reintroduced me
to the mysteries of language,
the miracles of speaking, the miracles of listening,
and the holy conversations
that develop among us in the company of
Father, Son, and Holy Spirit.

Contents

Acknowledgments

I was fortunate: I learned the language of faith at the same time I learned the English language. My language school was my family, my parents and my sister Karen and brother Kenneth, the best of teachers and the most congenial of classmates in the school.

This book had its inception in the J. Henderson Lectures, 1992, at Pittsburgh Theological Seminary. It developed further in courses on language, Scripture, and prayer at Regent College, Vancouver, B.C., from 1993 to 1998. It was tested out and matured in conversations with pastors at numerous retreats and conferences.

A succession of spiritual directors spanning fifty years as I moved across the country kept my words fresh and honest and personal: Reuben Lance in Montana, Pastor Ian Wilson in Baltimore, Sr. Constance FitzGerald, O.C.D., in Baltimore, Pastor Alan Reynolds in Canada. Jonathan Stine is a faithful friend who encourages reverence in the smallest details.

At about the time that I thought I knew what I needed to know and could go on to other things, my grandchildren began showing up at approximately two-year intervals and regularly restored a sense of wonder at the miracle of language. The book is dedicated to them.

Introduction

Language — given to us to glorify God, to receive the revelation of God, to witness to the truth of God, to offer praise to God — is constantly at risk. Too often the living Word is desiccated into propositional cadavers, then sorted into exegetical specimens in bottles of formaldehyde. We end up with godtalk:

> Knowledge of speech, but not of silence;
> Knowledge of words, and ignorance of the Word . . .
> Where is the Life we have lost in living?
> Where is the wisdom we have lost in knowledge?
> Where is the knowledge we have lost in information?[1]

*　　*　　*

My concern is that we use God's gift of language in consonance with the God who speaks. Jesus is the primary person with whom we have to do in this business. Jesus most of all. Jesus, the Word made flesh. Jesus who "spoke and it came to be" (Ps. 33:9) even "since the foundation

---

1. Excerpt from Part II of "Choruses from 'The Rock'" in *Collected Poems 1909-1962* by T. S. Eliot, copyright 1936 by Hought Mifflin Harcourt Publishing Company and renewed 1964 by T. S. Eliot, reprinted by permission of the publisher.

of the world" (Matt. 13:35). Jesus telling stories on the roads and around the supper tables in Galilee and while traveling through Samaria. Jesus praying in the Garden and from the Cross in Jerusalem. Jesus is God's Word to us in a variety of settings and circumstances. He engages in conversations with us in the language given to us in the Gospels. Those conversations are continued with us by the Holy Spirit just as he promised: "When the Spirit of truth comes, he will guide you into all truth . . . he will take what is mine and declare it to you" (John 16:13-14). He is also the person who prays to his Father and ours, "since he ever lives to make intercession for us" (Heb. 7:25).

* * *

Language and the way we use it in the Christian community are the focus of this conversation on the spirituality of language. Language, all of it — every vowel, every consonant — is a gift of God. God uses language to create and command us; we use language to confess our sins and sing praises to God. We use this very same language getting to know one another, buying and selling, writing letters and reading books. We use the same words in talking to one another that we use when we're talking to God: same nouns and verbs, same adverbs and adjectives, same conjunctions and interjections, same prepositions and pronouns. There is no "Holy Ghost" language used for matters of God and salvation and then a separate secular language for buying cabbages and cars. "Give us this day our daily bread" and "pass the potatoes" come out of the same language pool.

There is a lot more to speaking than getting the right words and pronouncing them correctly. *Who* we are and the *way* we speak make all the difference. We can sure think of enough creative ways to use words badly: we can blaspheme and curse, we can lie and deceive, we can bully and abuse, we can gossip and debunk. Or not. Every time we open our mouths, whether in conversation with one another or in prayer to our Lord, Christian truth and community are on the line. And so, high on the agenda of the Christian community in every generation is that we diligently develop a voice that speaks in consonance with the God who speaks, that we speak in such a way that truth is told and community is formed, and that we pray to the God and Father of our Lord Jesus Christ and not to some golden calf idol that has been fashioned by one of the numerous descendants of Aaron.

Preachers and teachers hold prominent positions in the Christian community in the use of language. Pulpit and lectern provide places of authority and influence in sanctuaries and classrooms that require careful, prayerful Christ-honoring speech in every sermon and lecture. But I am particularly interested here in the more or less out-of-the-way, unstudied, and everyday conversations that take place in kitchens and family rooms, having coffee with a friend, making small talk in a parking lot, or engaging in an intense, private discussion that could make or break a relationship. I want to attend to the words we listen to and speak as we go about the ordinary affairs of work and family, friends and neighbors, and provide them with an equivalent dignity alongside the language that we commonly associate with the so-called "things of God."

For the most part this is not high-profile language, not the language we use when we want to get something done or master a complex subject. It is language used when we are not dealing with one another in our social roles or our assigned functions. It savors subtleties. It relishes ambiguities. It consists in large part, using T. S. Eliot's phrase, in "hints followed by guesses." Emily Dickinson gives me my text:

Tell all the Truth but tell it slant —
Success in Circuit lies
Too bright for our infirm Delight
The Truth's superb surprise

As Lightning to the Children eased
With Explanation kind
The Truth must dazzle gradually
Or every man be blind — [2]

2. Emily Dickinson, *The Complete Poems*, ed. Thomas H. Johnson (Boston: Little, Brown and Company, 1955), p. 506. Reprinted by permission of the publishers and the

I want to tear down the fences that we have erected between language that deals with God and language that deals with the people around us. It is, after all, the same language. The same God we address in prayer and proclaim in sermons is also deeply, eternally involved in the men and women we engage in conversation, whether casually or intentionally. But not always obviously. God's words are not always prefaced by "Thus says the Lord." It takes time and attentiveness to make connections between the said and the unsaid, the direct and the indirect, the straightforward and the oblique. There are many occasions when the imperious or blunt approach honors neither our God nor our neighbor. Unlike raw facts, truth, especially personal truth, requires the cultivation of unhurried intimacies. Dickinson's "slant" and "gradually" are ways of getting past preconceptions, prejudices, defenses, stereotypes, and fact-dominated literalism, all of which prevent relational receptivity to the language of the other: the Other.

God does not compartmentalize our lives into religious and secular. Why do we? I want to insist on a continuity of language between the words we use in Bible studies and the words we use when we're out fishing for rainbow trout. I want to cultivate a sense of continuity between the prayers we offer to God and the conversations we have with the people we speak to and who speak to us. I want to nurture an awareness of the sanctity of words, the holy gift of language, regardless of whether it is directed vertically or horizontally. Just as Jesus did.

*   *   *

And so Jesus is my text for cultivating a language that honors the holiness inherent in words: the God-rootedness, the Christ-embodiedness, the Spirit-aliveness. The first part of the conversation, "Jesus in His Stories," will listen in as Jesus talks with the people of his day while strolling through wheat fields, having meals, sailing on a lake, answer-

---

Trustees of Amherst College from *The Poems of Emily Dickinson*, Thomas H. Johnson, ed., Cambridge, Mass.: The Belknap Press of Harvard University Press, Copyright © 1951, 1955, 1979, 1983 by the President and Fellows of Harvard College.

ing questions, dealing with hostility. The second part of the conversation, "Jesus in His Prayers," will immerse us in the way Jesus went about praying to his Father: prayers in Galilee, prayers in Jerusalem, prayers in Gethsemane, prayers on Golgotha. As we listen in on Jesus as he talks and then participate with Jesus as he prays, I hope that together we, writer and readers, will develop a discerning aversion to all forms of depersonalizing godtalk and acquire a taste for and skills in the always personal language that God uses, even in our conversations and small talk, maybe especially in our small talk, to make and save and bless us one and all.

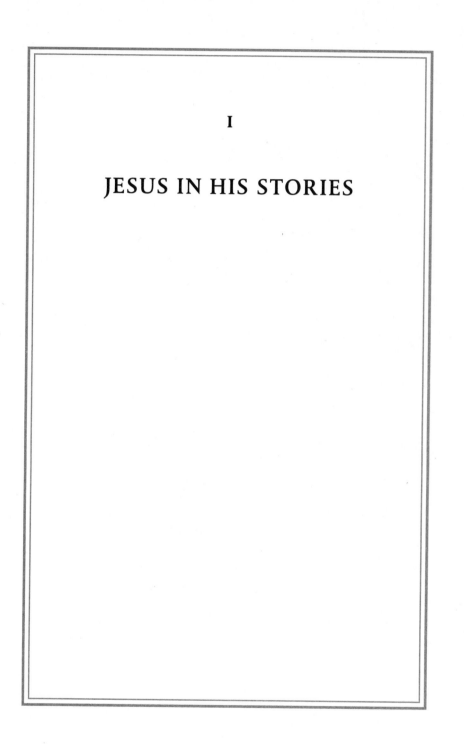

I

JESUS IN HIS STORIES

CHAPTER 1

Jesus in Samaria: Luke 9:51–19:27

It is a huge irony that Jesus, whose words create and form our lives, never wrote a word, at least not a word that was ever preserved. Those words he wrote in Jerusalem dirt using his finger for a pencil disappeared in the next rain shower. Notwithstanding, we know Jesus as a man of words. He is, after all, the Word made flesh.

But he didn't write. He spoke. He never had a publisher, never gave a book-signing, never dipped pen in an ink bottle. Language for Jesus was exclusively a matter of voice: "he spoke, and it came to be" (Ps. 33:9).

His words, of course, did get written — and published. Probably no single person's words have been reproduced in print in as many handwritten manuscripts and printed books as the words of Jesus. Still, it is important to keep that original oral quality in mind, that living voice of Jesus, the *spoken* words that came from his mouth and entered the lives of men and women through listening ears and believing hearts. Written words, important as they are, are a giant step removed from the speaking voice. A determined effort must be made to hear the speaking voice and listen to it, not just to look at it and study the written word.[1]

---

1. I expand considerably on this "determined effort" in *Eat This Book: A Conversation in the Art of Spiritual Reading* (Grand Rapids: Eerdmans, 2005).

*　　*　　*

Language is primarily a means of revelation, both for God and for us. Using words, God reveals himself to us. Using words, we reveal ourselves to God and to one another. By means of language, the entire cycle of speaking and listening, both God and his Word-created men and women are able to reveal vast interiors otherwise inaccessible to us.

This is important. It is important to reflect upon since it is not obvious. And it is important to continuously reconsider since our vast communications industry treats language primarily as either information or titillation, but not revelation. More often than not, when the word "God" is used in our society, it is reduced to a piece of information, impersonalized into a mere reference, or debased to blasphemy. George Steiner, one of our most perceptive writers on language, powerfully argues that conveying information is nothing but a marginal and highly specialized function of language.[2] But the language we learn in the company of parents and siblings and friends has its origin in the revealing God. All our speaking and listening take place in a language world that is formed and sustained by God's speaking and listening. The words that God uses to create and name and bless and command in Genesis are the same words we hear Jesus using to create and name and heal and bless and command in the Gospels. Jesus speaks, and we hear God speak.

The Conversational Jesus

Jesus' language, as reported to us by his evangelist witnesses Matthew, Mark, Luke, and John, is at times designated preaching and at other times teaching. Still, much of the time we find Jesus speaking in ways other than preaching and teaching. We find him speaking informally in conversational give-and-take while eating meals at someone's home

---

2. See George Steiner, *After Babel: Aspects of Language and Translation* (Oxford: Oxford University Press, 1998).

or with friends, strolling in fields or along a lakeshore, or responding to various interruptions and questions while going somewhere or other. It is this third use of language, the informal and casual, that interests me in the present context.

*   *   *

Preaching comes first. It is the kind of language that defines, both in meaning and in manner, what Jesus is about. The first words out of Jesus' mouth, as reported by Mark (who was the first to write a Gospel), were in preaching: "Jesus came to Galilee, proclaiming the good news of God, and saying, 'The time is fulfilled, and the kingdom of God has come near; repent, and believe in the good news'" (Mark 1:14-15). He concluded his sermon with an altar call that was answered by four fishermen. He was on his way.

Preaching is proclamation. Preaching announces what God is doing right here and now, at this time and in this place. It also calls hearers to respond appropriately. Preaching is the news, *good* news, that God is alive and present and in action: "Maybe you didn't know it, but the living God is here, right here on this street, in this sanctuary, in this neighborhood. And he is at work now. He is speaking right now — at this very moment. If you know what is good for you, you will want to get in on it."

All the Gospel writers give us a thorough orientation in Jesus' preaching, but Mark stands out as a first among equals: his punchy, urgent language keeps the here, the now, and the personal before us with great skill.

Preaching is language that involves us personally with God's action in the present. Preaching is conspicuous for conveying the personal and present. The listener is not permitted to suppose that the preached words are for anyone other than himself or herself. The listener must not try to get by with supposing that the preached words are about something that happened long ago or even yesterday, or that they are about what will happen in the future, whether near or far. Preaching reveals God in action here and now — for *me*. Whatever insipidities we have heard from preachers and their imitators, we can be sure that they didn't originate in Jesus.

That day when Jesus launched his public ministry in Galilee by preaching, he was the latest in a long tradition, more than a thousand years, of great preaching that had just been brought up to date by Jesus' cousin, John the Baptizer. After Jesus the tradition continued in Peter and Paul, Chrysostom and Cyprian, Ambrose and Augustine, Francis and Dominic, Luther and Calvin, Wesley and Whitefield, Edwards and Finney, Newman and Spurgeon. Preaching continues to be the basic language for conveying the revelation of God in Christ Jesus, spoken from street corners and pulpits all over the world: God alive, at work and speaking, here and now, for you and me.

Jesus also used language to teach. Unlike the teaching that we are accustomed to in our schools, lectures designed to do our thinking for us, Jesus' teaching sparkled with scintillating aphorisms. He wasn't so much handing out information as reshaping our imaginations with metaphors so that we could take in the living multi-dimensioned truth that is Jesus. All the Gospel writers present us with Jesus teaching, instructing us in detail what it means to live in this kingdom of God. But Matthew is the Gospel writer who provides us with the most extensive witness on Jesus' teaching. He gathers Jesus' teaching together into five great discourses (reminiscent perhaps of the Five Books of Moses?): The Sermon on the Mount (Matt. 5–7), Instructions to the Twelve Disciples (Matt. 10), Instructions for the Community (Matt. 18), Warnings against Hypocrisy (Matt. 23), Teaching on Last Things (Matt. 24–25).

Day-to-day living in this world where God is present and active for us and for our salvation involves cultivating a detailed sense of what is involved in every aspect of our lives. We often dichotomize our lives into public and private, spiritual and secular, cut up our lives into separate parts, and stuff the parts into labeled cubbyholes for convenient access when we feel like dealing with them. Teaching puts the parts together, makes connections, demonstrates relationships — "connects the dots," as we say. So Jesus teaches us, goes over the details of what we are up against, the decisions and discernments we need to make, the ways and means that are appropriate to living this kingdom life in which Jesus is king. Jesus' teaching, both then in Galilee and Jerusalem and now as it is reproduced by our teachers and professors, usually takes place in company with others, some who are brothers and sisters in obedience and others who turn out to be indifferent or even hostile.

In his teaching, just as in his preaching, Jesus lives out of a long tradition: the books of Moses climaxing in Deuteronomy, further on Proverbs and Ecclesiastes, and then the counsel and wisdom woven into the magnificent fabric of pastoral care we find in the prophets and priests of Israel. This teaching also continues in the church's life as our pastors and theologians train us in cultivating an intelligent and faithful obedience while dealing with politics, business affairs, family matters, personal failures and sufferings, living whole and integrated lives. Teaching resurrects dead words so they live again. It occupies a large field in the way we use language in this life of following Jesus.

Preaching and teaching are prominent uses of language among the people who speak and give witness, who pray and provide direction in the Christian community. We commonly set men and women apart, provide them with training in schools and churches, to be preachers and teachers. There is a lot to know. There is a lot to be wary of. We need preachers and teachers to keep us focused on God in Christ and alert us to the seductive idolatries that surround us. For the most part we are well provided with preachers and teachers who understand what is going on in the kingdom, who will not be easily distracted from the "one thing needful," and who are disciplined to faithfulness and the renewal of our minds. Preaching and teaching are fairly well defined in manner and content and usually take place in public places.

But there is a third kind of language that all of us participate in regardless of our role in the community, whatever our abilities and aptitudes. Earlier I described this language as "informal conversational give-and-take while eating meals at home or with friends, walking on the road between villages, or in response to interruptions by questions on the road to somewhere or other." In any weekly word-count of our use of language, this kind of speech far exceeds anything we speak or listen to that might be designated preaching or teaching. When Jesus wasn't preaching and when he wasn't teaching, he talked with the men and women with whom he lived in terms of what was going on at the moment — people, events, questions, whatever — using the circumstances of their lives as his text. Much as we do. Preaching begins with God: God's word, God's action, God's presence. Teaching expands on what is proclaimed, instructing us in the implications of the text, the reverberations of the truth in the world, the specific ways in which God's word shapes in detail the way we live our daily lives between birth and death. But unstructured, informal conversations arise from incidents and encounters with one another that take place in the normal course of going about our lives in families and workplaces, on playgrounds and while shopping for groceries, in airport terminals waiting for a flight and walking with binoculars in a field with friends watching birds. Many of the words that Jesus spoke are of this nature. Most of us are not preachers or teachers, or at least not designated as such. Most of the words that we speak are spoken in the quotidian contexts of eating and drinking, shopping and traveling, making what we sometimes dismiss as "small talk."

All the Gospel writers present us with Jesus using this kind of language, but the most extensive revelation of Jesus using this casual and unstructured language is in the Gospel of Luke. What Mark does for preaching and Matthew does for teaching, Luke does for the informal give-and-take language that takes place in the comings and goings of our ordinary lives.

Luke's Travel Narrative

At the center of Luke's Gospel (Luke 9:51–19:44), there is a ten-chapter insertion that features just this kind of informal language between Jesus, his followers, and other men and women he meets along the way. The section is framed by references to leaving Galilee (9:51) and then arriving in Jerusalem (19:11, 28, 41). Because of these framing references it is often designated the Travel Narrative. Most of the material in these ten chapters is unique to Luke.

Our first three Gospels follow a similar outline, with much of the arrangement and content similar. They do not exactly copy one another, for each Gospel writer has his own way of telling the story that brings out salient features that we would otherwise miss. In broad terms, Mark picks up on the kerygmatic, preached qualities of Jesus' language, and Matthew features the didactic, teaching qualities. But Luke has a particular interest in immersing us in the conversational aspects of Jesus' language. And so Luke interrupts the story line set down by his predecessors in Gospel writing, Matthew and Mark, and interpolates this long section of mostly original material at the center of his Gospel. The first nine chapters of Luke's Gospel tell the story of the Galilean ministry of Jesus, following the pattern set down by Matthew and Mark. The Galilean story lays the foundations for our lives in Christ. The final five chapters tell the story of the final week of Jesus' ministry in Jerusalem — Jesus rejected, crucified, and raised to new life — and also follow Matthew and Mark. The Jerusalem story consummates our lives in Christ: crucifixion, resurrection.

What Jesus said and did in the early years in Galilee has continuities with what took place in that last week in Jerusalem. The transition between the two places is narrated as a journey through Samaria, the country that separated Galilee from Jerusalem. Samaria was, if not exactly enemy territory, at least decidedly unfriendly territory. Samaritans and Jews had several hundred years of bad blood between them. They neither liked nor trusted one another. There was occasional violence, even bloody encounters. Josephus tells a story of an incident in which Samaritans murdered some Galilean pilgrims who were crossing through Samaria on their way to Jerusalem for a feast. Jewish guerrillas then attacked Samaritan villages in vengeance.[3] To get from Galilee to Jerusalem was a dangerous journey of about sixty or seventy miles — a three- to five-day trip by donkey or on foot.

It is while traveling through Samaria, going from Galilee to Jerusalem, that Jesus takes the time to tell stories that prepare his followers

---

3. Joachim Jeremias, *Jerusalem in the Time of Jesus* (Philadelphia: Fortress Press, 1969), p. 353.

to bring the ordinariness of their lives into conscious awareness and participation in this kingdom life. Jesus announces to his disciples that he is going to Jerusalem to be crucified, and he calls them to go with him. As they walk together those several days, he prepares them for their post-crucifixion and post-resurrection lives. There are dramatic events in the offing. Their lives are going to be changed from the inside out. But at the same time they are going to be dealing with the same people, the same routines, the same temptations, the same Roman and Greek and Hebrew culture, the same children and the same parents, the sometimes endless waiting, facing the indifference of so many about them, dealing with the maddening hypocrisies of the self-righteous, the stupidities of war, the absurdities of conspicuous consumption, and the lies of arrogant rulers. Everything will have changed and yet nothing will have changed. Jesus is preparing them to live in a world that neither knows nor wants to know Jesus. Jesus is preparing them (us!) to live a crucifixion and resurrection life patiently and without fanfare, obediently and without recognition. He prepares them in these Samaritan conversations to quietly and courageously do all this in continuity with the way Jesus did it and the way Jesus talked about it. He makes it clear that soon, when he is no longer physically with them, they most decidedly will *not* be on their own to carry out the work in any way they decide is best. The way he is doing it, the way of the cross, must be continued. But it is interesting and significant that Jesus doesn't use crisis language. He speaks conversationally, hardly raising his voice. Mostly he tells stories. Some of his followers (although not all) will never forget these stories.

A kind of intimacy develops naturally when men and women walk and talk together, with no immediate agenda or assigned task except eventually getting to their destination and taking their time to do it. Matthew and Mark waste no time in getting us from Galilee to Jerusalem. Luke slows us down, takes his time. Luke takes the opportunity to use this setting of a relaxed, walking road trip to expand and develop the spontaneity of unstructured conversations while Jesus and his disciples walk from Galilee to Jerusalem — Jesus answering questions, Jesus talking around the supper table, Jesus talking things over with his friends, Jesus telling stories. What Matthew and Mark each take care of in two chapters, Luke stretches into ten chapters. He immerses us in the way Jesus uses language as he deals with the ordinary and the occasional. Jesus unhurried — continuously interruptible. This is the way Jesus uses the language when he is not preaching and teaching. And this is the way we use language at the times not formally set aside for what we might call "religious" talk.

*   *   *

Two things interest me in the Travel Narrative. First, it deals with what takes place "in between" the focused areas of Jesus' life and ministry, Galilee and Jerusalem. Jesus and his disciples are traveling through the unfamiliar and uncongenial country of Samaria. Unlike Galilee and Jerusalem, Samaria is not home ground to Jesus and his companions. They are away from their familiar Galilean synagogues and their beloved Jerusalem temple. They don't know these people and have little in common with them, neither synagogue nor temple nor an agreed upon Scripture. They are outsiders to this country and this people.

There is an analogy here to what is experienced in the life of the Christian "between Sundays." The Jesus life is commonly preached and taught in Sunday worship. The Sunday sanctuary is the appointed time and place for giving our attention to what it means to worship and follow Jesus in the company of the baptized, the men and women and children who find and realize who they are not in themselves but in the company and work of Father, Son, and Holy Spirit. It is a set-aside, protected time and place for prayer and prayerful listening among men and women who are "on our side." We pretty much know, although not in detail, what to expect. The structure, at least, and most of the people are predictable. But between Sundays we spend most of our time with people who are not following Jesus as we have been, who do not share our assumptions and beliefs and convictions regarding God and his kingdom. The circumstances — family needs, work responsibilities, inclement weather, accidents and windfalls — are, at least to the casual eye, thoroughly secular. Anything might be said;

anything can happen. More often than not the "anything" *is* said and *does* happen. Not much of it seems to derive from or be connected with the sermon text we listened to in Sunday worship. Samaria is the country between Galilee and Jerusalem in which we spend most of our time between Sundays. None of us can anticipate what will be said to us or happen to us while we're there.

Some of us try to confine our Christian identity to what takes place on Sundays. In order to preserve it from contamination from "the world," we avoid as much as we can conversation beyond polite small talk with the Samaritans. Others of us memorize phrases from Sunday sermons and teaching and then try to insert them into pauses in the conversations or circumstances over the next six days. But it doesn't take us long to realize that these tactics are unsatisfactory. Or if we don't realize it, the Samaritans surely do.

The designation "Travel Narrative" is not entirely satisfactory because while the ten chapters clearly begin and end with references to travel from Galilee to Jerusalem, there is no clear itinerary or chronology of the trip. The journey itself seems to serve as a kind of grab bag of stories and incidents in which we see Jesus adapting and improvising his language to fit each person and circumstance on the terms that are presented to him. The Travel Narrative has Jesus speaking in informal, non-structured language, much of it not explicitly "religious," in the course of the relaxed and spontaneous incidents that occur "on the way" through Samaria.

What we begin to sense is that what began as a "Travel Narrative" has developed in the telling into a metaphor, a metaphor for the way Jesus uses language between Sundays, between the holy synagogues of Galilee and the holy temple in Jerusalem, places and times in which language about God and his kingdom are expected. But Samaria wasn't "holy" in the same sense, wasn't congenial to the Jesus who was being revealed in Galilee and Jerusalem. Luke gives us Samaria as a metaphor for the way Jesus uses language with people who have very little or maybe no readiness to listen to the revelation of God, and not infrequently are outright hostile. This is the way Jesus uses language when he isn't, as we would say, in church.

*   *   *

The second thing of interest in the Travel Narrative is how frequently Jesus tells stories, the mini-stories we name parables. Jesus, in these ten chapters, mostly tells stories. Ten of the stories in this middle section of Luke's Gospel are unique to Luke. All of the Gospel writers feature Jesus telling stories — "he did not speak to them except in parables" (Mark 4:34) — but Luke outdoes his brother evangelists. And it is precisely in this Travel Narrative that the ten parables not mentioned in the other Gospels are clustered.

Is there a reason for this? I think there is. The parable is a form of speech that has a style all its own. It is a way of saying something that requires the imaginative participation of the listener. Inconspicuously, even surreptitiously, a parable *involves* the hearer. This brief, commonplace, unpretentious story is thrown into a conversation and lands at our feet, compelling notice. A parable is literally "something thrown alongside of" (*para*, alongside, plus *bolē*, thrown) to which our first response is, "What is *this* doing here?" We ask questions, we think, we imagine. "Parables appear in quick, precise strokes. A parable is feeble; almost all the power is in the one who hears it."[4] And then we begin seeing connections, relations. A parable is not ordinarily used to tell us something new but to get us to notice something that we have overlooked although it has been right there before us for years. Or it is used to get us to take seriously something we have dismissed as unimportant because we have never seen the point of it. Before we know it, we are involved.

Most parables have another significant feature. The subject matter is usually without apparent religious significance. They are stories about farmers and judges and victims, about coins and sheep and prodigal sons, about wedding banquets, building barns and towers and going to war, a friend who wakes you in the middle of the night to ask for a loaf of bread, the courtesies of hospitality, crooks and beggars, fig trees and manure. The conversations that Jesus had as he walked on

---

4. Jean Sulivan, *Morning Light* (New York: Paulist Press, 1988), p. 64.

Samaritan roads were with people who had a different idea of God than what Jesus was revealing, or maybe not much of an idea at all. This was either hostile or neutral country. Parables were Jesus' primary language of choice to converse with these people, stories that didn't use the name of God, stories that didn't seem to be "religious." When we are in church, or a religiously defined time and place, we expect to hear about God. But outside such times and places, we don't expect to. In fact, we don't want to. If we wanted to deal with God we would go to God's house. The people we meet "on the road" and "between Sundays" expect to deal with things on their own terms, meanwhile keeping God in his place where he belongs. So, keep *Jesus* in his place — in Galilee and Jerusalem. "This is Samaria! I have my hands full dealing with family and business, society and politics. I'm calling the shots here. I'll do things my own way."

Samaritans, then and now, have centuries of well-developed indifference, if not outright aversion, to God-language — at least the kind used by synagogue and church people. They have their own ideas on God and how to run their lives and nothing but cool contempt for the messianic opinions of outsiders. Samaritans are well defended against the intrusions of God-language into their affairs, particularly when it comes from Jewish (or Christian) lips. So as Jesus goes through Samaria he is very restrained in his use of explicit God-language. Preaching and teaching are not eliminated, but they do recede to the margins. Jesus circles around his listeners' defenses. He tells parables. A parable keeps the message at a distance, slows down comprehension, blocks automatic prejudicial reactions, dismantles stereotypes. A parable comes up on the listener obliquely, on the "slant." The Samaritan listens, unsuspecting. And then, without warning, without the word being used: God! John Dominic Crossan says that the parable is an earthquake opening up the ground at your feet.[5]

It interests me greatly that throughout these several days when Jesus is walking with his disciples, parables are his primary language of

---

5. John Dominic Crossan, *The Dark Interval: Towards a Theology of Story* (Niles, Ill.: Argus Communications, 1975), p. 57.

choice. We know that the end is coming: crucifixion and resurrection. We know that there is not much time left before Jesus leaves his disciples and they are going to have to carry on in his place. Every step they take through Samaria to Jerusalem increases the urgency. This is the last time these Samaritans are going to see him, listen to him. Why in the world is Jesus telling unpretentious stories about crooks and manure? Why isn't he preaching the clear word of God, calling the Samaritans to repentance, offering them the gift of salvation in plain language? As the end approaches, his language becomes less, not more, direct. As the stakes increase, his language becomes even more relaxed and conversational than usual. Instead of high decibel rhetoric, calling for decisions before it is too late, he hardly, if at all, even mentions the name of God, choosing instead to speak of neighbors and friends, losing a lamb, and the courtesies of hospitality.

I find this interesting because it is in such contrast to what so often occurs among us. It is common among many of us when we become more aware of what is involved in following Jesus and the urgencies that this involves, especially when we find ourselves in Samaritan territory, that we become more intense in our language. Because it is so much more clear and focused we use the language learned from sermons and teachings to tell others what is eternally important. But the very intensity of the language can very well reduce our attentiveness to the people to whom we are speaking — he or she is no longer a person but a cause. Impatient to get our message out, we depersonalize what we have to say into rote phrases or a programmatic formula without regard to the person we are meeting. As the urgency to speak God's word increases, listening relationships diminish. We end up with a bone pile of fleshless words — godtalk.

*   *   *

Spiritual masters are particularly fond of the parable, for there is nothing more common than for people who want to talk about God to lose interest in the people they are talking to. Religious talk is depersonalized into godtalk. Godtalk is used to organize people in causes that no longer involve us, to carry out commands that no longer command us. When the words of Jesus become the stuff of arguments, verbal tools for manipulation, attempts at control, the life drains out of them and there they are, a raked-up pile of dead leaves on the ground. Just then, the master drops a parable into the conversation. We stumble over it, no longer able to cruise along in the familiar word ruts. The parable forces attention, participation, involvement.

Luke's Travel Narrative is an immersion in the distinctive parabolic, storying language of Jesus on the road through Samaria as he walks from Galilee, where we took up the life of following Jesus, to Jerusalem, where we will find our maturity and completion, embracing Jesus on the cross and embraced by Jesus in resurrection. Samaria for us becomes an orientation in the ordinary, the everyday, the place where the habits and character of a Jesus follower are formed among people who have no interest nor give any encouragement to following Jesus. Luke's Travel Narrative saturates our imaginations with the way Jesus uses language in this inhospitable stretch of road between the Galilean proclamation of the presence of the kingdom, where we got our start in following Jesus, and the Jerusalem crucifixion and resurrection that so decisively and dramatically completes the story.

The Holy Spirit in Our Conversations

Luke's Travel Narrative develops an awareness that the Holy Spirit is as present in our spontaneous and casual conversations as in formal preaching and intentional teaching. Because our spontaneous and casual conversations have no immediate focus on what we sometimes refer to as "the things of God," it is easy to miss the "word of God" implications when we aren't aware that we are talking to or about God. When we are in a sanctuary listening to a sermon on John 3:16 or sitting in a classroom taking notes on a lecture on Isaiah, it is fairly obvious that we are listening to and speaking language that God uses to reveal himself and that we use to participate in that revelation. But how about when we are telling someone about a report we just heard on the radio, or when we're reading a letter received from a family member that morning, or when we express worries about a neighbor down the street? Can these words also be revelatory, also be ways of participating in God's presence and action in times and places not clearly signposted "sacred"? Do we witness to Jesus when we do not use the name of Jesus? Do we convey trust in God when we do not know we are doing it? Do we confess sin when we are not in a confessional or on our knees? Do we praise with an exclamation or gesture, unaware that we are in the company of angels singing "Holy, Holy, Holy"? One night when Nicodemus was puzzled by the unconventional, nonreligious way in which Jesus was talking about God's kingdom, Jesus told him, "The wind blows where it chooses, and you hear the sound of it, but you do not know where it comes from or where it goes. So it is with everyone who is born of the Spirit" (John 3:8). Nicodemus had no idea what he was talking about. A great deal of Spirit-inspired, or Spirit-accompanied, language takes place when we do not know it, whether it comes from our own mouths or the mouths of others.

So we need reminding. We need guidance. We need friends who are capable of hearing the Holy Spirit's whispers in what we are saying — and sometimes between the lines in what we are not saying. And we need to be such friends to our friends. These friends ordinarily have no assigned role in one another's lives. Often they do not know that they are doing anything at all that might be named "spiritual." Nathaniel Hawthorne was blunt in his assertion on these matters: "His instruments have no consciousness of His purpose; if they imagine they have, it is a pretty sure token that they are *not* his instruments."[6]

I am interested in cultivating the fundamentally holy nature of all language, including most definitely the casual, spontaneous, unself-conscious, conversational language that occurs while we're sitting in a rocking chair before a fireplace on a wintry day, strolling on a beach, or having coffee in a diner — conversations while we're walking through Samaria. I am interested in discerning the voice of God in

---

6. Quoted by David Dark, *The Gospel According to America* (Louisville: Westminster/John Knox Press, 2005), p. 52.

the conversations that we engage in when we are not intentionally thinking "God."

All of us have wide experience in this language. But not all of us are practiced in bringing our experience to awareness, naming what we have heard or said. Sometimes we notice in retrospect. We meet a friend while shopping and stop to talk for a while — a minute or two at most. A few hours later we realize that something said was revelatory, a realization of grace, a perception of beauty, a sense of presence in which we develop an awareness that "God was in this place and I did not know it." Sometimes the triggering word or phrase comes almost offhandedly. Sometimes the realization is sparked by a tone of voice or a gesture. Almost never by intention. The fact is that almost all words are holy and God speaks to and through us by the very nature of language itself.

What I want to say is that the Holy Spirit conveys in and through our language words of Jesus' peace and love and grace and mercy when we are not aware of it — at least not at the time it is taking place. And all of us get in on it simply by virtue of the fact that we talk and listen to a lot of different people, in a lot of different settings, on most days of our lives. Paying attention to Jesus telling stories in Luke's Travel Narrative is as good an orientation in this dimension of language that I know of.

*   *   *

There is an ancient discipline of honoring the careful attention we give to just such language, language that we use in personal discourse conversationally, language that takes its place alongside of preaching and teaching as essential to formation-in-community in the Christian life. It goes under the heading of "spiritual direction." It will be obvious to those familiar with this tradition and its practice that what I write here is deeply influenced by it. From early on in the church's life, alongside the practice of public preaching and teaching there has been the corresponding practice of spiritual direction. In spiritual direction the language used in the proclamation and teaching of the gospel is worked out in one-on-one conversations that take seriously the uniqueness of each person and the actual circumstances in which that person lives. It won't do to lump souls into categories and then herd them into one of three or four companies that can be dealt with efficiently by formula.

As we grow into maturity in Christ our distinctiveness is accentuated, not blunted. General directions, useful as they are, don't take into account the details that face us as holiness takes root in the particular social and personal place we are planted. We need wise personal attention from someone who knows the ropes, who knows the subtleties of sin and the disguises of grace. Especially, we need personal attention given to our prayers, for prayer is the practice by which all that we are, all that we believe and do, is transformed into the action of the Spirit working his will in the details of our dailiness. Prayer consists in the transformation of what we do in the name of Jesus to what the Holy Spirit does in us as we follow Jesus.

Spiritual direction is one person intentionally and prayerfully immersing himself or herself in the casual ordinary life of any ordinary Christian. But the practice is neither ordinary nor casual. The Christian community has a history of recognizing wise, experienced persons who can direct the rest of us. "Father" *(abba)* and "mother" *(amma)* are the most widely used designations. The qualifications for doing this work are not formal, but there is a consensus in the church that the qualifications are nevertheless quite rigorous. A knowledge of theology is basic, and long experience in prayer is prerequisite.

So we find a person who is practiced in discerning the Spirit's language and we ask him or her to meet with us occasionally or regularly — a spiritual director. Often these persons, these "fathers" and "mothers," are members of contemplative orders in monasteries or convents. Sometimes they are associated with retreat houses. Occasionally they are placed in congregations. These spiritual directors keep alive a long tradition in the church of Christ. Sometimes they are pastors and priests. Sometimes they are laypersons. They maintain visibility and provide definition to what so often takes place in obscurity and in the shadows of the more public discourse of preaching and teaching. By their presence, and sometimes in their writings, they call our attention to and give dignity to the way language continues to be revelatory in our most casual conversation.

We need a few of these men and women in the community, who are intentional in getting us to pay attention to the words we are using when we don't think we are saying anything of significance. We need alert listeners to give dignity to those stretches in our lives when we are not aware of participating in anything we think might be embraced by the kingdom of God.[7]

*   *   *

Without diminishing or marginalizing the strategic role of such designated spiritual directors, I want at the same time to extend the awareness of what they model into the ranks of both the laity who aren't aware of the ways the Holy Spirit breathes through our most casual conversations and the clergy who are only aware that they are speaking the word of God when they are preaching or teaching. Out-of-the-way conversations that take place out of the public ear and eye, in fact, occupy a prominent place in the way we learn to use and pay attention to language that conveys Spirit. My concern is derivative from the well-defined and necessarily rigorous traditions of the spiritual director, but I am attempting something much more modest — maybe something in regard to spiritual direction like what happened to the man who was astonished when he realized at the age of forty that he had been speaking in prose all his life.

Any Christian can, and many Christians do, *listen* and help us *listen* to the undercurrents in our language, the unspoken and unheard, the silences that undergird so much of the language that we use unthinkingly. These conversations can cultivate a sensitivity to the ways

7. The foundational and far and away the best exposition of this practice is in Martin Thornton, *Spiritual Direction* (Cambridge: Cowley Publications, 1984). Thornton is an Anglican and writes out of that tradition. But what he writes can easily be translated into whatever tradition we occupy. A thorough grounding in the early development of the practice is accessible in Irenee Hausherr, *Spiritual Direction in the Early Christian East*, trans. Anthony P. Gythiel (Kalamazoo, Mich.: Cistercian Publications, 1990).

of the Holy Spirit, encourage an embrace of ambiguity, extend a willingness to live through times when there is no discernible "direction" at all. With such listening, we get used to living a mystery and not demanding information to footnote everything that is going on. There are certainly skills to be cultivated, especially in this American society in which virtually everyone talks too much and listens hardly at all. I am only insisting that any of us is capable of doing this simply by virtue of our baptism and incorporation in the company of men and women in whom the Spirit breathes, as the Spirit brings to remembrance the words of Jesus (John 14:26) in the conversations of men and women who listen and give answer to the Word made flesh.

To avoid presumption and blurring the lines that set apart the learned and disciplined men and women who embody this ancient practice of the church, I will not use the term "spiritual direction" for the kind of conversation that I am encouraging as we walk on our various Samaritan roads. All the same, "I would," to adapt Moses' words in regard to Eldad and Medad in the wilderness, "that all the Lord's people were spiritual directors" (Num. 11:29).

*   *   *

An unscheduled conversation in the sanctuary at Shiloh between the old and nearly blind priest Eli and young Samuel is a classic instance of such unpremeditated conversation. It was night and Samuel was in bed. He heard a voice calling his name, "Samuel! Samuel!" Eli was the only other person in the sanctuary, and so Samuel naturally assumed that Eli was calling for him. He jumped out of bed and ran to Eli: "Here I am, for you called me." Eli said that he hadn't called and told him to go back to bed. This identical exchange took place three times. After the third time, the priest discerned that it was the Lord who was calling Samuel and told him that if it happened again he was to pray, "Speak, Lord, for your servant is listening." It did happen again, a fourth time, and Samuel said, as instructed, "Speak, Lord, for your servant is listening." And a prophet was born.

Eli, an incompetent pastor at best, nevertheless was able to identify the voice of God in what Samuel assumed was the voice of his priest, and so he redirected Samuel into a life of prayer in which he was formed into a prophet of God (1 Sam. 3:1-18).

Another informal, scriptural conversation — not preaching, not teaching — that alerts us to the way story-language does its revelational work indirectly occurs in Paul's letter to the Galatians. Paul is giving witness to his conversion and his lengthy, painstaking integration (seventeen years!) into the Christian community. In his report, he refers to his conversations with Peter (Cephas) in Jerusalem over the course of a fifteen-day visit. The Greek word he uses to describe the conversations is *historeō*. It is a word that came to refer to "history" of a nation or a people, but it had a more informal and personal sense when Paul used it, something more casual, as in "swapped stories." The German scholar Friedrich Büchsel suggests "visit in order to get to know."[8] They were not preaching and not teaching but simply getting acquainted, telling one another their stories and discerning in the conversation the ways in which God was preparing and developing Paul for his vocation as Apostle to the Gentiles in the Christian community. We can easily imagine Peter and Paul sitting in a courtyard, getting acquainted under an olive tree with glasses of iced tea, trading stories. Paul tells of his Damascus Road encounter with Jesus followed by the three days of blindness. Peter counters with his Caesarea Philippi confession cut short by Jesus' devastating rebuke, "Get behind me, Satan." Paul tells what it was like to hold the coats of his fellow persecutors as they stoned Stephen to death. Peter offers his night of ignominy in Caiaphas's courtyard when he denied Jesus. And on and on, fifteen days of story-telling as they got to know one another as brothers in Jesus, discovering intimacies of the Spirit as they opened their vulnerable hearts to one another.

But the showcase use of this language is Jesus in his stories. Jesus' parables were mostly nonreligious in explicit content. His parables used homely language from everyday life and were typically occa-

8. *Theological Dictionary of the New Testament*, ed. Gerhard Kittel, trans. Geoffrey W. Bromiley, vol. 3 (Grand Rapids: Eerdmans, 1965), p. 396.

sioned by a specific circumstance. There is an off-the-cuff, spontaneous, unpremeditated quality to them.

Jesus used parables a lot. When he wasn't preaching and wasn't teaching, he spoke in parables. Jesus' characteristic way of using language was to tell stories: "he told them many things in parables" (Matt. 13:3). Jesus tells stories and we listen to God tell stories. And, almost inevitably, we find ourselves in the stories. Jesus in his stories is Jesus using language in the ways that we have come to recognize broadly as spiritual direction.

The Zebedees

An arresting incident prefaces this lengthy excursus into conversational storytelling in the Travel Narrative. It features the Zebedee brothers, James and John.

When Jesus decided that it was time to go to Jerusalem, he was faced with a difficulty. The way to Jerusalem passed through Samaria, and Samaritans held rather strong, negative opinions about Jews. Jews felt the same way about Samaritans. The racial and religious prejudice was longstanding. And so when Jesus sent some of his companions on ahead into Samaria to arrange for accommodations, they were rebuffed. They returned to Jesus and reported that they were unable to secure bed and board. They had encountered considerable antipathy in the village. They were not welcome (Luke 9:51-53).

The Zebedee brothers, James and John, were outraged. Nicknamed "sons of Thunder" *(Boanerges)*, these two didn't take insults sitting down. The brothers were short-tempered firebrands. Angry at the inhospitality, they wanted to call down fire from heaven and incinerate the rude Samaritans. They had biblical precedent for their violent impetuosity. Hadn't Elijah the Tishbite done this very thing, called down fire from heaven eight hundred years earlier, and in this very Samaritan country (2 Kings 1:10-12)? Only a few days before in the transfiguration on Mt. Tabor, the thunder brothers had seen Jesus in conversation with Elijah. They were now on an Elijah-authorized mission in Samaritan country; why not use the old Elijah fire to take care of the old Samaritan problem?

Jesus said, "Nothing doing." His rebuke was peremptory and non-negotiable. It was no part of their task as disciples to destroy the opposition. Christ followers don't bash the people who are not on our side, either physically or verbally.

Several years ago, I was driving down a stretch of road that I knew well. I was just in time to see a bulldozer take out a house at the side of the road. It took the yellow machine about twenty seconds to smash the house into kindling. I had observed that house with appreciation for the twenty-six years that I had been pastor in that community. The small, well-kept house was accompanied by a large, well-kept garden that was planted and tended with devotion. Straight rows of corn and beets and carrots. Always cleanly weeded. And by midsummer (which it was that day), flourishing with food, ready to be picked and cooked and eaten. But recently a development company had purchased the land in order to build a shopping mall. A house and garden are an offense to a shopping mall. And there is an easy technological solution: the bulldozer. The living beauty of the house and garden had no cash value in competition with the ugliness and asphalt of the mall, and so the bulldozer was sent in to eliminate it. At the time I saw it happen, I remember thinking, "The Zebedees are at it again."

When the company of Jesus, on its way to Jerusalem to establish definitively the kingdom of God, came up against the offending inhospitality of Samaritans, the Zebedee brothers had (or thought they had) the technological means to wipe them out of the way — not a Caterpillar Bulldozer for them but the equally effective and spiritually superior technology of Elijah Fire.

A surprising number of Christians, oblivious to Jesus' unqualified rebuke, continue to sign up with the Zebedees. Full of zeal as they follow Jesus, they will not tolerate interference. Violence follows. They do it in their families, in their churches, among their friends. Over the course of hundreds of years they have killed Jews and Muslims, communists and witches and heretics, and, closer to home, Native Americans. Most of the violence, maybe all of it, begins in language. Jesus warned us that it might: "You have heard that it was said to those of ancient times, 'You shall not murder'; and 'whoever murders shall be liable to judgment.' But I say to you that if you are angry with a brother or sister, you will be liable to judgment; and if you insult a brother or sister, you will be liable to the council; and if you say, 'You fool!' you will be liable to the hell of fire" (Matt. 5:21-22).

So all of us, no exceptions, need a thorough schooling in the language of Jesus, the way he talked with those who followed him, *and* the way he talked with those he met as he traveled through Samaria. The trip that began with the Zebedee brothers determined to call down fire from heaven to kill the impudent Samaritans ended a few days later when the Romans killed Jesus for disturbing the peace. Threatened violence at the outset, accomplished violence at the end. But between the times, a gentle, listening language of suggestion, language that invites participation, language that doesn't say too much but leaves room for mystery. Stories.

*   *   *

My intent in the pages that follow in the first part of this book is to observe, in turn, the ten parables unique to Luke that he places in the Travel Narrative. I want to recover facility in using this storying way of words, this signature language of Jesus, the parable, for use in our own travels through our own American Samaria, this country so largely indifferent to Jesus and the language of Jesus.

CHAPTER 2

The Neighbor: Luke 10:25-37

The first story Jesus tells on the road through Samaria features, appropriately, a Samaritan. But before Luke tells the story, he supplies two incidents that take place on that Samaritan road that links Galilee to Jerusalem.

*   *   *

A man says to Jesus, "I will follow you wherever you go." Jesus tells him that they won't be staying in the best hotels. Apparently that had never occurred to the man. We never hear from him again. Jesus then says to a second man, "Follow me." This man agrees but insists on conditions. He has something important that he has to do first. Jesus dismisses him. Following Jesus isn't something we put off until we have first done what we want to do. Then a third man steps up and says that he is ready to follow Jesus — but not quite yet. Jesus says, in effect, "Never mind. It's now or never." It turns out that the man is not ready after all.

Jesus has barely begun his journey through Samaria to Jerusalem before he has picked up three followers. But they haven't gone a dozen paces before each of them has dropped out.

We get the message: following Jesus doesn't take place on our terms. We follow Jesus on his terms. This is not an auspicious launch for the Travel Narrative. Three potential followers and each a dropout (Luke 9:57-62).

The three dropouts are replaced by a contrasting group, a group characterized by immediate and obedient response (Luke 10:1-24). Jesus appoints seventy-two others and sends them out in thirty-six pairs as a vanguard to prepare the way through Samaria for him. There is good work to be done — Jesus speaks of a plentiful harvest — and they are ready to begin the good work. But as good as it is they must not be naïve about the conditions. They are not to expect an open-hearted welcome. Jesus warns of "wolves." He advises austerity, no lavish strategies: keep things simple, direct, courteous, personal. Opposition is to be expected. Not everyone is going to be enthusiastic about these trespassing foreigners with their "kingdom of God" talk.

Jesus concludes his instructions to the seventy-two with a sternly phrased reprimand of men and women who reject the good news of the kingdom of God that has "come near." He lets loose with a fiercely denunciatory message of judgment on men and women who reject the good news of the kingdom of God "come near." Refusal to repent carries serious consequences. But it is significant that when Jesus names names, it is Galilean, not Samaritan towns that he cites: Chorazin, Bethsaida, and Capernaum. These are the three small towns, the "evangelical triangle," in which Jesus spent most of three years in calling and teaching disciples.

By using the names of the Galilean hometowns of his followers as core concentrations of the unrepentant, Jesus is indirectly countering an indiscriminate lumping of Samaritans with the stereotypical "bad guys." "Expect hostility," Jesus is telling them, "but don't think that inhospitality to God 'come near' is a Samaritan thing. It is no different from what goes on among your families and neighbors back home. Don't treat these people with a chip on your shoulder. They are no more likely to either accept or reject your witness than any of the good Jews you grew up with." Jesus doesn't take the anticipated hostility lightly. But neither does he take it as a personal affront.

And off they go. When the returns from their mission start pouring in, one word, "joy," characterizes the reports. Everything is working. The Jesus works and the Jesus words performed and preached and taught by the seventy-two have Jesus results. The seventy-two are absolutely astonished at what takes place among the Samaritans — "surprised by joy." This is heady stuff. Jesus confirms their excitement: He "sees Satan fall from heaven like a flash of lightning," joins them in rejoicing "in the Holy Spirit," and thanks the "Father, Lord of heaven and earth" for the harvest. "Rejoice" (*agalliaō*), the verb that powers Jesus' confirming words, conveys an exuberance we see expressed in dance and cartwheels. And in Samaria of all places!

But he also introduces a word of caution: "Do not rejoice at this, that the spirits submit to you, but rejoice that your names are written in heaven" (Luke 10:20). There is danger that we will become overly excited at what we see going on around us and neglect the center, our heaven-inscribed identities, out of which the work develops. Not what we do, but who we are "in heaven," anchors the joy.

There is a huge exuberance in getting in on the work and words of Jesus. But there is also this single sentence of caution embedded in the joy.

This side-by-side contrast in personal response to Jesus, the three dropouts and the avant-garde, exuberant seventy-two, provides a realistic orientation in what we can expect as we travel through Samaritan country: disappointing defections, clearly articulated instructions, "wolves," insider participation in the work of Jesus, great joy, and disciplined optimism.

*   *   *

Just then a religion scholar stood up with a question to test Jesus. "Teacher, what do I need to do to get eternal life?"

He answered, "What's written in God's Law? How do you interpret it?"

He said, "That you love the Lord your God with all your passion and prayer and muscle and intelligence — and that you love your neighbor as well as you do yourself."

"Good answer!" said Jesus. "Do it and you'll live."

Looking for a loophole, he asked, "And just how would you define 'neighbor'?"

Jesus' answer is the first parable in the Travel Narrative.

Jesus answered by telling a story. "There was a man traveling from Jerusalem to Jericho. On the way he was attacked by robbers. They took his clothes, beat him up, and went off leaving him half-dead. Luckily, a priest was on his way down the same road, but when he saw him he angled across to the other side. Then a Levite religious man showed up; he also avoided the injured man.

"A Samaritan traveling the road came on him. When he saw the man's condition, his heart went out to him. He gave him first aid, disinfecting and bandaging his wounds. Then he lifted him onto his donkey, led him to an inn, and made him comfortable. In the morning he took out two silver coins and gave them to the innkeeper, saying, 'Take good care of him. If it costs any more, put it on my bill — I'll pay you on my way back.'

"What do you think? Which of the three became a neighbor to the man attacked by robbers?"

"The one who treated him kindly," the religion scholar responded.

Jesus said, "Go and do the same." (Luke 10:25-37 *The Message*)

*   *   *

The story is provoked by a conversation with an unnamed person who is identified only by his work. He is a lawyer, a *nomikos*. The law that he was identified with professionally was not secular law but God's law, the law of Moses, the Torah. A more accurate designation among us would be "religion professor" or "Bible scholar." The work of a lawyer, defending and interpreting the law of God, was honored and responsible work in the first century. Then, as now, the Scriptures were quoted and misquoted by anyone who wanted divine authority for his or her program. The lawyers, these Bible scholars, were responsible among other things for keeping their communities alert to the possibilities of religious craziness and/or deceit. Many are the religious leaders who deceive and seduce in the name of God. We can't be too careful in these things.

This Bible scholar is taking his work seriously, testing Jesus against the authority of Scripture. There is no reason to suppose that there was any hostile intent in the testing — *ekpeiradzō* can simply mean test in the sense of "test for authenticity," with no sense of entrapment.

The story is told in the context of a crowd of people who are following Jesus, many of them probably out of curiosity. The just-returned seventy-two have come back from an extraordinarily successful mission in Samaritan territory, a country that among Jews had a reputation for heresy. Men and women are gullible. It is easy to fool people (especially Samaritans?) in the name of God. It is important to have knowledgeable and discerning people around, especially in matters of religion and the Bible. A Jewish Bible scholar with responsibility for making sure that the truth is *true* happens to be there that day when the seventy-two come back rejoicing. By training and habit he asks himself, "Is this the real thing?"

The man is doing important work. No one wants an untested Messiah. The stakes are too high. We don't want to risk our lives on what may turn out to be a fraud. We know from experience that there is an incredible amount of religious fraud taking place in the world. We want our Messiah tested inside and out, examined and cross-examined. So the lawyer steps forward "to test Jesus."

This was neither the first nor the last time that Jesus was tested. Luke tells us that Jesus, just before he began his public ministry, was tested by the devil in the wilderness. The testing was comprehensive and rigorous — and hostile. The devil's testing was a seductive tempting, tempting him to be a crowd-pleasing, glamorous celebrity-Messiah. He met the test. He said no to the devil. Matthew and Mark preceded Luke in reporting this testing. Jesus was also tested near the conclusion of his public ministry in the garden of Gethsemane. This testing was even more comprehensive and rigorous than the first, the ultimate test: Will Jesus go to the cross, sacrifice his life for the salvation of the world — or not? The testing was agonizing. Jesus met the test. Matthew and Mark also report this testing.

At the Last Supper Jesus said something to his disciples that only Luke reports: "you are those who have stood by me in my trials" (Luke 22:28).[1] "In my trials" catches my attention: it seems that there were more tests put to Jesus than just the agonistic wilderness test at the beginning and the agonizing Gethsemane test at the end. Among these other tests was this one that only Luke reports, the test given by the Bible scholar in the early days of travel through Samaria. As the test is conducted, we observe something significant regarding the way Jesus uses language — not proclaiming, not interpreting, but conversing. Respectful give-and-take. Neither confrontational nor condescending. A conversation that invites (and achieves) participation.

There are five segments to the conversation.

Segment 1. The Bible scholar asks his test question, "What must I do to inherit eternal life?" Maybe this is his standard test question, one that he asks every religion teacher who is a stranger. It is not a bad question. All of us want to live something more than an animal existence, and it is in this "more" that our character and values show themselves. The way we go about living this "more" tells a lot about our wisdom and our motives and our goodness.

And putting the question in the first person is smart. The Bible scholar disguises his question as a request for advice. He is no amateur in this business. He knows that if you pretend to ask for counsel, the person you are examining is disarmed, drops defenses, doesn't feel anxious. If you interrogate a person accusingly, you are going to get far less than if you ask for personal advice. All of us have a hard time resisting the giving of advice. A question, quite apart from its content, usually honors us with respect. Anyone who asks for directions of any kind usually gets far more than he or she asks for.

Yes, I think this Bible scholar has done this before. He knows

---

1. "Trial," "test," and "temptation" all come from the same word in Luke's Greek, *peirasmos.* How it is translated depends on the context.

what he is doing and has perfected his technique. And he probably has a notebook at home full of the answers that he has been given to his question.

But he is no match for Jesus. Jesus answers his question by asking a question, "What's written in God's Law? How do you interpret it?" (I once saw an interview conducted with Elie Wiesel, the Jewish novelist and writer on spirituality. The interviewer said, "I have noticed that you Jews often answer questions by asking another question. Why do you do that?" To which Wiesel replied, "Why not?")

The ground shifts. This is no longer an objective examination, a multiple-choice question in which the answer can be marked in an appropriate square. A relationship is begun; dialogue is initiated. It is no longer a superior questioner and inferior answerer. The dialogue develops collegiality. Did the Bible scholar begin this conversation with just the least amount of haughtiness, or with an impersonal and policing rectitude? If so, it is suddenly gone. The tables are turned. Jesus' question levels the playing field.

*　　*　　*

Segment 2. The Bible scholar answers Jesus' question by summarizing the law of Moses in the classic style: love God and love your neighbor — a meld of Deuteronomy and Leviticus. It is not original, but it is accurate. Jesus gives him a good grade: "Good answer! Do it and you'll live."

The most notable feature in this segment is that the positions of the scholar and Jesus are reversed. In the course of testing Jesus, the Bible scholar finds himself no longer administering the test but personally involved in the test. In the act of testing Jesus he finds himself tested by Jesus. The examiner has become the examinee. The Bible scholar who set out to give Jesus a test on orthodoxy gets his own orthodoxy tested. This is an oral examination conducted out in the open, perhaps on the road or in the village square. The result is reassuring. He passes. In fact, they both pass, Jesus and the scholar. They are now on equal footing, both certified as orthodox, both competent in teaching the ways of God.

*　　*　　*

Segment 3. The scholar, instead of feeling relaxed and companionable with Jesus as we might expect, both of them now assured of the other's orthodoxy, asks another question: "And just how would you define 'neighbor'?"

Luke ascribes a motive to the scholar's question: "wanting to justify himself" (NRSV). The scholar is feeling uneasy. He is "looking for a loophole." We feel the need for justification only when we sense that we are not quite in the right. Maybe there is more to life than orthodoxy. Self-justification is a verbal device for restoring the appearance of rightness without doing anything about the substance. If we sense that we are being criticized by another, we jump in with a defense or an excuse. Most of us do this quite a lot. We don't like being thought bad or inadequate or stupid. One of the standard ploys of defensiveness is to seize the offense to put the other person on the defense, to take attention off of my weakness or fault and shift attention to the other person.

What is the scholar's weakness or fault that he wants to avoid dealing with, that he wants to distract attention from? There is nothing wrong with his knowledge or thought processes. He knows the Torah thoroughly and can quote it accurately. There is nothing wrong with his professional competence. We have observed that he conducts his examination of Jesus with considerable skill. If he thinks well and works well, what is left? Well, maybe the way he *is*, the way he lives, the way he loves. Maybe it has to do with his unwillingness to be vulnerable in a relationship that might involve him in suffering (which all relationships do involve), unwilling to engage in the demands of loving in which all that is distinctively human is put to the test. Maybe he refuses to risk himself in the uncertainties and vulnerabilities of a *relationship* with men and women and God, and especially the paramount personal relationship, love. Maybe he wants to keep rigid control. Maybe his heart is atrophied.

The scholar starts this conversation with confidence. He is in charge. He is the guardian of biblical truth. He intends to judge whether Jesus is competent to teach and lead disciples. One way in

which the examination could have ended was in a simple pronounce-
ment of pass or fail. Or, it could have developed into an argument, a
theological debate with the bystanders as the jury.

What actually happened was not, I think, anticipated by the
scholar. Caught by surprise in this unaccustomed position of being
himself examined, he tries to regain his original position of being in
control by asking another question. He is uncomfortable with being
on a par with Jesus; he wants to be in charge of Jesus. He isn't used to
being in a personal relationship of mutuality. He wants to be impersonally in control.

And so he attempts to regain control of the conversation by asking a question that will put Jesus on the defensive: "And who is my
neighbor?" Even as he is asking the question he must have been congratulating himself — "brilliant recovery!" "Neighbor" is a notoriously
difficult category to define in practical terms. If the scholar had asked,
"And who is God?" he and Jesus could have traded a few Scripture quo-
tations and that would have been the end of it. It would have been a discussion between equals. But he wants to regain the high ground, so instead of asking for a definition of the revealed God, he introduces the
shadowy "neighbor." Defining the neighbor would have been good for
an all-day discussion, with the bystanders slowly drifting off as hunger
pulls them to their suppers.

The Bible scholar is a veteran in the religion business. He knows
that a person can hide undetected for a long time, maybe even for a
lifetime, behind religious questions. Has he been doing this all his life
— leading Bible studies, asking probing questions, upholding the
truth of Scripture, fulfilling religious functions — and never been
found out?

But Jesus finds him out. And it is a parable that does it, this de-
servedly famous story that is commonly named "The Good Samaritan."

The story is told on a Samaritan road, but it is told *to* a Jewish religious professional. And it is most likely overheard by other Jews
who are accompanying Jesus from Galilee to Jerusalem. There must
have been quite a crowd of them — how many besides the seventy-
two who had been sent on the mission? I imagine a substantial con-

gregation of Galilean Jews traveling through unfriendly Samaritan country with Jesus.

The significance of the setting is clarified by three observations. One, Jesus tells his story to a man whom his Jewish listeners would think of as a good Jew. Two, the story features a man who in the Jewish imagination of the day would be stereotyped as a bad Samaritan. Three, the story itself is set not on the Samaritan road on which they were walking but many miles south on the Jericho road out of Jerusalem, a road in Jewish territory. A good Jewish scholar, a good Jewish road, and a "bad" Samaritan.

Jesus creates the story. A man is walking from Jerusalem to Jericho. It is a long walk of seventeen miles descending 3,300 feet through wilderness badlands to the fertile Jordanian plain. The road twists and turns through canyons and arroyos pockmarked with caves. This is a road famous for harboring brigands. Robbery is common, murder not infrequent.

Jesus does not make the ethnic identity of the man explicit, but given the context we assume he is a Jew. He is waylaid by brigands who take everything he has, literally the clothes off his back, beat him nearly to death, and leave him for the vultures to finish off. It happens all the time even now, on city streets and country roads all over the world. Luckily, just then a priest comes by. But the luck is short-lived. The priest can't be bothered with him. Then a Levite comes by — another chance! But he fares no better at the hands of the Levite than at the hands of the priest. The man is three times forsaken — by the robbers, the priest, and now the Levite.

Given the conversation just recorded between the Bible scholar and Jesus, we can't help assuming that the priest and the Levite also know that double command that the Bible scholar has just recited, and know it just as well as he does. The three men, priest and Levite and Bible scholar, are fellow professionals in matters of Torah. They are responsible for keeping the law of Moses regarding God and neighbor remembered and in working condition in the Jewish community.

Just then a Samaritan shows up and takes care of the robbed and beaten Jew, and not in a perfunctory way. He disinfects the man's wounds, anoints them with healing oil, bandages him up, puts him on his donkey, takes him to an inn, and pays for his keep. A Samaritan, the stereotypical bad person in the Jewish imagination, loves his Jewish "neighbor."

A simple story, simply told while walking through Samaritan country.

* * *

Segment 4. The entire conversation between Jesus and the Bible scholar turns on questions. First the Bible scholar's question, "Teacher, what do I need to do to get eternal life?" Then Jesus' question, "What's written in God's Law? How do you interpret it?" And now a third and final question by Jesus, "What do you think? Which of the three became a neighbor to the man attacked by robbers?"

The Bible scholar, not Jesus, provides the conclusion to the story: "The man who showed him mercy." Jesus' story did not define the neighbor. It created a neighbor.

Jesus' story puts a full stop for all time to all the variations on the question, "Who is my neighbor?" From that time and right down to the present, the question is, "Will I be a neighbor?" As Heinrich Greeven puts it, "One cannot define one's neighbor; one can only be a neighbor."[2]

* * *

Segment 5. The leading word, hovering silently but insistently, in this conversation between Jesus and the Bible scholar is a verb in the imperative: "love." That love command, although not repeated, reverberates continuously through the details of the conversation.

"Love" as a noun is a vast and complex subject. Philosophers and theologians write thousands upon thousands of pages exploring its

---

2. *Theological Dictionary of the New Testament*, ed. Gerhard Friedrich, trans. Geoffrey W. Bromiley, vol. 6 (Grand Rapids: Eerdmans, 1968), p. 317.

cultural expressions, its emotional intricacies, its psychological nuances. But there is surprisingly little of that sort of thing in our Scriptures. Love is not a subject to be discussed by our prophets and priests, our apostles and pastors, our praying-poets and our wise sages. The word is used as a noun often enough, but most significantly in our Scriptures it is as a verb that it springs into life. Not "God is love" but "God so loved the world. . . ."

The moment the noun "love" becomes a verb it ceases to be a subject to be discussed or understood or explored. It enters our lives. And when the verb is spoken in the imperative, it comes to life in an act of obedience. It goes into action, gets embedded in a story, and in the story reveals its true nature. Used as a verb in a story, it very soon becomes apparent whether the noble and glory-resonating word is being used to ennoble and glorify souls or is being used as a cover for manipulative greed, cynical power, or depersonalizing lust in a world emptied of neighbors.

Jesus speaks the final and definitive words in this story, both of them verbs in the imperative: *"go . . . do."*

No more questions. No more answers. No more godtalk. Go and love. No more detached discussions of Scripture interpretation, no more using religion (or Jesus!) as a way to avoid or dismiss the actual men and women who are in our lives. Something is going on, and I am told that I can get in on it. No, I am in fact told, *"Get in on it!"*

Stories do that: create the imaginative conditions in which we intuit an imperative command to leave the slovenly world of detached and impersonal discussions and become obedient participants in life, obedient followers of Jesus, neighbors to everyone we meet on our way to Jerusalem.

We are curious. Did the Bible scholar become a neighbor and "go and do" the love command that he knew so well? We don't get an answer to that question. We only get to know our own responses and our own stories.

CHAPTER 3

The Friend: Luke 11:1-13

Life is personal. By definition. All parts of it: language, work, friends, family, flowers and vegetables, rocks and hills, Father, Son, and Holy Spirit — the works. When any part of life is abstracted from the particular, formulated into a generalization, bureaucratized into a project, reduced to a cause, life itself is killed, or at least diminished considerably. When any one of us quits being personally present to our child, our spouse, or our friend, life leaks out. A failure to be hospitable to a stranger blocks life. A withdrawal of attention from a conversation breaks the flow of life. Habitual indifference to the glory of a dogwood in blossom disrupts the intricate, underlying creation-congruities that deepen participation in glory, living in and to the glory of God.

Jesus is our primary witness to the primacy of the personal: "I came that they may have life, and have it abundantly" (John 10:10) — not bare survival rations but extravagance, *perisson.* Jesus is our primary revelation that God is personal, extravagantly personal. When we deal with God, we are not dealing with a spiritual principle, a religious idea, an ethical cause, or a mystical feeling. We are dealing personally with Jesus, who is dealing personally with us. Everything we know about God we know through and by means of Jesus. And Jesus is nothing if not personal — a living body and soul, who eats bread and fish and drinks water and wine. Jesus speaks and listens. Jesus is born into a family whose names we know, and he has a personal name, a name that was as common in his culture as Bill and Jane are in ours. Jesus weeps. Jesus gets angry. Jesus touches and is touched. Jesus bleeds when he is cut. Jesus dies. Jesus is totally at home in his body and with his family, at home with us in our bodily-ness and our families. He is not abstracted from any of it; he is not isolated in any detail. He is present totally, relationally, intimately.

What the biblical revelation tells us, a revelation that is summed up and completed in Jesus, is that we can't become more like Jesus (more pleasing or acceptable to God) by becoming less human, less physical, less emotional, less involved with our families, less associated with socially or morally undesirable people. We don't become more spiritual by becoming less human.

*   *   *

Jesus' first story in the Travel Narrative creates neighbors of us all, neighbors to men and women we never had any idea were our neighbors. We had no idea they were our neighbors because we used language to stereotype them into bloodless cardboard caricatures — "Samaritan," for instance, or some other ethnic or racial, moral or religious term of dismissal. Once we have dehumanized them by a simple trick of language, it doesn't even occur to us to love them. How can you love a piece of cardboard? Obeying God's command to love our neighbors is made far more manageable when most of the people we don't know or like are excluded from the command. Jesus' story re-humanizes, re-personalizes, re-*neighbors* us and everyone we meet. Having become a neighbor through Jesus' story, we find another neighbor to love at every turn of the road.

The second story in the Travel Narrative brings God into personal focus. We depersonalize people by stereotyping them. We depersonalize God by generalizing him — God as an idea, God as a force, God as a dogma. But since we can't love an idea or a force or a dogma, we effectively remove love from the biblical command "Love God" and replace it with verbs such as "acknowledge," "respect," "consider," "defend," "study" — all verbs that require little, if any, personal relationship.

So Luke, as he composes his Travel Narrative, recounts a Jesus story that does for a depersonalized God what the Samaritan story did for all our depersonalized neighbors. Jesus immerses us in a way of language that keeps us thoroughly and absolutely personal in our approach to God, which is to say, in our prayers.

Prayer may well be the single aspect of our language most in danger of losing touch with the sheer grittiness of our humanity. We lose touch with our humanity when we deprive God of his humanity. Children pray in spontaneous honesty. Catastrophe and crisis very often take us to the bedrock of our humanity, where our language is purged of pretense and piety and we pray from the gut. But apart from childhood and crisis, while we are on the road through the secular Samaritan ordinary, our prayers have a way of being abstracted from the homely and distinctive details that are part and parcel of our ordinary and daily life. Prayer more often than not is practiced in religiously defined and protected settings, Galilee and Jerusalem. And more often than not it is formulated in pious clichés picked up hanging around churches or borrowed from prayer books.

But there is nothing clichéd or borrowed in Jesus' story. Jesus tells this story to get us immediately and personally present to our God in the same way that his earlier story did with our neighbor.

> One day he was praying in a certain place. When he finished, one of his disciples said, "Master, teach us to pray just as John taught his disciples."
> So he said, "When you pray, say,
>
> Father,
> Reveal who you are.
> Set the world right.
> Keep us alive with three square meals.
> Keep us forgiven with you and forgiving others.
> Keep us safe from ourselves and the Devil."

Then he said, "Imagine what would happen if you went to a friend in the middle of the night and said, 'Friend, lend me three loaves of bread. An old friend traveling through just showed up, and I don't have a thing on hand.'

"The friend answers from his bed, 'Don't bother me. The door's locked; my children are all down for the night; I can't get up to give you anything.'

"But let me tell you, even if he won't get up because he's a friend, if you stand your ground, knocking and waking all the neighbors, he'll finally get up and get you whatever you need.

"Here's what I'm saying:

Ask and you'll get;
Seek and you'll find;
Knock and the door will open.

"Don't bargain with God. Be direct. Ask for what you need. This is not a cat-and-mouse, hide-and-seek game we're in. If your little boy asks for a serving of fish, do you scare him with a live snake on his plate? If your little girl asks for an egg, do you trick her with a spider? As bad as you are, you wouldn't think of such a thing — you're at least decent to your own children. And don't you think the Father who conceived you in love will give the Holy Spirit when you ask him?" (Luke 11:1-13 *The Message*)

*   *   *

The story is told in circumstances in which Jesus has been praying, and his disciples ask him, "Lord, teach us to pray" (Luke 11:1). Jesus responds by giving them a brief prayer and then telling a story.

This is the only time in the Gospels that the disciples ask to be taught, the only time that Jesus is addressed by his disciples in the verbal imperative: "teach us." Jesus taught daily. He taught in field and synagogue and temple. The disciples for a considerable time through the Galilean years have observed Jesus praying. Now they ask, "teach *us.*" They have had the introductory courses in living Jesus' way and are now eligible for an upper-level elective. And what do they choose? Prayer. "Teach us to pray."

Is this not significant? They don't ask to be taught better behavior — no petition here for a course on ethics. They don't ask to be taught to think more accurately about God — no request here for a seminar in theology. They don't ask for a course in strategic planning for bringing in the kingdom. They have been living with Jesus for something like three years, watching what he does and listening to what he says. Somehow they have come to the realization that following him does not mean imitating what he does nor repeating what he says. It means cultivating a relation with God the way they observe Jesus doing it. They want to work out of the God-personal, God-relational, God-love-fueled center the way they have seen Jesus doing it. They want instruction and training in this source action, in this most deeply human and humanizing act. They want to do well what Jesus does best: "Teach us to pray."

Jesus responds by giving them a brief model prayer, telling a simple parable, and then connecting the prayer and the parable with some comments about parents and children so that the prayer and parable cross-fertilize. The comments get our imaginative juices flowing. And then Jesus steps back and lets the prayer and parable do their work in us.

*   *   *

The model prayer that Jesus gives them is surprisingly, maybe even insultingly, brief. They ask to be taught to pray. They have sifted through the possibilities of what they want from Jesus. They have narrowed the options down to this one request, teach us to pray. They have arrived at the heart of the matter and are motivated to engage in this central action that undergirds and shapes and motivates Jesus' life. They sign up and assemble. Jesus begins to teach. He has barely started before he is finished. The prayer he teaches them is composed of thirty-eight words. Prayed slowly and meditatively it takes a mere twenty-two seconds. And then it's over. Class dismissed.

What is going on here? They thought they had signed up for a graduate-level seminar on prayer, and suddenly they are out on the streets again without so much as cracking a book or getting a definition written down. If any had had pencils poised and ready, they would have had, at best, a page of notes.

But there is no sense of surprise expressed in the text as we have it, no evidence that the disciples felt shortchanged. Maybe it is our ideas of teaching that are deficient. And especially teaching on prayer.

Uninstructed by Jesus, our idea of teaching is dominated by explanations. When we go to school we expect to get things defined, have them explained, acquire a lot of information that we can put to use. We are taught to read, taught to count, and then tested on what we are taught by being asked to repeat it back. The more complex the subject matter, the longer it takes to learn it.

But this is, properly speaking, not education but schooling. The things that matter most to us are not learned this way, things like walking, for instance, and speaking. And loving and hoping and believing. We require teachers for these complex and wonderful tasks but not schools, not explanations, not definitions. We need to be around the people who do it, who are engaged in the action and are a little ahead of us in the process, but we would never think of going to school to be instructed in them. That would be like going to school to learn how to ride a bicycle, a school in which we never saw or even touched a bicycle.

Frequenting a place of worship is a good way to learn to pray; attending a workshop on prayer is not. Associating with a person who you know prays is a good way to learn to pray (whether you talk about prayer or not); reading another book on prayer is not. Praying requires these kinds of education and can be acquired only through this kind of teaching, the kind of teaching at which Jesus is the master. And for right now, looking with curiosity and wonder at this prayer/parable/comment sequence in the words and presence of Jesus in St. Luke's Travel Narrative is a good way to learn prayer.

*　　*　　*

The prayer/parable/comment combination makes it clear that prayer is personal speech. The prayer model begins with a vocative noun, "Father" — focused personal address. And the parable begins with a vocative noun, "Friend" — focused personal address. These vocatives insist on direct personal address, not "to whom it may concern," not a call to prayer by means of a mass-produced flier. The comments that follow use a conversation between a child and parent to emphasize the personal dimensions of prayer. The final comment returns to the Father that launched the prayer model, but this time it is "heavenly Father." The first word in the prayer is "Father," the last line in the parable features "Father."

The prayer/parable combination, each opening with vocative nouns — "Father!" "Friend!" — trains us in personal direct address. A vocative is not general address. It targets a particular person in order to give a personal message. The vocative emphasis on the personal is extended by the use of verbs in the imperative. Each verb in the prayer is voiced in the imperative, five of them: *hallowed, come, give, forgive, bring not* (I am using the more familiar RSV translation of the prayer now). Another five verbs in the imperative dominate the parable: *lend me*, don't *bother* me, followed up by *ask, seek, knock*. Imperatives are commands or orders from one person to another. They are addressed by one person to another person and anticipate a personal response. These imperatives are supplemented by the references to the child who asks his parent for a piece of fish or an egg, an asking that implies a verb originally in the imperative.

Imperatives are verbs that connect persons in such a way that the way things are gets changed. Something comes into being that is not now in being. As a form of speech, instead of describing what is, or supposing that something might or might not be the way it is, it reaches into the future so that something new can take place. The imperative has no time for impersonal language — magical incantation, for instance, or technological propaganda, or programmatic manipulation.

Jesus teaches us to pray. By using nouns in the vocative and verbs in the imperative he gets us involved personally in the action of the God who acts personally in our lives. Prayer is action. Prayer is not a passive giving in to the way things are. There are many other dimensions to prayer, to be sure, and we will learn about them soon enough.[1] But this is where we begin. This is where Jesus begins.

Jesus deepens our sense of the personal in prayer by using the terms "Father" and "friend." "Father" and "friend" are designations that exclude the impersonal. The dynamics of prayer as personal are developed in parabolic detail in the story of the friend coming to his friend at midnight and asking for three loaves of bread so that he can receive another friend hospitably. The term "friend" is used to refer to each person in the story: the friend in bed who is being asked for the bread (v. 5), the friend who arrives hungry at midnight (v. 6), and the friend who asks for the bread (v. 8). Everyone in the story is designated "friend." Three friends.

Not everything in the story goes smoothly just because they are all friends. The friend in bed disclaims friendship initially before submitting to its claims. But everything that takes place takes place between friends and has a responsive, relational core to it. Our relation to fathers and friends is essentially personal. None of us is indifferent to fathers and friends. It makes no difference in this regard whether they treat us well or ill. However they treat us, we take it personally. Most of us spend our entire lives dealing with our fathers (and mothers) and friends, and these dealings are among the most profound we will ever have. Our identities and our developing characters are formed in personal relationship. We are biological, quite; we are psychological, true; we are political, yes; we are economic, certainly. But the foundation of all of this is the personal.

What this means is that prayer can be learned only in the vocabulary and grammar of personal relationship: Father! Friend! It can never be a matter of getting the right words in the right order. It can never be a matter of good behavior or proper disposition or skillful manipulation. It can never be a matter of acquiring some information about God or getting in touch with myself. It is a *relationship*, exclusively and unendingly personal. And so it is imperative that we watch our lan-

1. Part II of this book, "Jesus in His Prayers," will explore some of these many other dimensions of prayer.

guage, for the personal is constantly and increasingly in danger of suppression by the arrogant and blasphemous claims of technology, the very apotheosis of the impersonal.

*   *   *

And here is a detail that I find intriguing: bread holds a prominent place in both the prayer and the parable.

St. Luke's version of Jesus' model prayer is an edited version of what St. Matthew gives us. Jesus' prayer in Matthew is in the form of six petitions:

> Our Father in heaven,
> Hallowed be your name. (1st petition)
> Your kingdom come. (2nd petition)
> Your will be done,
>   on earth as it is in heaven. (3rd petition)
> Give us this day our daily bread. (4th petition)
> And forgive us our debts,
>   as we also have forgiven our debtors. (5th petition)
> And do not bring us to the time of trial,
>   but rescue us from the evil one. (6th petition)
> For the kingdom and the power and the glory are yours forever.
>   Amen.
>
> (Matt. 6:9-13)

Luke's edited version runs,

> Father, hallowed be your name. (1st petition)
> Your kingdom come. (2nd petition)
> Give us each day our daily bread (3rd petition)
> And forgive us our sins,
>   for we ourselves forgive everyone indebted to us.
>   (4th petition)
> And do not bring us to the time of trial. (5th petition)
>
> (Luke 11:2-4)

Luke shortens Matthew's version by deleting five items: a pronoun ("our"), two phrases ("in heaven" and "but rescue us from the evil one"), the third petition ("your will be done, on earth as it is in heaven"), and the doxology ("for the kingdom and the power and the glory are yours forever. Amen").

Luke's deletions have two effects: they tighten the focus, and they bring bread into the center. Now we have a five-petition prayer. In a series of five, the third item, "Give us this day our daily bread," is at the center and therefore stands out just a little from the others. The centering of bread in the prayer as the third of five petitions corresponds to the prominence of bread in the parable, also identified with the number three ("three loaves of bread"). Bread is further emphasized in Jesus' commentary as he speaks of a son asking his parent for fish and an egg, which, like bread, are common and basic foods.

I don't want to claim too much in these observations, but might it not be that Luke is subtly but powerfully teaching something absolutely foundational to understanding and practicing prayer, namely, that prayer deals with what is basic to our humanity? It is not an add-on. It is not a "spiritual" accessory to be indulged after we have insured our physical survival.

Luke is an artist. His art is in his words. His teaching is artful. He is not explaining. He is not cheerleading. He is doing what Emily Dickinson, who probably learned it from Jesus, who was a master of indirection, advised when she wrote, "Tell it slant. . . ."

By means of Luke's art and Jesus' teaching we find ourselves immersed in the daily conditions in which our lives in Christ are formed and nurtured: give me bread, lend me three loaves, pass the fish. We are poor. We don't have what we need to live. We are dependent on the Father, the Friend, for the very basics.

Left to ourselves, we are very likely to suppose after we have gotten a decent-paying job, secured a place to live, and arranged for health insurance — taken care of these and any other earthly necessities — that it might be time to start dealing with God and make provisions for heaven. We take up the heavenly agenda by learning how to pray.

We open our Bibles to see what Jesus has to say about it. We happen on Luke 11. What do we find? Jesus facing us with our poverty, our need for what we cannot live without — bread. Jesus telling us to ask our Father for bread. Jesus telling us a story about our Friend who will most certainly give us bread. What are friends for if not to give us and our friends what we need?

*   *   *

A realization and embrace of our basic neediness, our poverty, is a necessary precondition for the employment of the imperatives in the prayer and the parable. If the imperative is issued from wealth, it is nothing but wanting more, stark religious or spiritual consumerism. We command God to give us what we want, not what we need, using prayer to raise our standard of living.

St. Paul tells us that Jesus Christ, the revelation of God become human, "set aside the privileges of deity and took on the status of a slave, became *human!* Having become human, he stayed human. It was an incredibly humbling process. He didn't claim special privileges. Instead, he lived a selfless, obedient life and then died a selfless, obedient death — and the worst kind of death at that: crucifixion" (Phil. 2:5-8 *The Message*). In other words, when God became man, revealing to us our sheer humanity, he didn't come in the form of a superhuman, but "experienced the poverty of human existence more deeply and more excruciatingly than any other man could."[2] He became absolutely poor and of no account: "a root out of dry ground . . . no form or comeliness . . . despised and rejected . . . we esteemed him not" (Isa. 53:2-3 RSV).

When God became human in Jesus, he showed us how to become complete human beings before him. We do it the way Jesus did it, by becoming absolutely needy and dependent on the Father. Only when we stand emptied, stand impoverished before God can we receive what only empty hands can receive. This is the poverty of spirit in which Jesus blesses us (Matt. 5:3). When we listen to and follow Je-

---

2. Johannes Baptist Metz, *Poverty of Spirit*, trans. John Drury (New York: Paulist Press, 1968), p. 18.

sus, who lived in continual dependence on his Father, we become convinced of our poverty as men and women. We realize our absolute neediness. We are all beggars. Father, give us bread. Friend, lend us three loaves. Being human means that we are the poorest and most incomplete of all creatures. Our needs are always beyond our capacities. Johannes Baptist Metz writes of the "radical indigence of our humanity" and the "transcendental neediness" at the core of our humanity.[3]

We do not become less needy, less dependent when we pray; we become more needy, more dependent — which is to say, more human. When we pray we dive ever more deeply into the very human condition from which sin alienates us and Christ saves us.

*   *   *

Jesus concludes his teaching on prayer with this: "If you then, who are evil, know how to give good gifts to your children, how much more will the heavenly Father give the Holy Spirit to those who ask him!" (Luke 11:13).

Holy Spirit? We thought we were asking for bread for ourselves and for our friend. We thought we were asking for a fish and eggs. And we were. We are. But by introducing the term "Holy Spirit" into the conversation, Jesus anchors our understanding of the words and ways of God in the details of each and every hour of each and every day. Holy Spirit is God's way of being personally with us in all our listening and speaking and acting. God in all the particulars of our lives and our friends' and neighbors' lives. God comprehensively and personally present.

---

3. Metz, *Poverty of Spirit*, pp. 28 and 30.

CHAPTER 4

The Barn Builder: Luke 12:13-21

A theological question from a Bible scholar regarding "eternal life" got Jesus started on a story about a man who helped a stranger he found on the road who had been robbed and beaten nearly to death by bandits. Later, a request for teaching on prayer from his disciples produced a Jesus story featuring a man asking his friend for bread to feed an unexpected visitor.

Why does Jesus answer questions about heaven and requests for teaching about prayer — classic *spiritual* concerns — with stories about a wounded stranger and a hungry drop-in guest? Maybe because Jesus notices that a lot of our talk about "the things of God" is a way of avoiding the personal presence of God in the hurt and hungry people we meet on the road to Jerusalem? Maybe because he knows that our fondness for discussions on matters of heaven and prayer is a diversion from having to deal personally with our family and friends in whom God is present? Maybe because Jesus is trying to wean us from chattering godtalk? Here's another story that follows a similar pattern as Jesus moves a conversation from the supposedly "spiritual" to the apparently mundane. An unnamed person steps out of the crowd and addresses Jesus with this: "Teacher, bid my brother divide the inheritance with me" (Luke 12:13).

The man, it seems, is being defrauded by his brother of his inheritance rights and asks Jesus to help in righting the wrong. Jesus refuses to help him, disclaiming authority to do it: "Friend, who set me to be a judge or arbitrator over you?" The question is obviously rhetorical, requiring a negative answer. No one has appointed Jesus as the judge or arbitrator in this man's family affairs. But we can't help but think, "Really?" Jesus' refusal strikes us as odd because we know that rabbis were, and still are, judges in the Jewish community.

The man's request is not out of line. And coming so soon after the prayer and parable on prayer, this is even more odd. Here is a man doing exactly what Jesus urged us to do: "Ask . . . seek . . . knock. . . ." The man is praying, and praying just as Jesus taught him to pray — using the personal vocative ("Teacher!") and using a verb in the imperative addressed personally to Jesus, which is to say, God (whether the man recognized Jesus as God or not). But the consequence of his prayer is an abrupt dismissal. So much for prayer as formula. The man is following to the letter Jesus' teaching to his disciples on prayer. If prayer is a matter of getting the correct grammar addressed to the right person, this man certainly would have gotten his way.

Jesus has just exercised some elementary spiritual discernment. He discerned in the petition for justice the underlying sin of covetousness. There is nothing in the text to indicate that the man was not, in fact, being defrauded. His rights were being violated. And it is certainly not God's will that any of our rights be trampled under foot by others. Justice is essential to the kingdom of God and passionately insisted upon by all the Hebrew prophets from Isaiah to Malachi, by John the Baptizer as he prepared the way for Jesus, and by Jesus himself. The pursuit of justice and the cry for justice have impressive biblical precedent. So, there is nothing technically wrong in what the man asks for. He is asking for the very justice that Amos and Isaiah and Jeremiah had taught him was foundational in God's kingdom.

But Jesus discerns in the request not a passion for justice but a virus sin, the sin of greed, of covetousness. There is nothing more common among those of us who hang out in the company of the men and women who follow Jesus than using what everyone agrees is a good thing and essential to the kingdom of God to disguise our sin. Those of us who have committed ourselves to following Jesus and being taught by him are not conspicuously liable to overt sin. We do not want to sin. We do not deliberately set ourselves in the way of evil. But our good intentions are no sure protection from the wiles of the devil, the seductions of the tempter. Nearly all the sins that we get drawn into are packaged as virtues. We think we are asking for or doing something that is biblical and true and right. And, in fact, we are. Just like this man out of the crowd who had only a day or two before been taught how to pray and was now doing what he had been taught: Give me justice!

Virtually every temptation that comes to those of us who are committed to Jesus and have thrown ourselves sacrificially into a life of following Jesus comes in the form of something right and necessary and obviously good. The devil doesn't waste his time tempting us to do something that we know is evil. He hides the evil in something good and then tempts us with the good. We have been well warned that the devil comes as an angel of light. Why do we continue to live in such naiveté? The old camp song has it right: "The devil is a liar and a conjuror too, and if you don't watch out he'll conjure you."

One of the wonders of the world is the rampant sin that flourishes to applause in Christian communities and organizations. Ambition and pride and avarice are uncritically given places of honor and then "supported" with a proof text and sealed with prayer.

Jesus is not an uncritical prayer-answerer. He has been through this before. Those forty days and nights of desert temptation allowed no room for naiveté in these matters. Everything that the devil put before Jesus was wrapped in Scripture packaging. Jesus was not tempted by the obvious evil but by the apparent good. He saw through it and stood fast. And now he sees through this man's so very correct prayer — and stands fast.

We tell lies with the same words that we use to tell the truth. Words not only can reveal; they can conceal. Language is the way of revelation, unveiling reality; it is also a way of velation, veiling reality. We can't be too careful in these matters. "Friend . . . take care!" Is a cry for justice in fact a whine for a bigger slice of the pie? Is a campaign against political corruption fueled mostly by anger? Does a proposal for evangelism mask an idolatrous obeisance to King Number? And that "vision statement" cobbled together in a late night committee meeting — examined under the light of day, might it turn out to be a blueprint for bloated ambition?

Was this man's request to Jesus in a matter of justice a smoke screen obscuring something quite different? Jesus thought it was. His story blew the smoke away.

> Someone out of the crowd said, "Teacher, order my brother to give me a fair share of the family inheritance."
>
> He replied, "Mister, what makes you think it's any of my business to be a judge or mediator for you?"
>
> Speaking to the people, he went on, "Take care! Protect yourself against the least bit of greed. Life is not defined by what you have, even when you have a lot."
>
> Then he told them this story: "The farm of a certain rich man produced a terrific crop. He talked to himself: 'What can I do? My barn isn't big enough for this harvest.' Then he said, 'Here's what I'll do: I'll tear down my barns and build bigger ones. Then I'll gather in all my grain and goods, and I'll say to myself, Self, you've done well! You've got it made and can now retire. Take it easy and have the time of your life!'
>
> "Just then God showed up and said, 'Fool! Tonight you die. And your barnful of goods — who gets it?'
>
> "That's what happens when you fill your barn with Self and not with God." (Luke 12:13-21 *The Message*)

*   *   *

The story that Jesus tells ignores the man's "rights" and skewers the man's greed. But the story does it by indirection. Will the man out of the crowd recognize himself in the story of the barn builder? If he does, it will require the exercise of his imagination. For a parable is not an explanation. A parable is not an illustration. We cannot look at a parable as a spectator and expect to get it. A parable does not make a thing easier; it makes it harder by requiring participation, by entering the story, in this case by taking on the role of the barn builder.

But by not forcing recognition, the parable preserves dignity. If the man asking for Jesus' help is not a farmer but at the same time is a fierce literalist, he will not recognize himself in the story. He enters into the story only on his own volition. God does not impose truth from without. The truth of God is not an alien invasion but a loving courtship. By telling a story out of the ordinary stuff of our common life — in this case building a bigger barn — Jesus makes common cause with us. Building a barn is normal work for a farmer. No one would ever think of it as a moral failure. No farmer was ever reprimanded by his pastor or put in jail by the sheriff for building a barn. The story about the barn builder doesn't condescendingly explain or paternalistically diagram or moralistically condemn. It just sits there, unobtrusively in our imaginations — and then comprehension filters in. Did the man in the crowd wait around long enough to get it? Or because it had never even occurred to him to ever build a barn did he impatiently walk away and continue to shop around the neighborhood for a rabbi who would take up his cause?

*   *   *

Several years ago I was conducting a seminar in the interpretation of Scripture in a theological seminary. It was a graduate seminar. Our topic that day was Jesus' parables. All the participants were experienced pastors and priests. One of the priests, Tony Byrnne, was a Jesuit missionary on sabbatical from twenty years at his post in Africa. As we discussed the biblical parables, Father Tony told us of his experience with his Africans, who loved storytelling, who loved parables. His Jesuit order didn't have enough priests to handle all the conversions that were taking place, and he was put in charge of recruiting laypersons to carry out the basic teaching and diaconal work.

When he first began the work, whenever he would find men who were especially bright he would pull them out of their village and send them to Rome or Dublin or Boston or New York for training. After a couple of years they would return and take up their tasks. But the villagers hated them and would have nothing to do with them. They called the returnee a *been-to* (pronounced *bean-to*): "He's *bean-to* London, he's *bean-to* Dublin, he's *bean-to* New York, he's *bean-to* Boston." They hated the *bean-to* because he no longer told stories. He gave explanations. He taught them doctrines. He gave them directions. He drew diagrams on a chalk board. The *bean-to* left all his stories in the wastebaskets of the libraries and lecture halls of Europe and America. The intimate and dignifying process of telling a parable had been sold for a mess of academic pottage. So, Father Byrnne told us, he quit the practice of sending the men off to those storyless schools.

* * *

It doesn't take us long to realize that we are set down in a world prodigious in wealth. The Creator is incredibly generous. We are given what we need but also much, much more. We are given not just a few trees to shade us from the sun but entire forests of pine and beech and oak. We are given not just a few stars so that we can locate North and navigate our ships but skies full of pictures and stories. We are given not just a few birds to keep the insects under control but a huge ballet company of shapes and colors and songs pirouetting and cutting arcs through the air for our endless delight. Annie Dillard exclaims over "the creator's exuberance . . . the extravagant landscape of the world, given, given with pizzazz, given in good measure, pressed down, shaken together and running over."[1]

This wealth is also interior. God does not barely save us, doling out just enough grace to get us across the threshold of heaven. He is lavish. We find ourselves in the middle of a way of life that has as one of its characteristic words *blessing*: "my cup runneth over!"

With all this wealth in and around us, who needs God other than in a conventional way, a beneficent figure to whom we are taught to give thanks, like children receiving gifts from their grandparents, to make sure that the gifts will keep coming?

1. Annie Dillard, *Pilgrim at Tinker Creek* (New York: Harper's Magazine Press, 1974), p. 146.

*　　*　　*

Greed is a nearly invisible sin, a tiny parasite that makes its home in the intestines of wealth. In previous cultures and former times greed, though not confined to the rich, seemed to find its ideal host in affluence and opulence. The myth of King Midas is the classic warning. But in America, with our astonishingly high standard of living and nearly unlimited access to consumer goods, we are all vulnerable. The Christian who learns to enjoy all the goods of this earth as gifts of God is no less vulnerable than the person who assumes that he deserves everything he has because of his hard work. We are rich. We have more than we need. The moment we are wealthy, whether in goods or in God, we are liable to greed.

There is no avoiding this condition of wealth, whether we conceive it as a spiritual blessing from God or the material results of a capitalist economy. And all the time the greed virus is in our bloodstream. Sometimes there are enough Scripture antibodies (commandments, proverbs, parables) to protect us against infection. But there are other times when our defenses are lowered and our whole system is fatigued. We get the fever and runny nose of greed. It isn't long before we're thinking about building a bigger barn.

We quit thinking of wealth as love to be shared and begin calculating it as power to be used. We reinterpret our wealth and position as something we are in charge of and others as the poor that we must organize and direct and guide. As we do it, it feels good. We are in charge. We don't need others. We are in control. We know more than others, have more experience. We are doing so much good! We need a bigger barn. In order to be more effective in our use of what we have we accumulate more, extend our influence. We become very busy doing good, because when we are very busy we don't have time for building the much more demanding and difficult personal relationships of love. Building barns, which is so obviously a good thing, doesn't leave much energy left over for the time-consuming work of loving our neighbors, let alone our God.

We are well warned by Jesus. All the same, building barns continues to be a growth industry among us, some of us as servants of the Lord, others of us as slaves of a capitalist economy, and others yet serving both masters. Our neighbors and pastors admire us (but not usually our families). We get promotions. And nobody notices that we are sick, sick with the covet parasite. The very people who ought to be taking us to the doctor are making us sicker than ever.

Many of the expositors who study and teach the Ten Commandments have noticed a parallel between the first and the last commandment. The first is "You shall have no other gods before me." The last is "You shall not covet." The first commandment establishes our lives before God in undiluted worship so that we can love him without compromise. The last commandment protects our friends and neighbors from being depersonalized into objects of greed, *things* that we can love without loving them. Just as idolatry results in a pollution of our love for God, so covetousness results in a pollution of our love for one another. If we keep the first commandment well and the last commandment well, all the commandments between are protected: love God, love your neighbor.

The parable of the barn builder is an exposé of greed: using what we have to get more instead of giving away more; using our position or goods as a means for getting impersonal power rather than giving away love. The story is a small pebble in our shoe that gets our attention the moment that our life of love for God and others begins to work itself into the manipulation of power over others.

All our wealth is grace-wealth. We are never power-wealthy, money-wealthy, influence-wealthy. We are love-wealthy.

In a lively sequence of colorful comments, Jesus drives home the ramifications of the parable.

"Don't fuss about what's on the table at mealtimes or if the clothes in your closet are in fashion. There is far more to your inner life than the food you put in your stomach, more to your outer appearance than the clothes you hang on your body. Look at the ravens, free and unfettered, not tied down to a job description, carefree in the care of God. And you count far more.

"Has anyone by fussing before the mirror ever gotten taller by so much as an inch? If fussing can't even do that, why fuss at all? Walk into the fields and look at the wildflowers. They don't fuss with their appearance — but have you ever seen color and design quite like it? . . . If God gives such attention to the wildflowers, most of them never even seen, don't you think he'll attend to you, take pride in you, do his best for you?

"What I'm trying to do here is get you to relax, not be so preoccupied with *getting* so you can respond to God's *giving*. People who don't know God and the way he works fuss over these things, but you know both God and how he works. Steep yourself in God-reality, God-initiative, God-provisions. You'll find all your everyday human concerns will be met. Don't be afraid of missing out. You're my dearest friends! The Father wants to give you the very kingdom itself.

"Be generous. Give to the poor. Get yourselves a bank that can't go bankrupt, a bank in heaven far from bankrobbers, safe from embezzlers, a bank you can bank on. It's obvious, isn't it? The place where your treasure is, is the place you will most want to be, and end up being." (Luke 12:22-34 *The Message*)

*   *   *

Poverty is the condition in which we do not have what we need to live adequately, to discover our urgent need for God, and so acquire energy to learn the language of prayer. Wealth is the opposite condition: we have far more than enough, and in the process of building a barn that can handle the "more than enough" our language is emasculated of the personal and relational. We lose our basic sense of neediness, *God*-neediness, and lose both interest and fluency in the language of prayer. In our preoccupation with bigger barns, we forget about asking for bread for our friend. But as this story sinks into our imagination, making plans for building a huge barn suddenly seems like pretty small potatoes compared to asking for three loaves of bread for a friend.

CHAPTER 5

Manure: Luke 13:6-9

Here is a Jesus story that is odd in the extreme. Luke drops it into the Samaria Travel Narrative cold. Unlike the stories of the neighbor, the friend, and the barn builder, this parable has no triggering incident, no context. It arrives on the page "after the order of Melchizedek . . . without father or mother or genealogy" (Heb. 5:10 and 7:3 RSV). If Jesus' fondness for parables is because of the verbal energy they create to involve us in his life, to bring us from the sidelines into the game as participants, what "game" is Jesus playing here that he wants us in on? No context is provided to guide us in interpretation.

The first parable, The Neighbor, creates neighbors of us all. Neighbor is not a definition but a "new creature." Life in the company of Jesus is not a discussion group but an act of becoming. The second parable, The Friend, prevents us from developing a special vocabulary and grammar for speaking with God that is different from the language we use in speaking with one another. Prayer, speaking and listening to God, is no more "spiritual" than the words and silence we employ to get along in the world and with one another. The way we talk in the company of Jesus is no different than the way we talk in the company of our friends. Or, to put it a little differently, if we talk in the company of our friends differently than we talk in the company of Jesus, we desecrate language. The third parable, The Barn Builder, is a

whistle-blowing story — a story that arrests us in the very act of artic-
ulating high-minded concerns as a cover for base sin. It is a story that
penetrates verbal camouflage and tells us to quit it. Deception is rife in
and around the company of Jesus: be well warned. But what about this
fourth parable? The story is brief.

> "A man had a fig tree planted in his front yard. He came to it ex-
> pecting to find figs but there weren't any. He said to his gardener,
> 'What's going on here? For three years now I've come to this tree
> expecting figs and not one fig have I found. Chop it down! Why
> waste good ground with it any longer?'
> "The gardener said, 'Let's give it another year. I'll loosen the
> ground and dig in manure. Maybe it will produce next year; if it
> doesn't, then chop it down.'" (Luke 13:6-9, my trans.)

*   *   *

The violence of the command "Chop it down!" is a clue to the context.
Following Jesus doesn't make for smooth sailing. Traveling with Jesus
through Samaria on the way to Jerusalem is not a parade led by a brass
band and cartwheeling cheerleaders. Suspicion and hostility are per-
vasive throughout this trip, so perhaps it doesn't matter where Luke inserts the story; almost any place on the journey would serve as a suit-
able context. There are going to be fig trees without figs — an offense
to any serious farmer — at every turn in the road. But Luke places it
early on, so that it can be working in our imaginations all through the
journey.

*   *   *

The first experience Jesus and his followers have as they set out on the
journey is a taste of crude Samaritan hostility. When they attempt to
find a place to stay for the night, the Samaritans let them know in no
uncertain terms that they are not welcome. The Zebedee brothers, the
"thunder brothers," are outraged and want to kill them on the spot

with supernatural fire. Jesus rebukes them. But it leaves a bad taste in their mouths.

A day or so later, Jesus lets them know that things aren't going to get any better. Don't be under any illusions, Jesus tells them, that people are going to receive either me or you with open arms: "Do you think that I have come to give peace to the earth? No, I tell you, but rather division!" (Luke 12:51).

Twice before setting out on the journey Jesus told his followers what they had to look forward to: in the days to come he will be rejected and killed (Luke 9:22, 44). So they are well warned. He tells them the same thing again just before arriving in Jerusalem (18:31-33). And, of course, as we know so well, the opposition and hostility do their work: Jesus is killed.

Jesus meets hostility at many turns in the road. Early in the journey he is accused of being in league with the devil: "Some of them said, 'He casts out demons by Beelzebul, the ruler of the demons'" (Luke 11:15). Samaritan country is not a friendly country. Differences over the meaning of God and the nature of the spiritual life erupt into violence more often than not. Religious wars are common and uncommonly bloody. The potential for violence provoked around Jesus is evident from the very beginning. So Luke makes sure that we pay attention to the response Jesus makes to violence ("Chop it down!") by placing a blunt, unadorned, uninterpreted Manure Story in the Samaria narrative.

*   *   *

Jesus is not a word in a book to be read and studied. He is not a word to be discussed. Jesus is the "Word made flesh." He is the living Word, a live voice, God's Word that took on human form and lived in an actual country, Palestine, in real time, the first century, and ate meals of bread and fish and wine with named people (Mary and Martha, Peter and Andrew, James and John, for a start). In order to respond rightly to this voice, this Word-made-flesh, we must listen and answer in our actual neighborhoods, while eating meals of tuna casserole and spinach salad, and in the company of people who know us and whose names we know (our spouses and children, friends and fellow workers, for a start). Nothing in general. Nobody anonymous. No disembodied or unvoiced words.

The Christian community and its leaders know this well. We know that without vigilance we can easily erode into faithlessness, drift into unthinking betrayal, lose this responsive, obedient, person-to-person, voiced relationship with Jesus and with one another. And so we are encouraged to develop a language of participation, of following, of listening with the intent of obeying, of being on guard against depersonalizing godtalk.

In the process we recognize how significant Jesus' parables are in keeping our language involved and participatory — not a language *about* but a language *with* — getting us in on and keeping us alert in acts of justice, loving kindness, and walking humbly with our God (Mic. 6:8). The parables are basic verbal defenses against disengaged complacency.

Parables release the adrenaline of urgency into our bloodstream. God is active in the world and our neighborhood. There is much to do. We are invited into the action. There is exhilaration in being in on the action, *God's* action. But there are other times when restraint is called for. There are occasions when not-doing is commanded, and more often than not it has to do with our intuitively violent response to hostility. Hostility provokes a swift succession of thoughts: "God's enemy is my enemy. I am on God's side. I am going to defend his cause and his honor with any weapon at hand." And of course words are always at hand. And then Jesus intervenes and says, "No."

Jesus' commands are energizing: "Repent and believe. . . . Follow me. . . . Go and do likewise. . . . When you pray, say. . . . Child, arise. . . . Put out into the deep and let down your nets. . . ." But sometimes his commands stop us in our tracks. It is as important not to do what Jesus forbids as it is to obey what he tells us to do — Jesus rebuking Peter: "Get behind me" and "Put your sword back into its sheath" (Mark 8:33 and John 18:11). And in this Manure Story, "Sir, let it alone. . . ."

Throughout our twenty-plus centuries the Christian community has achieved a broad consensus regarding Jesus' commands to his followers — not unanimous, to be sure, but considering the circumstances a surprising readiness to at least pay attention when he commands us to love God and love our neighbors. Even if not obeyed, the commands are not dismissed as of no account. But more often than not, Jesus' prohibitions are ignored. As in this parable, "Let it alone...." It is a strange thing, perhaps, but given a certain level of motivation and maturity it is easier to do things than to not do things. We want to be in on the action. We don't like being put on the sidelines. A yes is more congenial to our spirit than a no.

So much of the time it is not complacency that threatens but its opposite, impetuosity. We see something that is wrong, whether in the world or in the church, and we fly into action, righting the wrong, confronting sin and wickedness, battling the enemy, and then we go out vigorously recruiting "Christian soldiers."

Just then Jesus' Manure Story, long dormant in our imaginations, springs to life and does its work among us. Instead of goading us into action, it takes us out of the action. We have just come across something that offends us, some person who is useless to us or the kingdom of God, "taking up the ground," and we lose patience and either physically or verbally get rid of him or her. "Chop him down! Chop her down! Chop it down." We solve kingdom problems by amputation.

Internationally and historically, killing is the predominant method of choice to make the world a better place. It is the easiest, quickest, and most efficient way by far to clear the ground for someone or something with more promise. The Manure Story interrupts our noisy, aggressive problem-solving mission. In a quiet voice the parable says, "Hold on, not so fast. Wait a minute. Give me some more time. Let me put some manure on this tree." Manure?

*   *   *

Manure is not a quick fix. It has no immediate results — it is going to take a long time to see if it makes any difference. If it's results that we are after, chopping down a tree is just the thing: we clear the ground and make it ready for a fresh start. We love beginnings: birthing a baby, christening a ship, the first day on a new job, starting a war. But spreading manure carries none of that exhilaration. It is not dramatic work, not glamorous work, not work that gets anyone's admiring attention. Manure is a slow solution. Still, when it comes to doing something about what is wrong in the world, Jesus is best known for his fondness for the minute, the invisible, the quiet, the slow — yeast, salt, seeds, light. And manure.

Manure does not rank high in the world's economies. It is refuse. Garbage. We organize efficient and sometimes elaborate systems to collect it, haul it away, get it out of sight and smell. But the observant and wise know that this apparently dead and despised waste is teeming with life — enzymes, numerous microorganisms. It's the stuff of resurrection.

There are many things that we must not do, *cannot* do, if we are to be faithful to Jesus. Violence is high on the list — taking things into our own hands, getting rid of the offender along with the offense.

*   *   *

Jesus' parable contains a nugget of memory of what had been played out in history over seven hundred years earlier in this same Samaritan country through which Jesus was walking when he told this story. God's people were faced with invasion by the ruthless Assyrian conqueror Tiglath-Pileser III, who had set out to create a huge empire. As it turned out, he had an easy time of it in Palestine and took over most of its cities. In just a few years, two kings later (the year was 721 B.C.), Sargon II finished the job by destroying the northern capital, Samaria, and hauling off the cream of the population, 27,000 in number, deporting them to various sites in upper Mesopotamia, where they ultimately lost their identity. We never hear from them again.

It was the policy of the Assyrian kings at that time to replace the deported population with conquered peoples from other places who then mingled with whoever had been left behind. It was a brutal, heartless strategy designed to eradicate all traces of national sentiment capable of nurturing resistance. In the course of succeeding years, people deported from Babylon, Hamath, and other places (2 Kings 17:24) were brought in and resettled in Samaria. These foreigners brought their native customs and religions with them, and, together with others brought in still later, mingled with the surviving Israelite population. These are the people we know in the time of Jesus as the Samaritans, a mixed-blood people with a centuries-long accumulation of brutality and ignominy.

At the time of the Assyrian invasion of Samaria, Isaiah was preaching vigorously in Jerusalem that God's people must not meet sword with sword. They must not fight fire with fire. But they wouldn't listen. They "refused the waters of Shiloah that flow gently" (Isa. 8:5). George Adam Smith, the great Scottish pastor and scholar, summarized Isaiah's message at this time in the history of the Hebrew people like this: "We are not warriors but artists . . . after the fashion of Jesus Christ who came not to condemn . . . but to build life up to the image of God."[1]

When he saw the war party make preparations by getting war horses from Egypt, Isaiah warned them:

> Doom to those who go off to Egypt
>   thinking that horses can help them,
> Impressed by military mathematics,
>   awed by sheer numbers of chariots and riders —
> And to The Holy of Israel, not even a glance,
>   not so much as a prayer to GOD.
>
> (Isa. 31:1 *The Message*)

They were obsessed with getting horses. Isaiah countered with

> thus said the Lord GOD, the Holy One of Israel,
>   In returning and rest you shall be saved;
>   in quietness and in trust shall be your strength.
>
> (Isa. 30:15 NRSV)

1. Quoted by Brevard Childs, *The Struggle to Understand Isaiah as Christian Scripture* (Grand Rapids: Eerdmans, 2004), p. 287.

"Forget about cutting down the Assyrians. Let me handle the Assyrians." And then this:

> GOD's not finished. He's waiting around to be gracious to you.
>   He's gathering strength to show mercy to you.
> GOD takes the time to do everything right — everything.
>   Those who wait around for him are the lucky ones.
>
> (Isa. 30:18 The Message)

But Israel wouldn't listen. They had no patience with manure. Their response to the Assyrian threat was "Cut it down." In their impatience, both they and their witness to God's salvation were destroyed.

*　　*　　*

Manure. The Psalms are prayers worked into the soil of our lives to shape our imaginations and obedience so that we live our lives congruent with the way God works in the world and in us, works in a world of violence and antipathy without becoming violent. One of the most repeated sentences, repeated because we are so impatient to "cut it down and get on with it," is "O give thanks to the Lord for he is good; / His steadfast love endures forever" (Pss. 106:1; 107:1; 118:1; and others). His love never quits.

Manure. God is not in a hurry. We are repeatedly told to "Wait for the Lord." But that is not counsel that is readily accepted by followers of Jesus who have been conditioned by promises of instant gratification, whether American or Assyrian. Eugen Rosenstock-Huessy, one of our great modern Isaianic prophets who had extensive experience with violence in two World Wars, wrote, "The greatest temptation of our time is impatience, in its full original meaning: refusal to wait, undergo, suffer. We seem unwilling to pay the price of living with our fellows in creative and profound relationships."[2] Like Isaiah, he also was ignored.

---

2. Eugen Rosenstock-Huessy, *The Christian Future* (New York: Harper & Row, Torchbook Edition, 1966), p. 19 (first published in 1946).

Manure. Silence. Manure means reentering the conditions of "Let it be done to me," submitting to the silent energies that change death into life, the energies of resurrection. Language consists in equal parts of speaking and silence. The art of language requires skills in not speaking quite as much as skills in speaking. Much mischief and misunderstanding result from talking that is not embedded in much listening. When we listen we are silent. I like Saul Bellow's comment, "The more you keep your mouth shut, the more fertile you become."[3] Silence is the manure of resurrection.

God is a God who acts. We are constantly called on to pay attention to "his wonderful works to the children of men" (Ps. 107:31 KJV). But he is also the God who waits: "The Lord is not slow about his promise, as some think of slowness, but is patient with you, not wanting any to perish, but all to come to repentance" (2 Pet. 3:9). Even Samaritans? Even Samaritans. Anyone who spends any time at all walking through Samaria with Jesus simply must learn to put up with this slowness, "as some count slowness."

*   *   *

The Manure Story is free-floating throughout the journey through Samaria — as it is in the journey through America. It is ready for use whenever we come up against animosity, against antagonism and impetuous indignation and are prepared to counter the opposition with violence, whether verbal or physical. But the story comes to its most powerful and incisive expression in words Jesus spoke from the cross.

A few days after this story had entered the imaginations of the company of men and women who were following Jesus, Jesus entered Jerusalem. Before a week was out, he was hanging on the Golgotha cross.

Pilate and Caiaphas in an unholy alliance agreed that Jesus had to go: he was a threat to the precarious peace that the Roman army was trying to preserve. He was a threat to the highly profitable business

3. Saul Bellow, *It All Adds Up* (New York: Penguin Books, 1995), p. 310.

that Caiaphas and his Sadducean henchmen were running from the Jerusalem temple. He was "taking up the ground" needed for their own purposes. And so they killed him. They eliminated both him and his kingdom from this earth. Or so they thought. Jesus responded to their hostile violence with a word out of the Manure Story, this parable that he had told just a few days earlier on the road through Samaria. Hanging from the cross, Jesus' first words were a prayer: "Father, forgive them" (Luke 23:34).

Our translations obscure the identity of this word that Jesus prayed from the cross with Jesus' earlier word in the story of the Manure and the Fig Tree. The farmer's order, "Chop it down!" is echoed in the Holy Week "Crucify him!" Jesus' prayer to his Father, "Forgive them," is a verbatim repetition of the gardener's intervention, "Let it alone." The Greek word is *aphes.* In some contexts it means "Hands off. . . . Cool it. . . . Leave it alone. . . ." In other contexts having to do with sin and guilt it means "Forgive . . . Remit. . . ." It is the word used in the prayer Jesus taught us, "Forgive us our sins . . ." (Luke 11:4). Here the contexts of parable and prayer converge.

The violence intended for the fig tree is deflected by the gardener's "Let it alone." The violence visited on Jesus is countered by "Father, forgive them."[4]

For those of us who are up to our necks in manure, which is to say, up to our necks in forgiveness, it is perhaps important to note that the forgiveness Jesus prayed for us was not preceded by any confession or acknowledgment of wrongdoing by the crucifixion crowd or any of us since. Preemptive forgiveness. Jesus prays that we be forgiven before we have any idea that we even need it, "for they know not what they do." No preconditions. Amazing grace.

---

4. I owe this insight to an observation by William Willimon in *Thank God It's Friday* (Nashville: Abingdon Press, 2006), p. 7.

CHAPTER 6

Table Talk: Luke 14:1-14

It was 1982, the fourth day of our first trip to Israel. After our El Al flight landed at Lod, we took a bus to Haifa and spent a couple of days on Mount Carmel exploring Elijah country. Then we took a bus to the kibbutz Nof Ginnosar on the shores of Lake Galilee, where we planned to spend a week walking through the towns, hills, and fields of Galilee. We took a day to settle in and made plans for Nazareth. We arrived by bus early the next morning.

We spent the day in Nazareth looking for Jesus. We walked up and down the narrow streets, took in the market fragrances, entered the tiny synagogue. We saw him everywhere: Jesus, eight years old, kicking a soccer ball in the street; the three-month-old Jesus on a bench near a well, nursing at his mother's breast; children in a court-yard celebrating the birthday of Jesus at six years of age, sitting on a makeshift throne with a crown on his head, the friends dancing around him, singing and throwing confetti.

It was a good day, full of sights and smells that filled our imagina-tions with details that Matthew, Mark, Luke, and John had forgotten to give us. We waited on a bench for the bus back to the kibbutz. After a half hour or so, a taxi driver who had been cruising back and forth all the time we were there pulled over and asked us where we were going. We told him. He said he would take us. We declined, told him we would wait for the bus. We were on a tight budget. A taxi seemed like an unaffordable luxury. But when we had sat there for over an hour, the prospect of a bus steadily declining, the taxi driver pulled up again with his offer and we took it.

We had hoped to go the next day to the valley of Jezreel and some of the archeological sites in the area. I asked our driver how we could get there, where the bus routes went. He told me that he would take us — no buses went where we wanted to go. He presented the situation as hopeless, except for him. The price for the day seemed exorbitant, but we finally agreed. Conversation was amiable. His name was Sahil, a Palestinian born and raised in Nazareth. Another Jesus? He said he would pick us up at seven in the morning and would bring a picnic lunch for the three of us.

The next day, after strolling through the ruins of Bethshan, I wanted to find Shiloh, a little more than twenty-five miles further south. Sahil had never heard of it, but it would certainly be well marked and I thought we could find it. It wasn't well marked and we never did find it. And then it was time for the picnic lunch that Sahil brought. We pulled off into an open field and spread the lunch of cucumbers, tomatoes, and pita bread on the ground. A Bedouin leading a camel on a rope came by. He asked us for some food. Sahil without hesitation gave him well over half of what we had there on the ground. The man went on his way with his free and very generous lunch. I asked Sahil why he had given it to him, no questions asked — and so much!

"Muhammad commands it. A man is hungry, you feed him."
"And that's it?"
"That's it."

That was our introduction to Middle Eastern hospitality.

*   *   *

It didn't occur to me that day while we were being hosted at lunch by Sahil in that field somewhere in the vicinity of Shiloh and witnessing his hospitality to a stranger, not until I was writing this book in fact, that this was the same Samaritan country that had so rudely stone-walled Jesus and his disciples when they entered it on their way to Jerusalem. In contrast, our first experience in Samaria was of hospitality.

Samaritan inhospitality supplied the opening incident in the Samaria Travel Narrative that Luke composed. Perhaps it should not surprise us to find that hospitality is a prominent theme in the Travel Narrative metaphor that Luke uses to immerse us in a culture and among a people who don't share the assumptions and practices of Jesus.

Jesus taught in the synagogues and preached in the temple, but settings of hospitality seemed to be Jesus' venue of choice for dealing with kingdom matters. All the Gospel writers give us his table talk, but there is more of it in Luke, stories of Jesus in conversation at meals. The table is the focal point of hospitality in all cultures. Eating and talking go together. Luke makes the most of it.

Sometimes Jesus is host: feeding the five thousand (Luke 9:10-17), hosting the last supper (22:14-23). Sometimes he is the guest: at dinner at Levi's house (5:27-32), twice at supper with Pharisees (7:36-50 and 14:1-14), in the home of Mary and Martha (10:38-41), at the home of Zacchaeus (19:1-10), at the third resurrection appearance (24:36-43). And sometimes, as at the Emmaus supper, you can't tell the difference between host and guest (24:28-35).

And then there are the four hospitality stories that Jesus wove into his table talk. All occur in the Samaritan Travel Narrative: getting a meal together for the unexpected friend at midnight (Luke 11:5-8), the feast welcoming the prodigal (15:11-32), the Sabbath meal teaching on humility (14:1-14), the rude excuses to the great dinner invitation (14:15-24). The first three stories are unique to Luke, the fourth a variant telling of a story as Matthew gives it to us in his Gospel (22:1-10).

*   *   *

In the simple, everyday act of sitting down with others at meals, Jesus aroused enormous hostility. There were rigid ritual rules in the world Jesus lived in that were inviolable. Jesus violated them. There were strong prohibitions against eating with unsavory people — outsiders such as tax collectors, prostitutes, and people who didn't keep up the appearances of religious propriety ("sinners"). Jesus ate with them. As things developed, eating with "sinners" became one of the most characteristic and attention-getting facets of Jesus' regular activity. The Pharisees in particular were fierce in their observance of these rules and fierce in their criticism of Jesus.

At a meal with some of these Pharisees Jesus tells a hospitality story that turns the tables on his critics. His story is a stinging rebuke of the inhospitality of those on the frontlines of enforcing the hospitality codes of their culture.

*   *   *

One time when Jesus went for a Sabbath meal with one of the top leaders of the Pharisees, all the guests had their eyes on him, watching his every move. Right before him there was a man hugely swollen in his joints. So Jesus asked the religion scholars and Pharisees present, "Is it permitted to heal on the Sabbath? Yes or no?"

They were silent. So he took the man, healed him, and sent him on his way. Then he said, "Is there anyone here who, if a child or animal fell down a well, wouldn't rush to pull him out immediately, not asking whether or not it was the Sabbath?" They were stumped. There was nothing they could say to that.

He went on to tell a story to the guests around the table. Noticing how each had tried to elbow into the place of honor, he said, "When someone invites you to dinner, don't take the place of honor. Somebody more important than you might have been invited by the host. Then he'll come and call out in front of everybody, 'You're in the wrong place. The place of honor belongs to this man.' Red-faced, you'll have to make your way to the very last table, the only place left.

"When you're invited to dinner, go and sit at the last place. Then when the host comes he may very well say, 'Friend, come up to the front.' That will give the dinner guests something to talk about!

What I'm saying is, If you walk around with your nose in the air, you're going to end up flat on your face. But if you're content to be simply yourself, you will become more than yourself."

Then he turned to the host. "The next time you put on a dinner, don't just invite your friends and family and rich neighbors, the kind of people who will return the favor. Invite some people who never get invited out, the misfits from the wrong side of the tracks. You'll be — and experience — a blessing. They won't be able to return the favor, but the favor will be returned — oh, how it will be returned! — at the resurrection of God's people." (Luke 14:1-14 *The Message*)

*   *   *

Jesus is invited to a Sabbath meal by a leader of the Pharisees. Others, presumably all Pharisees except for Jesus, are also invited. We can easily imagine that having just worshiped together at the synagogue they are now walking to the leader's home for the celebrative Sabbath meal. They had all been called to worship God in the synagogue. They are now called to eat a meal together in the home of one of their leaders. Sabbath worship and Sabbath meal mirror each other — times of relaxed, joyful receptivity, receiving what God generously gives in creation and salvation, and now sharing that bounty with one another in the hospitality of a meal and good conversation.

Sabbath. A day to open our hearts and mouths and take it all in. We are needy creatures. We need food and drink, shelter and clothing. And God. None of us are sufficient to ourselves. We are plunged into this vast and intricate world of interdependencies and receive, receive, receive. Receive from generous breasts, from the Grand Tetons of nature and grace, from creation and covenant.

But it sometimes happens that as we find our way around the country of faith and acquire a few habits of discipleship, the sense of need begins to atrophy. We know our way around. We feel at home. We are no longer babes at the breast; we are grownups helping out, entrusted with a few responsibilities.

Unaware, we are in a perilous place: we are as dependent upon

God as ever, but our feelings of dependence are not as sharply experienced. We are now insiders, and day by day acquiring a feeling of competence. Is it possible to retain a raw appetite for righteousness while we are experiencing so many satisfactions? Are we like children engrossed in play who have to be called in to meals and refuse to come to the table because we aren't hungry?

The Pharisees accompanying Jesus to the Sabbath meal that day aren't thinking about the meal. They are engrossed in being Pharisees. They aren't hungry. The symbiotic relation of receiving life from God in worship and sharing life with one another at table has been broken.

They know about Jesus, and they know he is not one of them. His reputation has arrived ahead of him. When they leave the place of worship they forget about worship. They are preoccupied with what comes next. They are going to have to eat a meal with this man who has a reputation for eating with sinners, sinners who ignore Sabbath and never go to synagogue. Jesus probably has no idea of how to keep Sabbath properly. They are obsessively suspicious. Luke's phrase, "watching his every move," seethes with hostility. The conversation that Sabbath day as they walk from synagogue to dinner table is anything but congenial. They are not amiably discussing the Scripture readings or sermon. They are not relishing the freedom and spaciousness of this gift day of immersing themselves in God's goodness. They are watching Jesus for any infraction of the taboos clustered around Sabbath-keeping that will invalidate his teaching.

Jesus generously gives them what they are looking for. There is a man sitting beside the road who is "hugely swollen in his joints." The antique name for the condition is dropsy. Doctors now name it edema, the retention of water in the joints, making movement awkward and painful. Jesus asks them if it's okay to heal him. The Pharisees sense that they are being baited. They don't answer.

Jesus accepts their silence as permission. He heals the man and sends him on his way. He then exposes the silliness of their obsessive Sabbath policing by bringing them into the world of common sense: wouldn't they rescue a child from drowning in a well on the Sabbath? Or even an ox? They don't answer.

Jesus has asked them two questions. Is it lawful to heal on the Sabbath? Would you save a child from drowning on the Sabbath? The Pharisees have not answered either. Do they also have a rule against answering questions on the Sabbath?

*   *   *

The scene shifts: Jesus and the Pharisees are now sitting around a table eating the Sabbath meal to which they have been invited by their host. Jesus has just been treated with conspicuous rudeness on the road from the synagogue to the home where they are having dinner. And now, it seems, they are continuing their Sabbath rudeness with one another. Nobody is saying anything to anyone.

But Jesus observes that the actions of those at the table, both of guests and host, speak louder than words. The guests have been pushing and shoving for the place of honor at the table. The Sabbath meal, especially when it is at the home of one of the top leaders among the Pharisees, is a place where you can be recognized as an important person. The closer you are seated to the host, the more important you are. If you can snag a seat next to the host, you'll be the talk of the town that week.

But the host is no better than his guests. Jesus notices that everyone seated around that table is "important" in some way or another. That is probably why the competition to be noticed as *most* important, at least for that day, was so intense among them. The host has invited these particular guests because he has plans to use these "important" men. The guests assume that they are being honored by being invited to the Sabbath meal of this prominent Pharisee. In reality the host is cynically putting them under obligation. In their vanity over being invited and their zeal to be "most honorable," they don't notice the host's hidden agenda. He's a host who is not a host.

Jesus supplies all the table talk that day, supplies the words that fit their actions and makes a parable out of the occasion. He weaves their behavior into a scathing indictment of inhospitality: it is scandalously wrong to use a place of hospitality to promote oneself at the expense of others; it is insufferably wrong to use an occasion of hospitality to manipulate others. Hospitality is an exercise in humility: when we are guests we are in a position to receive. Hospitality is an exercise in generosity: when we are hosts we are in a position to give.

Jesus memorably scripts the collective actions of the guests and the host who have just desecrated this Sabbath meal and makes a parable of what has taken place. The Pharisees themselves, host and guests, are the parable, the Parable of Desecrated Sabbath Hospitality.

The practice of Sabbath hospitality that is all form and no content has just been used to destroy Sabbath hospitality. Will they hear the parable that they have become? It happens a lot: the practice of church that is all form and no content destroys a church; the practice of marriage that is all form and no content destroys a marriage; the practice of parenthood that is all form and no content destroys a family.

$$* \quad * \quad *$$

A Sabbath of inhospitality. Inhospitality to the unfortunate man with the swollen joints. Inhospitality among the guests. Inhospitality in the host. Preparing and sitting down at a meal is the most common and most congenial practice for engaging in openness, generosity, and receptivity. How does it happen that it so frequently becomes the opposite — like this dinner at the Pharisee's house?

It is important, I think, to keep our attention centered on the fact that the setting for this story is a Sabbath meal. Sabbath is the time set aside to do nothing so that we can receive everything, to set aside our anxious attempts to make ourselves useful, to set aside our tense restlessness, to set aside our media-satiated boredom. Sabbath is the time to receive silence and let it deepen into gratitude, to receive quiet into which forgotten faces and voices unobtrusively make themselves present, to receive the days of the just completed week and absorb the wonder and miracle still reverberating from each one, to receive our Lord's amazing grace.

But these strict Sabbath-keepers had their eyes first on Jesus to see what he was going to do, then on one another to see how they could take advantage of one another. They were betraying the Sabbath in the very act of "protecting" it.

Sabbath is one of the great gifts that God has given us. Every day of creation is "good" — good for receiving all that God has created, good for participating in the work of God, good for working in God's garden, good for naming and caring for what God has given, good for being a "helpmate" with and for another. But Sabbath is distinguished from the first six days of each week by being holy, a day set aside to be present to God, to assimilate and celebrate all the gifts of creation and salvation.

Sabbath is an actual day of the week. But it is also a sacrament of time extended into all settings of hospitality — most commonly breakfast, lunch, and dinner — times and places that are given to us to receive and assimilate and digest what we need to stay alive. We have received so much. We have so much to give. What are we going to do with it, with this largesse, with this bounty? "I will lift up the cup . . . !" (Ps. 116:13). Jesus' table talk at the dinner of Pharisees establishes a continuity between what we are freely given and receive in worship and what we freely give and receive at meals. His story brings us up short: worship is never just worship; meals are never just meals. Holiness permeates hospitality.

*   *   *

Jesus' parable keeps us alert to the lurking desecrations in Sabbath-hospitality, but also attentive to the possibilities, listening always for echoes of Jesus' table talk — the story he might make of *our* words and acts. We never know who is going to show up across the table from us, a host like Sahil or a guest like the traveler with the camel.

Benedict, the fourth-century founder of the monastic community at Monte Cassino in Italy, insisted that his monks always receive each guest as they would receive Christ. Benedictine hospitality has infiltrated communities of faith ever since.

Kathleen Norris tells a story said to originate in a Russian Orthodox monastery. An older monk tells a younger one: "I have finally learned to accept people as they are. Whatever they are in the world, a prostitute, a prime minister, it is all the same to me. But sometimes I see a stranger coming up the road and I say, 'Oh, Jesus Christ, is it you again?'"[1]

1. Kathleen Norris, *Dakota* (New York: Tichnor & Fields, 1993), p. 91.

CHAPTER 7

The Lost Brothers: Luke 15

When I was twenty-five years old and a graduate student in Baltimore, I entered Johns Hopkins Hospital for surgery on my knee. An old athletic injury, a torn cartilage in my knee, had recently been getting increasingly inconvenient and painful. I had put off tending to it for several years, but now I was having difficulty even getting across the street, and so I submitted to the verdict: surgery. The surgery involved a procedure that is done today with ease and almost no convalescence, but in those years there was an extensive incision and a painful recovery. The surgeon did his work with competence, fixed my knee, and left me with considerable pain that I was assured would diminish.

I was happy with the prospect of walking pain-free in a month or so. But then, while still in the hospital, I contracted a staphylococcus infection that nearly killed me. The knee healed within the prescribed month; the infection held on stubbornly for eighteen months. In those eighteen months I lost twenty of my 160 pounds under the assault of a series of boils up and down my back that put me in a league with Job. Every three or four days I would return to the hospital to have the boils lanced and treated. Job, indeed.

In the course of being treated for my infection, I learned a new word from my surgeon: *iatrogenic*. I became very fond of the word and used it every chance I got. Iatrogenic refers to a disease or illness that is contracted in the process of being treated by a physician. The physician treats you for one sickness, but the treatment, while healing you of that one sickness, makes you ill with another. *Iatros*, physician (or healer); *genic*, origin. So, *iatrogenic*, a disease or illness that originates in the process of being healed. The surgeon who was lancing my boils and binding up my wounds taught me the word. This word "iatrogenic," I thought, had a certain elegance. "Boils" was sodden and ugly in comparison. The pleasure of saying "iatrogenic" compensated somewhat for the pain from the boils.

Twenty years after my personal experience of an iatrogenic illness, Ivan Illich wrote a book on the alarming spread of iatrogenesis in North America. I came upon the book quite by chance. I remember wondering as I read it if I might be one of the few people in the country who didn't have to look up the word in a dictionary. Illich described iatrogenesis as an epidemic and used his book to substantiate his biting accusation that the medical establishment has become a major threat to the health of Americans.[1]

By this time I was a pastor. All that was left of those iatrogenic boils was an amused memory. But as I read Illich's book I became aware of something alarmingly similar in the American church that also qualifies as epidemic.

The Christian church is a Holy Spirit–formed community where salvation is proclaimed and sins forgiven; men and women are redefined by baptism in the company of Father, Son, and Holy Spirit; a life in Christ is formed; a eucharistic-shaped worship of God is enacted; and a holy life is practiced in a world of suffering, injustice, war, despair, addictions, and sin, both blatant and covert — a world at odds with both neighbor and God. It seems like quite a wonderful thing. It *is* a wonderful thing — all these people getting a taste of new life, Real Life, "ransomed, healed, restored, forgiven," and finding themselves participating in the holy operations of the Trinity.

But it doesn't take long for those of us who are in on this to realize that this new life isn't a finished life but a life in process. Many of

---

1. Ivan Illich, *Medical Nemesis* (New York: Random House, 1976).

us are slow learners. Many of us hang on to selfish immaturities for as long as we can, unwilling to grow up. Others of us slip back into old habits of disobedience as we look for shortcuts to holiness. Still others experiment with ways in which we attempt to stay in control of our lives and manipulate God to do for us what we can't do for ourselves. Not a few of us keep trying to find a way to deal with God without having to pay attention to our neighbors. When we take a good, long look at any congregation we see that most of the spiritual sins, moral and emotional, and the social disorders rampant in the general population continue to make their way, sometimes even flourish, among the elect.

This is common knowledge. We all experience it. That is why a corporate confession of sin is standard practice when Christians gather to worship. The language is blunt with no wiggle room: "we have erred and strayed from thy ways like lost sheep . . . we have left undone those things which we ought to have done; and we have done those things which we ought not to have done; and there is no health in us. . . . O Lord, have mercy upon us miserable offenders."[2]

"Miserable offenders" is subjected to a great deal of creative editing by our contemporaries, but if anything it is an understatement. Variations on this basic prayer of confession of sins occur in virtually all Christian congregations, at least until recently. It keeps us honest. It prevents idealizing or romanticizing or prematurely canonizing our fellow Christians into plastic saints. It prevents disillusionment when we discover that the man or woman that we have been "passing the

---

2. The complete prayer: "Almighty and merciful Father; We have erred, and strayed from thy ways like lost sheep. We have followed too much the devices and desires of our own hearts. We have offended against thy holy laws. We have left undone those things which we ought to have done; And we have done those things which we ought not to have done; And there is no health in us. But thou, O Lord, have mercy upon us miserable offenders. Spare thou those, O God, who confess their faults. Restore thou those who are penitent; According to thy promises declared unto mankind in Christ Jesus our Lord. And grant, O most merciful Father, for his sake; That we may hereafter live a godly, righteous, and sober life. To the glory of thy holy Name. Amen." *Book of Common Prayer* of the Episcopal Church in the USA.

peace" to for years is an adulterer or an embezzler. Every sin that originates outside the congregation, sooner or later, shows up within it.

But there is one form of sin that flourishes in religious communities in ways hardly possible outside of them — it *begins* in places of
worship. Religious communities provide the conditions for this spiritual disorder, this *sin,* far in excess to what is provided in the secularized world. The common name for the sin is self-righteousness. In order to take root it requires the soil of a community in which
righteousness is honored and pursued. Without a community in
which righteous ways are practiced, self-righteousness would not be
possible.

At the time when Illich was noticing that the medical establishment constituted a serious threat to the physical health of Americans, I
was taking up my work as a pastor and noticing what I had never taken
seriously before — that the religious establishment in which I now had
responsibilities constituted a serious threat to the Christian faith in the
form of self-righteousness. I was noticing that, unlike the sins that are
commonly noticed and repented of by a worshiping congregation,
self-righteousness is almost never recognized in the mirror. Occasionally in someone else, never in me.

This phenomenon is so common, so damaging, so unnoticed
much of the time, and therefore unremarked other than in its stereotyped cartoon forms, I thought it required a special naming,
"eusebeigenic," to call attention to it. I am forming the word on analogy with the medical term, "iatrogenic." The Greek word *eusebeia*
means godly, reverent, devout. It describes a person who is living a
godly life, full of faith and obedient before our Lord: *righteous.* It is always used in a positive way in Scripture.

But here's the thing: these people who are characterized by
eusebeia are in a position to sin and cause others to sin in ways that
non-*eusebeia* people — the people who couldn't care less about righteousness but are unapologetically out for more money, more pleasure, better sex, and a secure retirement — can't do. In other words,
there are some sins simply not accessible to the non-Christian, the person outside the faith. Only men and women who become Christians

are capable of and have the opportunity for some sins, with self-righteousness at the top of the list. Both capacity and opportunity for self-righteousness expand exponentially when we become openly professed Christians living in what we have all been told is a Christian country.

But since self-righteousness has become a shopworn cliché and rarely provokes self-recognition, we need all the help we can get to see how it works and how easily we can get infected inadvertently. Following the lead of Illich and his diagnosis of the iatrogenesis that is plaguing our health-care system, I propose the term "eusebeigenesis" to call attention to and sound the alarm regarding this so often socially approved sin in the Christian community.

The best protection against eusebeigenic sin is an acute awareness of our lost condition in which we so desperately and at all times need a Savior. But that is a difficult awareness to maintain when we walk into our workplace in a fresh cotton dress or a coat and tie and are greeted with "Good morning, pastor," or "Nice to see you, doctor," or "I just read your latest book, professor — you sure got it all together in that one." How do we cultivate a sharply imagined realization of "nothing in my hand I bring, only to the cross I cling" while in the other hand we are carrying our university diploma or Sunday school lesson plan or latest job assignment to lead a mission trip to Zimbabwe? After all, we are *Christians,* with credentials as Christ's chosen witnesses!

Eusebeigenic sin is difficult to detect because the sin is always embedded in words and acts that have every appearance of being righteous, *eusebēs* — godly, devout (in Hebrew, *tzadik*). Just as iatrogenic illness is most frequently picked up in a place of healing, a hospital or clinic or physician's office, eusebeigenic sin is most often picked up in a place associated with righteousness, a church or Bible study or prayer meeting.

*   *   *

Jesus tells a story, one of his very best, that involves us in a self-recognition of self-righteousness, the eusebeigenic sin we more or less innocently pick up by going to church. The story is artfully constructed and does its work by astonishing us with the fact that we are, in fact, lost. Knowing and meditating on this story is both cure and defense against self-righteousness.

Luke places the story at almost the exact center of his Samaria Travel Narrative, highlighting its central importance to those of us who are following Jesus to Jerusalem. Here's the story:

By this time a lot of men and women of doubtful reputation were hanging around Jesus, listening intently. The Pharisees and religion scholars were not pleased, not at all pleased. They growled, "He takes in sinners and eats meals with them, treating them like old friends." Their grumbling triggered this story.

"Suppose one of you had a hundred sheep and lost one. Wouldn't you leave the ninety-nine in the wilderness and go after the lost one until you found it? When found, you can be sure you would put it across your shoulders, rejoicing, and when you got home call in your friends and neighbors, saying, 'Celebrate with me! I've found my lost sheep!' Count on it — there's more joy in heaven over one sinner's rescued life than over ninety-nine good people in no need of rescue.

"Or imagine a woman who has ten coins and loses one. Won't she light a lamp and scour the house, looking in every nook and cranny until she finds it? And when she finds it you can be sure she'll call her friends and neighbors: 'Celebrate with me! I found my lost coin!' Count on it — that's the kind of party God's angels throw every time one lost soul turns to God."

Then he said, "There was once a man who had two sons. The younger said to his father, 'Father, I want right now what's coming to me.'

"So the father divided the property between them. It wasn't long before the younger son packed his bags and left for a distant country. There, undisciplined and dissipated, he wasted everything he had. After he had gone through all his money, there was a bad famine all through that country and he began to hurt. He signed on with a citizen there who assigned him to his fields to slop the pigs. He was so hungry he would have eaten the corncobs in the pig slop, but no one would give him any.

"That brought him to his senses. He said, 'All those farmhands working for my father sit down to three meals a day, and here I am starving to death. I'm going back to my father. I'll say to him, Father, I've sinned against God, I've sinned before you; I don't deserve to be called your son. Take me on as a hired hand.' He got right up and went home to his father.

"When he was still a long way off, his father saw him. His heart pounding, he ran out, embraced him, and kissed him. The son started his speech: 'Father, I've sinned against God, I've sinned before you. I don't deserve to be called your son ever again.'

"But the father wasn't listening. He was calling to the servants, 'Quick. Bring a clean set of clothes and dress him. Put the family ring on his finger and sandals on his feet. Then get a grain-fed heifer and roast it. We're going to feast! We're going to have a wonderful time! My son is here — given up for dead and now alive! Given up for lost and now found!' And they began to have a wonderful time.

"All this time his older son was out in the field. When the day's work was done he came in. As he approached the house, he heard the music and dancing. Calling over one of the houseboys, he asked what was going on. He told him, 'Your brother came home. You father has ordered a feast — barbecued beef! — because he has him home safe and sound.'

"The older brother stalked off in an angry sulk and refused to join in. His father came out and tried to talk to him, but he wouldn't listen. The son said, 'Look how many years I've stayed here serving you, never giving you one moment of grief, but have you ever thrown a party for me and my friends? Then this son of yours who has thrown away your money on whores shows up and you go all out with a feast!'

"His father said, 'Son, you don't understand. You're with me all the time, and everything that is mine is yours — but this is a wonderful time, and we had to celebrate. This brother of yours was dead, and he's alive! He was lost, and he's found!'" (Luke 15 *The Message*)

The story is sparked by Pharisees and Bible scholars murmuring critically against Jesus. The people to whom Jesus is talking at the time on this trip through Samaria are outsiders to the world of faith, "tax collectors and sinners" (NRSV), unsavory, disreputable people. The religious insiders, the Pharisees and Bible scholars, who lived uprightly and responsibly, are offended. They grouse, "He takes in sinners, hobnobbing with them at meals, treating them like old friends." The righteous complain that Jesus is treating the unrighteous, the Samaritan riff-raff, courteously and hospitably. Their complaints trigger the story.

This is not an isolated incident but a well-documented habit of Jesus, this easy and welcoming demeanor to outsiders, the men and women who are characteristically excluded from the society, especially the religious society, of the well behaved. The verbs in the story are in the present tense, carrying the implication that this is what Jesus does all the time. He is on easy terms with these people who live on the edge of respectability, at least religious and moral respectability. It is no great surprise, then, that those present who live responsible and respectable lives might be provoked to indignant murmuring.

The Greek word for what they are doing is *diegongudzon*, "murmur" (RSV), "grumble" (NRSV), "mutter" (NIV). Luke is the only New Testament writer to use this word; he uses it again in 19:7 in a similar context to describe people's response to Jesus' hospitable treatment of Zacchaeus, the rich tax collector of Jericho.

When Luke uses a word that none of his Gospel-writing colleagues use, it's a good idea to take a second look. Of the four Gospel writers, Luke employs the most extensive vocabulary. He is also the one who is most at home in the Septuagint, the Greek translation of the Hebrew Bible, the standard translation used by the early church. He is forever making allusion by his choice of words to those old, foundational Hebrew stories. And he does it here: the word "murmur" is used first in the Bible in Exodus 15:24 and 16:2.

In this Exodus passage the Israelites have been delivered from Egypt and are on their way to Canaan. After the exhilarating Red Sea crossing, they run into some hard traveling in the wilderness. After six pretty rough weeks, "the whole congregation of the people of Israel murmured [*diegongudzen*] against Moses and Aaron in the wilderness, and said to them, 'Would that we had died by the hand of the LORD in the land of Egypt, when we sat by the fleshpots and ate bread to the full; for you have brought us out into this wilderness to kill this whole assembly with hunger'" (Exod. 16:2-3 RSV).

Is Luke calling our attention to the similarity of context here? I think he is. The people murmur against Moses because he has led them through dangerous, unmapped, and difficult territory. They don't know where they stand. There are no road signs. They are longing for the security and safety of Egyptian slavery. The people murmur against Jesus because he is leading them through the unfamiliar and hostile country of Samaria, this wilderness of disreputable heretics and sinners. They are longing for the security and safety of moralism.

I am making an assumption here that I won't insist upon but that is supported by the context: these Pharisees and Bible scholars are followers of Jesus; they have entered the way of discipleship; they are on the way to Jerusalem with Jesus. And now they are having second thoughts — they're not sure they want to be associated with these lost souls, this Samaritan rabble.

The people of Israel murmured not because they were bad and evil but because they were good and scared. The Pharisees and Bible scholars murmur not because they are bad but because they are good and scared. The murmurers in both cases are reverent and devout worshipers of God, delivered from pagan superstitions and following God's leader. Both sets of murmurers can be given the adjective *eusebeia*, godly, righteous. But now something is taking place that turns everything topsy-turvy. Their self-image, righteous, by which they define themselves, is suddenly erased. They are disoriented, lost. They don't like the feeling and so they murmur, *diegongudzon*. Understandably so.

This is what provokes perhaps Jesus' most famous parable. The

Pharisees and Bible scholars are murmuring, with Israel murmuring in the far background. In the midst of this murmuring, this grousing and grumbling, Jesus drops this parable.

*　　*　　*

Four mini-stories (not three, which is the usual count) compose this parable. And they are arranged in a spiral of intensification.

The first story counts one hundred sheep: one out of one hundred is lost. The shepherd goes looking for the lost sheep, finds it, brings it home, and calls to his friends and family to rejoice with him.

The second story counts ten coins: one out of the ten is lost and the housewife goes looking for it, finds it, and calls her friends and family to rejoice with her.

The third story counts two sons: one out of the two is lost and the father waits for his return. The son does return, and the father throws a party of celebration.

This third is more elaborate than the first two: it includes details of the getting lost (the leaving), the conditions of lostness, the feelings of a broken relationship, the drama of the finding (the homecoming). We are drawn into the depth and passion of the lostness. A lost person gets more attention than a lost animal or a lost thing. But another difference is that the father doesn't go out looking for the son in the same way that the shepherd looks for a sheep and the housewife looks for a coin. He doesn't go looking at all, but he is looking all the same for when the son is returning. The father sees him a long way off and runs out to greet and welcome him.

Apparently we don't go looking for a lost son (or person) in the same way that we look for an animal or a coin. Something other than aggressive energy is required. Something no less energetic, yet passive — passive energy. There are situations in which our passivities take precedence over our activities.

Waiting provides the time and space for others to get in on salvation. Waiting calls a time-out, puts us on the sidelines for a while so that we don't interfere with essential kingdom-of-God operations that we don't even know are going on. Not-doing involves a means of detaching my ego, my still immature understanding of the way God works comprehensively but without forcing his way, without coercion. The restraint of passivity allows for the quiet, mostly invisible complexities and intricacies that are characteristic of the Holy Spirit as he does his work in us, in the church, and in this world for whom Christ died. "Renunciation — the piercing virtue" is Emily Dickinson's phrase for it.[3] It couldn't have been easy for the father to not go out looking for his son the way the shepherd looked for his sheep and the woman looked for her coin. Not all lost sons and daughters and friends and "unsaved" can be found by calling out a search-and-rescue team. Discernments are required.[4]

*   *   *

The changing ratio of the numbers intensifies expectation: one out of a hundred, then one out of ten, then one out of two. In each case there is a successful recovery of what was dear but lost. In each case there is a call to celebration, a glad rejoicing.

These simple, artless stories do their work in us. We applaud. We can all identify with the everyday dramatics — a lost dog or cat, a misplaced ten dollar bill, a lost or runaway child. Anticipation deepens: one out of a hundred, one out of ten, one out of two. Shepherds, housewives, parents. We cheer along with the people in the stories.

Were the grumbling Pharisees and Bible scholars applauding? Of course they were. Who could keep indignation smoldering through such stories? These are people who have been through lost-and-found stuff all their lives. They know what it's like to look hard for what is lost and then find themselves in a celebration at the finding. Every time it happens they determine never to lose anything again. From now on

3. Emily Dickinson, *The Complete Poems*, ed. Thomas H. Johnson (Boston: Little, Brown and Company, 1960), p. 365.

4. Important discernments on the "divinisation of our activities" and the "divinisation of our passivities" are given by Teilhard de Chardin, *The Divine Milieu* (New York: Harper & Brothers, 1960).

they are going to play it safe. They are not going to be careless with their lives. They know where everything is — especially the things that have to do with God — with a place for everything and everything in its place. Pharisees are people who have it all together. And what they have together primarily is their religion. They may have lost things in the past but no more. They keep a careful eye on things now. They have things, life, together. They are righteous, *self*-righteous. They are the stereotypes of those who are not lost and don't lose things.

And so the Pharisees, who have been murmuring about Jesus and his careless ways, for a moment are caught up in these stories and are not murmuring. Their imaginations have been enlisted as participants in lost-and-found experiences they know something about. The Pharisees are applauding the finding of the sheep, the coin, the son. Who wouldn't be?

*   *   *

Then, with their self-righteous defenses down, Jesus slips in a fourth story. This is the story of another lost son. But this son is triply lost: lost to his father, lost to his brother, and lost to the celebrating community. A son who has never done anything conspicuously wrong, who has kept the rules, who has worked hard on the farm. And then this: the father, who has spent years waiting for the return of the younger son, immediately goes out looking for this son, finds him, and urges, pleads with him, to join the celebration. The verb is *parakalei*. It is a coming-alongside word. A wooing, inviting, welcoming, encouraging word that draws us into the singing and feasting and congratulating community of the lost and found. This is the verb associated primarily with the Holy Spirit, the Paraclete — God coming alongside us, drawing us into the community of the lost and found.

Jesus doesn't provide a conclusion to this fourth story. The first three stories are told with a similar structure and an identical ending: *lost* followed by *search* followed by *found* followed by *celebration*. The fourth story follows an identical structure: lost, search, found. But there is no closure, no celebration. We are not told whether the older brother lets himself be found and participates in the celebration. It is the same lost-and-found story but without an ending. A story without an ending invites the listener or reader to provide the ending.

Here is mine. In the steady accumulation of lost-and-found stories, each succeeding story tightens the focus: one out of a hundred, one out of ten, one out of two — now it is down to one. All eyes are on the one, the remaining lost brother. Jesus stops talking. Silence.

What becomes of this final lost one? Is Jesus not going to finish the story? The silence develops suspense. The silence becomes uncomfortable, and then unbearable, and, finally, seismic.

In a shock of recognition, one of the murmurers — a Pharisee? a Bible scholar? — gets it: "I'm the brother. This is *me!* And my lostness exceeds all the other lostnesses. I'm the one. And I'm found! The Father has found me."

And then another, and another, and another, as the tectonic plates shift deep beneath their feet. All that is left of self-righteousness is rubble.

One after another, the murmurers abandon their secure, self-defined, crowd-approved status as righteous and join the company of the lost and found. They finish Jesus' story in a celebration of friends and neighbors and angels. No more murmuring.

Now we get it. Jesus told the first three mini-stories "on the slant" in order to bring in this fourth story of a lost person who has long since lost any sense of being lost, to get past the self-perceptions of the insiders in congregations who never think of *our* selves as lost. Aren't we the ones who are out looking for the lost, or organizing things in such a way that no one and nothing will get lost?

*   *   *

Self-righteousness in large part consists in a denial of our lostness. It is eusebeigenic and spawns a multitude of sins. It is difficult to recognize it as sin because we picked it up in such a respectable place, in the company of Christians sitting in a church pew, singing hymns and reading the Bible, working "in Jesus' name." The reality, exposed by Jesus' earthquake story, is that Jesus is out looking for us. We are as lost as any wandering sheep, as any dropped coin, as any prodigal son.

For as long as we hold on to any pretense of having it all together we are prevented from deepening and maturing in the Christian faith. For as long as we avoid recognition of our lostness we are prevented from experiencing the elegant profundities of foundness. For as long as we insist on maintaining safe moral grids in which we always know where we stand (and where everyone else stands!), these poses of self-sufficiency, we disenfranchise ourselves from the company of the found sheep, the found coin, the two found brothers, and the celebrating angels.

Eusebeigenic sin can be prevented. It is as simple as it is difficult: lay our competencies and skills daily on the altar. Re-enter each day the condition of lostness in which our Savior comes looking and finds us "just as we are, without one plea," and restores us to his flock, his purse, his family, with all the angels in heaven rejoicing.

Everywhere and at all times we learn to submit to the conditions of Jesus' story and the counsel of wise guides in the Christian way who tell us that we cannot create righteousness by our activities or our moralisms but must continuously re-enter what Kierkegaard called "the preparing power of chaos," what John of the Cross called "the dark night of the soul," and an anonymous English writer named "the cloud of unknowing."

CHAPTER 8

The Rascal: Luke 16:1-9

Jesus' story of the lost brothers — the prodigal and his brother — ranks near the top of all-time favorites, told and retold down the generations. In contrast, the story that immediately follows takes the prize for being most ignored — or if not just ignored, dismissed outright. Its very unpopularity provides it with a certain distinction that compels our attention.

Scholars, although not all, consistently have trouble with it. Rudolf Bultmann, whom many consider to be the master commentator of the twentieth century, declared the parable to be incomprehensible.[1] But even if not incomprehensible, it is certainly odd.

Here's the story:

> Jesus said to his disciples, "There was once a rich man who had a manager. He got reports that the manager had been taking advantage of his position by running up huge personal expenses. So he called him in and said, 'What's this I hear about you? You're fired. And I want a complete audit of your books.'
>
> "The manager said to himself, 'What am I going to do? I've lost

1. Rudolf Bultmann, *The History of the Synoptic Tradition*, cited by Kenneth E. Bailey, *Poet and Peasant* and *Through Peasant Eyes*, combined edition (Grand Rapids: Eerdmans, 1983), p. 86.

my job as manager. I'm not strong enough for a laboring job, and I'm too proud to beg. . . . Ah, I've got a plan. Here's what I'll do . . . then when I'm turned out into the street, people will take me into their houses.'

"Then he went at it. One after another, he called in the people who were in debt to his master. He said to the first, 'How much do you owe my master?'

"He replied, 'A hundred jugs of olive oil.'

"The manager said, 'Here, take your bill, sit down here — quick now — write fifty.'

"To the next he said, 'And you, what do you owe?'

"He answered, 'A hundred sacks of wheat.'

"He said, 'Take your bill, write in eighty.'

"Now, here's a surprise: The master praised the crooked manager! And why? Because he knew how to look after himself. Streetwise people are smarter in this regard than law-abiding citizens. They are on constant alert, looking for angles, surviving by their wits. I want you to be smart in the same way — but for what is *right* — using every adversity to stimulate you to creative survival, to concentrate your attention on the bare essentials, so you'll live, really live, and not complacently just get by on good behavior." (Luke 16:1-9 *The Message*)

*   *   *

At first reading (or hearing) the two stories seem to come from different worlds. The story of the lost brothers and their patient and compassionate father touches emotions deep within us. A father with two sons, both of whom treat him wretchedly. The younger son does so in a calloused, cruel betrayal, the elder in a cold, crusty, rigid, standoffish self-righteousness. The father receives them both in a poignant, compassionate, all-embracing, reconciling welcome. We love this story. We can't get enough of it. Rembrandt's painting of the story moves us still. But the second story evokes none of this heart-wrenching, familial pathos in us.

Nevertheless there are striking similarities in the two stories. In Luke 15 the son throws himself on the mercy of his father. In Luke 16 the manager throws himself on the mercy of his master. Both son and manager are in desperate straits and have nothing to show for themselves except their wasted and misspent lives. One has made a mess of being a son; the other has made a mess of being a manager.

Both son and manager betray a trust. The core identity of each has been squandered and they have nothing to show for it. Neither prodigal nor rascal offers an excuse. No rationalization, no extenuating circumstance, nothing.

The word *diaskorpidzō* (Luke 15:13 and 16:1 — "squandered," "wasted," "scattered") is used at a critical place in both stories. Whatever draws us into these stories it is not moral achievement. These are not stories that goad us to good works.

The son and the manager both experience "amazing grace." The son is not banned from the family. The manager is not jailed. They do not reap what they sowed. They do not get what they deserve. After a lifetime of doing it wrong, they finally get it right. The son gets an extravagant party from his father. The manager gets a surprising commendation from his boss.

And in both stories there is no proper "ending." We are not told what the elder brother does. We are not told what happens to the manager. The missing ending clamors for an ending, a resolution. We the readers, the listeners, are pulled into participation in a world of grace. What do we do? Well, we don't do anything. It's not what we expect from having wronged a parent or boss, and it's not what we expect from a religious teacher. The stories leave us not with an agenda to do something to make up for whatever we have done wrong, but with an invitation to receive everything from One who wills our wholeness, our well-being.

*   *   *

I got my first insight into the significance of this story one day when I was approaching Johns Hopkins Hospital in Baltimore looking for a parking place. I was a pastor coming to visit a parishioner who had recently had surgery. There was no parking garage in sight. The street was lined with parked cars. I circled the hospital three times and no parking place opened up. I remembered that I had friends who in that situation always prayed for a spot and so thought I'd give it a try. I prayed for a parking place. Twenty feet ahead of me a car pulled out. I parked and locked my car. I was most pleased. Not only had I experienced a minor miracle on the streets of East Baltimore, but I also had a story that I could tell to my friends certifying me as an effective pray-er.

After an hour or so with my convalescent friend in his hospital room, I took the elevator down and returned to the street, reminiscing on the providential supply of a parking place — a first for me — and anticipating with relish telling the story to my friends . . . only to realize that I had locked my keys in the car. I stood there, helpless, looking at my keys dangling from the ignition within the locked car.

I was stumped, hands in my pockets, wondering what I could do. Just then a young boy, an African American about ten years of age, came up to me and said, "Something wrong, mister?" I said, "Yes. I locked my keys in my car." He said, "I can help you." He took a piece of wire out of his pocket and in thirty seconds or less had the door opened, reached in, and handed me my keys.

I said, "I'm sure glad that I was here when you showed up." He grinned and said, "Is it worth a dollar to you?" I reached for my wallet. I praised him, "A dollar? — it's worth two dollars!" and handed him the money.

As I drove away, this Jesus story that has puzzled and even scandalized so many generations of readers — a crooked manager praised for an act of dishonesty, a rascal commended for being a rascal — surfaced from my subconscious imagination. Wasn't this what I had just experienced, this street-wise boy of Baltimore's inner city, at ten years of age an old pro at entering locked cars and asking for whatever he could pick up for spending money, using his skill at picking locks to stay alive in that bare-bones environment, and now praised by me for employing his questionable expertise and prowess in creative survival?

And had I not been rudely awakened out of my pious reveries of a miracle-producing prayer and anticipating, with a touch of self-righteousness, the applause of my friends as they noticed my newly found powers of prayer? That street of hard, unplanned, inner-city realities — "Can I help, mister?" — was juxtaposed against my planned pastoral prayers and psalms in the hospital room.

*   *   *

A few years later, as I was reading a book, my insight into Jesus' story at that Johns Hopkins curbside was confirmed and deepened. The book was written by Kenneth Bailey, then a professor at the Near Eastern School of Theology in Beirut. He has spent his vocational lifetime in the Middle East (Lebanon, Egypt, Syria, Iraq, and Palestine), not only teaching in the classroom but also immersing himself in the languages and customs of the peasants, whose way of life maintained strong continuities with the first-century world of the New Testament. His familiarity with that peasant culture yields fresh and, in some cases, unique breakthroughs in receiving Jesus' parables. For me, and for many of my friends, he has become the master teacher of Jesus' parables. Our most comprehensive New Testament scholar, N. T. Wright, has commented that Bailey "has been eyes to the blind" for all of us who read Jesus' parables.[2] He did it for me with his reimagining of Luke 16, the story of the rascal, which "praises a scoundrel [and] has been an embarrassment to the Church at least since Julian the apostate used the parable to assert the inferiority of the Christian faith and its founder."[3]

Using his precise understanding of the culture that informs the text, Bailey teases out the folk, peasant traditions of the culture and observes that the manager is a rental estate manager and the debtors are farmers who pay their rent in kind (oil and wheat are mentioned). When the manager is found to have been embezzling some of the funds that he is responsible for, he is fired on the spot. He does not pro-

2. N. T. Wright, *Jesus and the Victory of God* (Minneapolis: Fortress Press, 1996), p. 129.

3. Bailey, *Poet and Peasant*, p. 86.

test his innocence. He is silent and makes no excuses. His silence is an admission of his guilt. He does not try to figure out a scheme to get his job back. He gives his full attention to what he will do next.

But in that silence he realizes something that is the key to understanding the story: he is fired but not punished. He is not required to pay back what he has embezzled. He is not jailed. In fact, he is not even scolded. Bailey summarizes the scene: "This servant has experienced two aspects of his master's nature. He is a master who expects obedience and acts in judgment on the disobedient servant. He is also a master who shows unusual mercy and generosity even to a dishonest steward. The thoughtful listener/reader of the parable would not miss either of these facts."[4]

So what will he do? He needs a job. He considers digging ditches and rejects that. He considers begging and rejects that. But who will hire him? His public image is in ruins. And then he comes up with a plan. But what is the plan? We are not told the plan — the silence builds dramatic tension.

This is Bailey's conjecture, a conjecture that fits both the peasant culture and the wider biblical context. The manager's plan "is to risk everything on the quality of mercy he has already experienced from his master. If he fails, he will certainly go to jail. If he succeeds, he will be a hero in the community."[5] In the moments of that silence, his entire life turns around. He enters into and experiences a world he has never before known — a world of grace. He has lived, apparently quite successfully, by his wits, by shrewd calculation. But it has been a very cramped, small world. Now he sees another and much larger way.

Here is how it works. Nobody as yet knows that he has been fired. So he calls in the debtors one by one. The manager is an estate manager in charge of overseeing the rentals of land to farmers who pay in kind (olive oil, wheat), say at harvest time. These are well-placed men in the community who have had long-standing associations with the master. They assume that the manager has an important message from the

4. Bailey, *Poet and Peasant*, p. 98.
5. Bailey, *Poet and Peasant*, p. 98.

master, and the manager lets them assume that. He is in a hurry — "write quickly" — he has to get this over before the master knows what he is doing. If the debtors know that there is deception involved they probably won't cooperate — that would mean breaking faith with the master and he would no longer rent land to them. The debtors assume that the bill-changing is legitimate, an order from the master carried out by the manager, who (they would also assume) had talked the master into it: a bonus. The debtors are delighted with the generous bonus from the master, arranged by the manager.

When the master realizes what has happened, he has two choices. He can go back to the debtors and tell them it was all a mistake, tell them it was a scheme cooked up by the manager who had already been fired. That would, of course, anger the debtors, and their enthusiasm over his generosity would change into cursing over his stinginess. Or, he can say nothing, accept the praise, and let the manager, rascal though he is, enjoy his popularity.

He thinks it over. He *is*, after all, a generous man — he didn't throw the manager in jail. Generosity in a nobleman in the East is a prized virtue. The manager's scheme is a kind of backhanded compliment to the master. He was passing on the generosity of the master to the farmers. The manager "knew the master was generous and merciful. He gambled everything on this aspect of his master's nature. He won. Because the master was indeed generous and merciful, he chose to pay the full price for his manager's salvation."[6]

"The rascal" emerges as a somewhat jaunty metaphor for the surprising improbability of grace, not unlike my ten-year-old friend on that East Baltimore street. One writer uses the term "picaresque" for him.[7] This story that has been worked over endlessly by men and women trying desperately to find some edifying moral lesson here, in order to save Jesus from commending a crook for being a very clever crook, becomes a story of embracing salvation, the kind of story that is at the very core of Jesus' good news.

6. Bailey, *Poet and Peasant*, p. 102.
7. Dan Otto Via Jr., *The Parables* (Philadelphia: Fortress Press), p. 160.

*   *   *

One more thing: the word "prudence." "The master commended the man for his *prudence*" (RSV); the manager "acted shrewdly" (NRSV and NIV), "had done wisely" (AV), "knew how to look after himself" (*The Message*). The Greek word is *phronimos*; the Hebrew word is *chokmah*.

The Greek and Hebrew words are commonly translated as "wise." They are common in the Old Testament, especially Psalms and Proverbs, setting before us in memorable metaphors and proverbs the kind of life that develops out of a lifetime of attentive alertness to the ways of God. There is an equivalent vocabulary in all languages, words that mark what it means to live well, live the good life, the moral life, the spiritual life, the Christian life. There are extensive wisdom traditions in all religions and cultures.

But these words, common and useful as they are, also tend to collect an air of stodginess about them. They are sober words, serious words. They come into our languages out of deep experience and mature reflection but also, through no fault of their own, get associated with the elderly who have most of their living behind them and are in a position to counsel and advise the rest of us how not to make a mess of our lives. Other words — words like "nice" and "polite" and "well-behaved" — become used in similar contexts. In the process they lose their luster. "Nice" as an adjective doesn't have pizzazz. "Polite" lacks zest. A Quaker girl named Prudence is half-sister to a prude. But when these words lose their place in the Jesus life and have to make it more or less on their own, they can become stuffy. Novelists always have a much more difficult time making a good person attractive and interesting than they do a scoundrel or a rogue.

Jesus' story of the rascal rescues this cluster of wisdom words that often get dulled into a kind of smugness and dull propriety by naming the rascal as prudent. "Prudent" in our language connotes caution and carefulness, playing it safe, not rocking the boat. The story about the rascal describes the behavior of a man who narrowly escapes a lifetime of self-serving calculation and discovers himself reveling in a huge world of generosity — of God. God is the one with whom he now has to do. The generous action of God defines his life, not his obsessive scheming, embezzling, and cooking the books.

Jesus came to save our souls. He also came to save our words. Word and words are at the very core of God's revelation of himself to us. If the words are damaged through careless or malicious usage, or are left in bad repair, or pick up barnacle encrustations from hanging around in bad company, the sharp details of the Jesus revelation are blunted. Careless language in the service of Jesus is responsible for an enormous amount of mischief, rivaling outright lying as an impediment to hearing and responding to the message of God's good news to us.

And so constant and vigilant attention is required to keep our language in good repair. Words wear out. They lose texture, and the colors fade. They need refurbishing, rehabilitating, renovating. Whether from overuse or misuse, once-vigorous words frequently end up blunted and dull. Those of us who use language have a responsibility for returning them to sharpness, cleaning them up, scrubbing off the grime of inappropriate associations. Most of us are more attentive to keeping the dishes and knives and forks clean that we use to eat our meals than to keeping in good repair the words we use to speak our love and promises, our commitments and loyalties.

In the wittily profound *Screwtape Letters* by C. S. Lewis, the master demon Screwtape writes to his apprentice demon Wormwood that one of the important departments of hell is the Philological Arm. "Our Father Below" has a team of skilled grammarians who diligently work away at eroding and then ruining words. They have a special interest in working on the words that the Christian community uses in its conversation and witness. We can observe in our contemporary world how they have done a pretty good job on "repent" by introducing cartoon figures of bent-over men carrying sandwich-board posters on city street corners, and on the word "saved" by squeezing it into a password that gets you into heaven, and by reducing "making love" to sexual intercourse.

"Prudent" and the cluster of wisdom words that surround it are too vital to be consigned to wallflower usage. But they do need refurbishing. Jesus manages to get these words alive and kicking again, not by sending us to a dictionary and tracing their origin, but by putting them in a story where we can't miss the robust nature that bursts out in surprised response to Jesus.

CHAPTER 9

The Invisible Man: Luke 16:19-31

Observant readers of St. Luke's Greek have noticed a detail, a mere phrase, that links the three Jesus stories in chapters 15 and 16, the story of the lost brothers, the story of the rascal, and the story of Lazarus and the rich man. The linking phrase clearly but unobtrusively connects the second and third stories with the first. The first set of "lost" stories in chapter 15 is introduced as a parable: "So he told them this parable . . ." (Luke 15:3). These stories are Jesus' response to the grumbling of scribes over his hospitality to outsiders, to sinners. But after the introductory lost sheep and lost coin parables, each of the primary stories that follows, the father and his sons, the rich farmer and his rascal manager, and Lazarus and the rich man, is introduced by a phrase that Luke, and only Luke, uses in the New Testament:[1] "There was a man who had two sons . . ." (15:11), "There was a rich man who had a manager . . ." (16:1), and "There was a rich man who was dressed in purple . . ." (16:19). The common phrase is *anthrōpos tis* — "a certain man."

What we observe is that, after introducing the grouping of stories

---

1. See Joel Green, *The Gospel of Luke*, New International Commentary on the New Testament (Grand Rapids: Eerdmans, 1997), p. 587, and Joseph A. Fitzmyer, S.J., *The Gospel According to Luke (X–XXI)*, Anchor Bible Commentary (New York: Doubleday, 1985), p. 886.

in chapters 15–16 with the term "parable," Luke introduces each main story with something like, "And now here is another story of the same sort — *a certain man* . . ." with the implication that they are all intended to reinforce one another. Each story features central characters who are lost in various ways: by being alienated from a parent (the two sons in turn by hotheaded profligacy and cool contempt), the rascal by squandering the trust of his master, and the wretched beggar pushed to the extreme outer-darkness margins of sickness and poverty.

Then in each story a visitation of grace reverses the plotline. The younger brother responds appropriately in repentance. We don't know how the older brother responds, but we know that he is generously welcomed to the party and we find ourselves hoping that he will also repent and join in. The response of the rascal is not explicit, but the implicit evidence is that he radically changes his life, from conniving against his master to sharing the largesse of his master with others.

Wretched Lazarus doesn't himself do anything but finds something done to him — he is raised from the dehumanized squalor of dogs licking his wounds to life in "the bosom of Abraham," experiencing that from which he has been so long excluded by the self-indulgence of the rich man, who now sees Lazarus as if for the first time and, even though it is too late for him, wants to see his five brothers have a chance to repent. The rich man's five brothers, like the elder brother in the first story, are left, at least narratively, in limbo. We don't know whether they will repent. There are undertones of resurrection in each story.

The common elements in each story accumulate: something has taken place in and around Jesus that reverses "the way things are." The exile conditions in which the characters (and Israel) have lived for so long are about to end; people are being faced with an appropriate response, namely, to repent. The imperative command "Repent!" is implied throughout Jesus' storytelling, though it is not explicit after the first uses of it in the opening days of Jesus' preaching (Matt. 3:2 and 4:19). But a reference to repentance holds a prominent place in the Lazarus story (Luke 16:30).[2]

---

2. There are nine occurrences of "repentance" in Luke, but none in the impera-

These observations free the final, Lazarus, story from being tethered for too long as a story about the afterlife, what happens when we die and find ourselves consigned to either the fires of Hades or the bosom of Abraham. As N. T. Wright argues in clear-sighted exegesis, "the parable is not, as often supposed, a description of the afterlife, warning people to be sure of their ultimate destination. . . . The reality is uncomfortably different . . . rather what was happening to both rich and poor *in the present time.* Jesus' welcome of the poor and outcast was a sign that the real return from exile, the new age, the 'resurrection', is coming into being; and if the new age is dawning, those who want to belong to it will have to repent."[3]

So what new insights does this third repentance story, the story of Lazarus, contribute to its predecessors?

Maybe first of all, a caution. The rich are an easy target in any concern, secular or spiritual, for social reform and economic justice. They furnish endless models for cynical and comic caricature. That possibility is not excluded from the Lazarus story, but given the tenor of Jesus' storytelling, my inclination is to focus on Lazarus. He is the one person in the story, after all, who is dignified with a personal name.

*   *   *

"There was once a rich man, expensively dressed in the latest fashions, wasting his days in conspicuous consumption. A poor man named Lazarus, covered with sores, had been dumped on his doorstep. All he lived for was to get a meal from scraps off the rich man's table. His best friends were the dogs who came and licked his sores.

---

tive, all of them in the Samaria Travel Narrative section in which Jesus is telling these stories (Luke 10:13; 11:32; 13:3, 5; 15:7, 10; 16:30; 17:3, 4), underlining the thematic centrality of repentance as Jesus is recruiting followers to participate with him on the way to Jerusalem and in the work of the kingdom.

3. N. T. Wright, *Jesus and the Victory of God* (Minneapolis: Fortress Press, 1996), p. 255.

"Then he died, this poor man, and was taken up by the angels to the lap of Abraham. The rich man also died and was buried. In hell and in torment, he looked up and saw Abraham in the distance and Lazarus in his lap. He called out, 'Father Abraham, mercy! Have mercy! Send Lazarus to dip his finger in water to cool my tongue. I'm in agony in this fire.'

"But Abraham said, 'Child, remember that in your lifetime you got the good things and Lazarus the bad things. It's not like that here. Here he's consoled and you're tormented. Besides, in all these matters there is a huge chasm set between us so that no one can go from us to you even if he wanted to, nor can anyone cross over from you to us.'

"The rich man said, 'Then let me ask you, Father: Send him to the house of my father where I have five brothers, so he can tell them the score and warn them so they won't end up here in this place of torment.'

"Abraham answered, 'They have Moses and the Prophets to tell them the score. Let them listen to them.'

"'I know, Father Abraham,' he said, 'but they're not listening. If someone came back to them from the dead, they would change their ways.'

"Abraham replied, 'If they won't listen to Moses and the Prophets, they're not going to be convinced by someone who rises from the dead.'" (Luke 16:19-31 *The Message*)

*　　*　　*

Lazarus is an invisible man. The rich man is very visible and very audible indeed, resplendent in his fashionable clothing, with the sounds and aromas of a perpetual party issuing from his trophy home — laughter and dancing and lavish meals. Nobody can miss the presence of the rich man in that village. Every appearance, every bit of gossip, every rumor adds weight to his importance. His very existence gives distinction to the whole community. His celebrity status, much like a championship sports team, confers luster, even if secondhand, on all the ordinary, undistinguished, dull, but enviously admiring spectators who by their very ordinariness are excluded from his magic circle.

And Lazarus is invisible. Nobody sees Lazarus. In his invisibility he shares the fate of the poor, the sick, the exploited, and all "the wretched of the earth." Every society finds ways to shut its eyes, put fingers in its ears, and by the extravagant use of deodorants and garbage trucks to get rid of the smell of decay, uncleanness, stench, and squalor. We put our sick in hospitals, our elderly in nursing homes, our poor in slums, and our garbage in landfills. We are never entirely successful in keeping them out of sight and smell and sound, but we do our best. Every once in a while a novelist or poet, a journalist or preacher, tries his or her best to stick our nose in it. But by and large, by averting our gaze, tuning out the sounds, and sanitizing the environment, we manage pretty well not to see or hear or smell or touch Lazarus.

I have a good friend, Karen, who was a journalist for our small town newspaper. A number of years ago an exhibit of the magnificent treasures of the ancient Egyptian king, Pharaoh Tutankhamen, was on tour in the United States and came to the Smithsonian Museum in Washington, D.C., only fifty miles from our town. She arranged with her editors for an assignment to cover the exhibit. It was big news at the time. Many of our neighbors were making their pilgrimage to see the treasures. But she also had a private agenda. It was a time when many were working hard to insure access for the disabled in public buildings. Charla, a young girl in our congregation who would spend the rest of her life in a wheelchair, provided Karen with a weekly visual reminder as they worshiped together of how important it was to take care of this too long ignored basic need of so many in our land. Karen decided to combine her journalistic assignment with her growing passion to do something about the needs of the disabled. She rented a wheelchair, borrowed a set of crutches, and engaged her husband to drive her to the Tutankhamen exhibit and to push her in her wheelchair through the crowded rooms of the exhibit. She wanted to experience, if only for a few hours, what our friend Charla and so many thousands of others had to put up with every day of their lives. The corridors of the museum were swarming. There were long lines of people waiting for brief looks at some of the more spectacular items of jewelry and sculpture, King Tut's equivalents of the parable rich man's "purple and fine linen." Karen in her rented wheelchair was duly impressed by these artifacts from the conspicuous consumption of the Egyptian royalty, but what absolutely astonished her was that in the five hours of being wheeled through that museum, not once, *not once,* did anyone look at her directly or speak to her. Men and women alike averted their eyes. They only had eyes for what was left of the dead rich man. She was an invisible person. Lazarus in a wheelchair.

Neither Karen nor I noticed it at the time, but years later in a casual conversation we did: the feature story that Karen wrote for our local newspaper that week was a retelling of the rich man and Lazarus story, not a story about what happens after we die, but a story that is repeated with variations all around us every day.

*　　*　　*

A few years before Jesus told this story he called out in his inaugural sermon, "The kingdom of God is at hand; repent" (Mark 1:15 RSV). Israel's long exile is over. He is gathering the exiles to participate in a new way of life, a new rule, a radical reversal of "the way things are." He is on his way to Jerusalem, recruiting followers along the way to participate with him in the new rule, the new kingdom way of doing things. He is welcoming anyone with "ears to hear," but he is also being as explicit as he can be that he is completing the agenda of what Isaiah of the Exile four hundred years or so earlier had preached as good news to his congregation of exiles:

> "The Spirit of the Lord is upon me,
>   because he has anointed me
>   to bring good news to the poor."

(Luke 4:18)

Jesus also included the blind and dumb and lame in his kingdom agenda, but it is significant that he begins with "the poor" — the out-

114

sider, the outcast, "whosoever will may come," without regard to status or reputation or qualification. Jesus lays the groundwork for inclusiveness among the "whosoever" by naming the unnamed, making visible those whom no one sees, giving a voice to the ones who are never listened to. Lazarus for a start.

The Lazarus story smashes to smithereens our stereotypes of the men and women we assume provide the leadership vanguard of Jesus' kingdom mission. Jesus is on the hunt for followers who will participate with him in establishing his kingdom rule. His first recruits take most bystanders by indignant surprise. The rich, powerful, and influential are by no means excluded — the rich man Joseph of Arimathea and the influential rabbi Nicodemus are named and numbered among Jesus' followers — but there is no suggestion in the Gospel stories as written that Jesus was going after "the brightest and the best." St. Paul underlines this way of Jesus in his unflattering appraisal of those called: "God deliberately chose men and women that the culture overlooks and exploits and abuses, chose these 'nobodies' . . ." (1 Cor. 1:28 *The Message*).

This is in contrast to the widespread and virtually unchallenged American strategy to target influential and accomplished men and women for kingdom work — men and women, as we say, with "proven leadership qualities" or at least "leadership potential." Wherever did we come up with that? Certainly not by reading the stories that Jesus told and the stories that were told about him.

*   *   *

It is characteristic of language that accurately tells stories (and the ones Jesus told are nothing if not accurate) that those stories are never isolated and complete in themselves but always organic to a larger story, a meta-story, a comprehensive story that accounts for everything that is. Story is a verbal witness to the coherence of life, the interconnectedness of beginning, middle, and end. While the large story, the meta-story, does not include everything, nothing is in principle left out.

But not all "stories" are stories. Illustrations and jokes, for instance, have a superficial appearance of story but are not. They are the grin of Lewis Carroll's Cheshire cat, the trivialization of story. And despite their frequent use by preachers in sermons and journalists for the sake of human interest and entertainment, they are fragments of life, however delightful, without precedence or consequence, snapshots without foreground or background, like Melchizedek "without father or mother, without genealogy, without beginning of days or end of life . . ." (Heb. 7:3 NIV). Ripped out of the complex story of God's revelation, the illustration or joke has a very short shelf life.

But story, as such, always operates in the context of a meta-story, and at least implicitly it develops recognition and awareness and, if we are willing, participation in a reality larger, more healthy (holy), and ultimately significant. Story enlists our imagination to grasp more than our immediate feelings and surroundings — other lives, other circumstances, other possibilities. Once we are free of being stuck in the mud of our sinful, self-absorbed, self-contained "miry clay" of ego, our imaginations can be a catalyst for faith that the Spirit uses to create something out of nothing, the assurance of things hoped for, the conviction of "things not seen . . . that the worlds were prepared by the word of God, so that what is seen was made from things that are not visible" (Heb. 11:1-3). Or, to put it another way, faith is "the firm foundation under everything that makes life worth living . . . our handle on what we can't see. . . . By faith, we see the world called into existence by God's word, what we see created by what we don't see" (Heb. 11:1-3 *The Message*). In the act of faith we become willing participants in the full story, the ways and work of God, the story that Jesus named "The Kingdom." Every honest story told along the way provides access into this evolving, expanding story of God's ways with us, and ours with God. The Bible is full of them. Our lives are full of them.

*   *   *

In telling the story of Lazarus, Jesus uses an old Egyptian folktale of which there were variations in Palestine well known in Jesus' time. The basic story line tells of the journey of the god Si-Osiris to the underworld where he observed the fate of a rich man and a commoner, portrayed as a reversal of fortunes, the rich man's funeral unattended and the commoner buried in great pomp. Retellings of this basic story occurred in Palestine. Jesus' hearers would have been familiar with the folktale, into which Jesus inserted the names of Abraham and Lazarus, customizing the Egyptian story for his Jewish and Samaritan listeners.

Jesus also retells the story in such a way as to shift its meaning from the afterlife to this present life. He does it by adding an epilogue to the old folktale that radically changes its intent. We start out assuming that we are listening to a story about Lazarus. But when the story is finished we realize that Lazarus was just a setup: this is a story about the rich man's brothers. *This* is the conclusion. We had no way of anticipating this (nor did Jesus' listeners) but now we get it: *this* is where the story had been going all along. What is to become of the five brothers?

Jesus' story made the invisible Lazarus visible to the very people who only had eyes for the rich man in the crowd and his entourage of hangers-on. So would his hearers likewise see themselves in the five brothers? And would they respond to Jesus' inaugural imperatives — "Repent!" (Matt. 3:2) and "Come, follow me" (4:19) — that quietly reverberate in the interstices of all Jesus' stories on this metaphorical road through Samaria?

Joachim Jeremias, one of our premier students of Jesus' parables, suggests that a better name for the Lazarus story would be "The Parable of the Six Brothers."[4] Or, maybe, "The Parable of the Five Brothers," picking up the ambiguity surrounding the elder brother of the prodigal and extending it into the Lazarus story. Did the elder brother repent and join the resurrection celebration — or not? Will the five brothers repent and join the resurrection celebration — or not?

The theme of resurrection is unmistakably present in this subversive re-telling of the old Egyptian folk story, subverting it from a moral and ethical lesson on the rich and the poor and on speculation about the afterlife to an eye-opening realization that the resurrection is taking place all around Jesus. But it takes an act of repentance to pry open

4. Joachim Jeremias, *The Parables of Jesus* (New York: Charles Scribner's Sons, 1963), p. 186.

those eyes. If you only have eyes for the rich man, you will remain blind to Lazarus.

Since this is the only parable in the Gospels in which a person is given a name, the story in John of the raising of the man who carries this same name, Lazarus, comes up for attention. The early church father Origen is the first we know of to suggest a connection. Is there any relation between the folktale Lazarus and the friend-of-Jesus Lazarus? There is no certain answer to the question, but just asking the question serves to keep the dynamics of repentance before us. When the rich man asks Abraham that Lazarus be sent to warn his five brothers because "if someone goes to them from the dead, they will repent," Abraham tells him, "If they do not listen to Moses and the prophets, neither will they be convinced even if someone rises from the dead" (Luke 16:30-31). Here are our two words: "repent" and "rise" (resurrection).

The parable of Lazarus states that resurrection in itself will not produce repentance; the raising of the actual Lazarus is confirmation. Worse, not only did his resurrection fail to compel repentance, it provoked further obduracy — murderous disbelief. The raising of Lazarus, even though some believed, turned out to be the last straw that set in motion the plot that issued in Jesus' crucifixion. "So from that day [the day that Lazarus was raised] on they planned to put him [Jesus] to death" (John 11:53).

And neither did the resurrection of Jesus from the dead ten days or so later result in anything like a nationwide revival of repentance.

*   *   *

"Repent" is among the stock imperatives in the spiritual life. It is not a difficult word to understand. But it is a most difficult word to *hear*. Repentance is a complex thing. The command itself is straightforward. It is an old word in the life of faith. It simply means "turn around" or "change your mind." The word is without ambiguity. Just do it. Personally, but not individualistically. In the biblical story repentance cannot be narrowed down to something private, such as being sorry for your sins and ready to make amends. The call is to return to God and the ways of God with his people. To return to the Story and everything and everyone in the Story. It has to do with entering a new way of life, taking up membership in the kingdom of God. Jesus is calling men and women to join him in a way of life that wills inclusion in the kingdom. Following Jesus in the way of the cross provides the most succinct metaphor. "You must revise your life" (Rilke).

Tacking on a recommended devotional practice to your already busy life will not do it. Making a set of resolutions will not do it. Feeling sorrow and penitence deep in your heart over a misspent life is a start but hardly sufficient. Moods can be cultivated. Emotions are easily manipulated. What must be abandoned in our understanding of repentance is the "lonely post-Enlightenment individual bent on a quest for private salvation."[5]

A number of years ago my wife and I were driving in the Rocky Mountains through a national park on a narrow road cut into the side of the mountain. We came to the scene of an accident where a motorcyclist had plunged off the road down a precipice of several hundred feet. A couple of the police and park rangers kept the traffic moving, while others were working a complex system of ropes and pulleys to retrieve what was left of the motorcycle and its rider.

Everyone, of course, was curious, but we were prevented by the police and rangers from stopping and looking around. But just beyond the scene of the accident, the road looped around to where we could look back across the ravine to what had taken place, about a hundred and fifty yards away. I stopped the car, and we got out with our binoculars to see what we could see. A policeman back at the scene of the accident spotted us and, using a bullhorn, commanded across the ravine, "Get back in your car! There is nothing to see." But I knew that there was something to see and I wanted to see it. I didn't obey immediately (although my law-abiding wife did). I didn't think I was breaking any law by just looking through binoculars. Then the command was repeated, "Get back in your car! There is nothing to see." And then again. Reluctantly, with the encouragement of my wife, I obeyed.

5. Wright, *Jesus and the Victory of God*, p. 257.

That is the end of the story as it happened. We drove on, our curiosity unsatisfied. But the story, as stories often do, keeps playing itself out in my imagination. As a parent, pastor, and interpreter of Scripture, I take a special interest in imperatives. The imperative is the briefest, clearest, and least ambiguous way to formulate a verb. And for anyone who cares about living well and is responsible for others living well, imperatives are a stock-in-trade in our language: eat your cereal, clean up your room, love God, love your neighbor. An imperative gets your attention, is easily understood, doesn't require explanation. And, in the short term at least, is usually effective.

The officer's command on that mountain road that day did all of that: got my attention, got me into my car, and got me moving. What it did *not* do was make me a participant in what was going on. Nor was it designed to — it intended the opposite, to eliminate my participation from what was going on. But what I am interested in is not the isolated imperative that gets my attention and gets me moving, but how it develops into indicatives and subjunctives, imperfects and perfects, a full range of involvement in a sentence, in *life*.

What would have happened, for instance, if that police officer had sent one of his subordinates to me and said, "We need some help in retrieving this body. All you are doing looking through those binoculars is getting in the way. Would you help us? We need some help on these ropes."

I can't imagine not doing that. It wouldn't be much, just holding or pulling on a rope. And it wouldn't require any skill. Then I would be in the story, not an in-the-way spectator to it.

*   *   *

What I am trying to get a feel for is that while imperatives are absolutely essential for getting our attention and getting us doing or not doing something, they don't function as intended until they get us into the story.

The effectiveness of the imperative is not usually increased by repetition or amplification. It does its proper work when it gets us into the story. And in the case of the imperative "Repent!" it gets us into Jesus' Kingdom Story, with all its complexities, mysteries, and possibilities for love and obedience.

We learn a lot from the way Jesus does it. As he makes his way through Samaria he doesn't simply repeat his inaugural sermonic "Repent!" over and over and louder and louder as he approaches Jerusalem. He mostly tells stories that invite us in as participants in the world of resurrection. For people, like so many Samaritans then and Americans now, who don't even know there is a story, Jesus, patiently and without raising his voice, tells story after story after story. Stories that get us into The Story.

CHAPTER 10

The Widow: Luke 18:1-8

It interests me greatly that, in contrast with the preoccupations of my contemporaries, in the biblical story there is very little, if any, interest in prayer as a thing in itself. And most certainly not in the story of Jesus. No systematic instruction in how to pray, no lectures on prayer, no speculation in the dynamics of prayer (how it works), no classifications that sort out the kinds and occasions of prayer.

We have men and women praying all over the place. The Psalms are our most comprehensive documentation of prayer. And Jesus, holding the center position, is our most representative exemplar of prayer (Part II of this book will take this up). But there is very little on prayer as such, as a subject that we can isolate, study, and practice. What we have is simply people at prayer, people praying.

As we follow in the steps of our praying ancestors, we do not find them stopping off along the way to hold a seminar on prayer, or conducting controlled experiments to demonstrate the efficacy of prayer. They are preparing for the way of the Lord, following "the Jesus Way." They don't take time out to pray. Praying is what they are doing as they are preparing, as they are following.

Which is to say that there are no ahistorical expositions of prayer — all prayer is embedded in person and place and time. It is not the kind of thing that can be approached as an abstraction. Coming to prayer apart from the revealed God to whom we pray and apart from the actual, lived conditions of the person who prays is unheard of in the biblical revelation.

*   *   *

Two of Jesus' uniquely Lucan Samaritan stories have to do with prayer. The first, the story of the friend (Luke 11:1-13), puts prayer in the homely setting of ordinariness: a man asks his friend for a loaf of bread for a friend of his who has just arrived at the inconvenient hour of midnight. There is nothing we would call "spiritual" about this, but it is incontrovertibly *personal*. We are dealing with conversation between *friends* who presumably know one another's names. They are, after all, neighbors. Everything in the story and its commentary is rooted in the personal: the term "friend" is used four times, "child/children" four times, and "Father" once — all personal, relational terms. Prayer is language used relationally in relation to the Trinity. Persistence (*anaidia*) is bold, unapologetic perseverance in asking for what we need. After all, the Father *is* our friend and no "stranger."

The second story is quite different. Here there is no emphasis on the personal. The story is about a widow petitioning a judge. Not two neighbors who are on easy, friendly terms with one another, but an impersonal relation in a court of law where relations are determined by a matter of justice. A nameless widow and a faceless judge.

But a common thread links the two stories. The first mentions the "persistence" of the friend asking for bread, and the second prefaces the story by announcing its purpose, emphasizing our "need to pray always and not to lose heart." "Not to lose heart" (*mē engkakein*) parallels the earlier "persistence." As we are coming close to the end of this metaphorical Samaritan journey, maybe this aspect of prayer needs to be given some emphatic bold print. Prayer is not an option; it is fundamentally necessary. Prayer is not a pious interlude; it necessarily permeates life at all times and places.

*   *   *

Jesus told them a story showing that it was necessary for them to pray consistently and never quit. He said, "There was once a judge in some city who never gave God a thought and cared nothing for people. A widow in that city kept after him: 'My rights are being violated. Protect me!'

"He never gave her the time of day. But after this went on and on he said to himself, 'I care nothing what God thinks, even less what people think. But because this widow won't quit badgering me, I'd better do something and see that she gets justice — otherwise I'm going to end up beaten black and blue by her pounding.'"

Then the Master said, "Do you hear what that judge, corrupt as he is, is saying? So what makes you think God won't step in and work justice for his chosen people, who continue to cry out for help? Won't he stick up for them? I assure you, he will. He will not drag his feet. But how much of that kind of persistent faith will the Son of Man find on the earth when he returns?" (Luke 18:1-8 *The Message*)

*   *   *

Widows in the ancient world were women without personal resources. When in need, they had to depend on the hospitality of the village. This widow was in need of justice. Someone had wronged or defrauded her. She had no one who was rich or powerful or influential enough to stand up for her. She had, as we say, "nothing but a prayer." She went to the village judge and asked for help. There were laws, after all, to protect such as she, and it was his job to enforce them. The judge ignored her just as he ignored God. The judge was contemptuous of her, just as he held everyone else in town in contempt. Some judge.

But the widow refused to quit. She kept after him. She pounded on his door in the middle of the night. She accosted him in the street. She badgered him relentlessly. He felt like he had bruises all over his face and two black eyes (the literal meaning of the verb, *hupopiadzō*) from her pummeling. Finally, he gave in. He gave her the justice she asked for.

It's a story about prayer: we "need to pray always and not to lose heart" (Luke 18:1 NRSV); it is necessary "to pray consistently and never quit" (*The Message*).

*   *   *

Most people, maybe all, at one time or another, pray. And many — who knows how many? — quit. And why shouldn't they? If they don't get what they ask for, if they don't get what they think of as an "answer," why keep at it? The remarkable thing about prayer is not that so many people pray, but that some of us keep at it. Why do we keep at it? Why do we keep praying when we have so little to show for it? Anyone who has made a practice of prayer knows the feeling, overwhelming sometimes, that prayer is a leaky bucket. You go to the river to get a pail of water and by the time you get home the water is gone, the bucket empty, and all there is left to show for your effort is a damp trail soon to be wiped out by the sun.

Little wonder that Jesus concluded his story with the aphorism: "And yet, when the Son of Man comes, will he find faith on earth?" Which is to say, "will he find men and women who are still praying, who have not given up, who have not lost heart?" This "faith" is not a generalized abstraction but a way of life that is expressed in persistent prayer. The word "faith" in Greek has a definite article, *the* faith, the faith-life that embraces and prays all the practices of faith and sticks with Jesus as he welcomes and invites followers into the kingdom.

The reality is that those who stick it out in this following-Jesus-faith-life, praying what we live and living what we pray, have learned how to handle what our uninstructed feelings would interpret as God's non-response, God's silence.

We have learned by experience that God's silence in the face of our prayers is not due to some inadequacy on our part, some technical glitch in the way we pray that can be fixed if we can just get our hands on the right prayer manual. God's silence is a common and repeated experience among all who pray. If there is anything like an official prayer book for prayer it is The Psalms. These are the prayers that provide us access to the complex and intricate world of language that our praying ancestors used to respond to God's word to them. And it turns out that God's silence is part of it. People who pray are deeply experienced in God's silence.

> Why, O LORD, do you stand far off?
>   Why do you hide yourself in times of trouble?
>
> (Ps. 10:1)

> How long, O LORD? Will you forget me forever?
>   How long will you hide your face from me?
> How long must I bear pain in my soul,
>   And have sorrow in my heart all day long?
> How long shall my enemy be exalted over me?
>
> (13:1-2)

> My God, my God, why have you forsaken me?
>   Why are you so far from helping me, from the words
>   of my groaning?
> O my God, I cry by day, but you do not answer;
>   and by night, but find no rest.
>
> (22:1-2)

> Rouse yourself! Why do you sleep, O Lord?
>   Awake, do not cast us off forever!
> Why do you hide your face?
>   Why do you forget our affliction and oppression?
>
> (44:23-24)

> How long, O God, is the foe to scoff?
>   Is the enemy to revile your name forever?
>
> (74:10)

> Will the Lord spurn forever,
>   and never again be favorable?

Has his steadfast love ceased forever?
　　Are his promises at an end for all time?
Has God forgotten to be gracious?
　　Has he in anger shut up his compassion?

　　　　　　　　　　　　　　　　　　　(77:7-9)

How long, O LORD? Will you be angry forever?

　　　　　　　　　　　　　　　　　　　(79:5)

Turn, O LORD! How long?

　　　　　　　　　　　　　　　　　　　(90:13)

"Why, why, why?" "How long, how long, how long?"

People who pray know what it is like to hear nothing in response. People who pray don't get what they ask for when they ask for it. People who pray ask "How long?" and "Why?" a lot.

The significant thing, though, is that these psalmists, our prayer masters to whom we apprentice ourselves in prayer, kept on praying despite the silence. We know they kept on praying because we have their prayers gathered together in The Psalms to immerse us in the world of prayer. Generation after generation of Jews and Christians continue to pray and sing these same psalms, praying and singing the "Why?" and "How long?" questions, praying and singing through the silences.

Like that widow who did not lose heart. Why do we do it?

*　　　*　　　*

We do it because we know who God is and what he is like. God has revealed himself in word and act as the God who creates, the God who saves, and the God who elects a people to give witness in word and act to his words and acts of creation and salvation. God made a cosmos and saw that it was "very good." God saved men and women lost to his ways and alienated from his love. God elected a people as a "kingdom of priests" (Exod. 19:6 NIV) to be a "light to the peoples" (Isa. 51:4), witnesses showing and telling the ways of God to the whole earth, welcoming everyone we meet to join the company.

A good God, a rescuing God, a welcoming God. The revelation is given in story after story after story over nearly two thousand years. God speaks to us, he involves himself in our lives, he involves us in his life. This all takes place in named people and named places. It is all personal and local. We never get to know the whole story — it is too large and complex for one thing. Given that this is God that is doing the revealing, there are necessarily many mysteries that we will never comprehend. (A god you can understand is not God.) But they are good, light-filled mysteries, not ominous, evil-tinged mysteries. Words like "steadfast love," "faithfulness," "blessing," "forgiveness," and "grace" are used lavishly throughout the God-revealing stories and prayers, meditations and reflections. The unanswered questions we raise (the "Why?" and "How long?" questions), along with whatever silences occur, once we see them integrated into the all-embracing story of the good, rescuing, welcoming God, rather than diminishing our basic trust, extend it beyond the margins of what we are able to take in.

The sketch of the evil judge in Jesus' story is everything that we know God is *not*. Because we have been immersed in all these centuries of story and song, prayer and reflection, we recognize at once that this judge is an evil and grotesque parody of the God who is revealed to us. The sketch of the evil judge gives a shock of fresh realization to everything that we know that God is not and who we know that God is. By now, having kept company with Jesus, we know the character and work of the God who is with us, the God with whom we have to do.

That is why we keep praying and do not lose heart. We do it because we know that God is everything that the evil judge is not. We know that neither silence nor absence is evidence of contempt or indifference.

*   *   *

And here's another reason that we keep praying and do not lose heart. We know that this kingdom business is urgent business — we've heard it from Jesus' own lips. Kingdom is not a matter that comes up for discussion from time to time. Kingdom is what is going on all the time, whether we are aware of it or not. But it is Jesus' intent to make us aware of it. Kingdom requires a total renovation of our imagination so that we are able to see what our eyes do not see, so that we are capable of participating in what will not be reported in tomorrow morning's newspaper.

As Luke leads us along in the company of Jesus on this metaphorical journey through Samaria, immediately previous to telling the story of the widow, he prepares our imaginations to understand the context of the story. He does it by introducing (in Luke 17:20-37) a radical reorientation on the nature of time and place, *kingdom* time and place, so that when we listen to Jesus tell the story of the widow we will recognize that persistence in prayer is something very different than just gutting it out no matter what. Persistent prayer is the only kind of prayer that is congruent with what we might term a "kingdom" understanding of the way God works in time and place.

The Pharisees jump-start the teaching by asking when the kingdom of God is coming. "Kingdom of God" is the term that Jesus used frequently as a metaphor for the all-inclusive work of God's rule, God's dominion that Jesus is both proclaiming and enacting.[1] The Pharisees want to know "when?"

Is there a tinge of skeptical sarcasm to the question? As if they are saying, "You keep talking of this kingdom of God. We're getting a little tired of the talk. Show us. When are we going to see it? Are we ever going to see it?"

Jesus' answer is "Right now. It's not something you can see in the way you see an elephant on the street. It's right here. You are in it. The kingdom of God is in formation right here. It's not one of the wonders of the world like the pyramids that you can visit by taking a camel to Egypt. Quit looking around and asking 'when?' Pay attention to who you are and who I am. For a start, maybe try praying."

---

1. Luke uses the term "kingdom of God" 51 times, 27 times in this Samaritan section.

Jesus then elaborates on his answer to the Pharisees by teaching his disciples more on the subject. He repeats what he says to the Pharisees by insisting that the kingdom of God is not an event the way a football game is an event that you can visit by buying a ticket and watching the action from the stands. He employs apocalyptic language to shake them out of their routine ways of thinking. Apocalyptic language is a language of the imagination. Apocalyptic language is extreme language, attention-getting language. Typically, it deals with the catastrophic, with earthquakes and eclipses, with death and hell, dragons and devils — end-of-the-world kinds of things. Also with angels, archangels, and heavenly splendors. It is particularly useful in waking up people who are sleepwalking through this world of wonders. It is language that enables us to see what can't be captured with a camera, to hear what can't be electronically recorded.

Apocalyptic language can be understood as referring predictively to upcoming doomsday events: judgment, second coming, nuclear holocaust, whatever. But the very same language can also be understood metaphorically to convey a sense of urgency. Knowing Jesus' fondness for metaphor and knowing the historical context in which he is working, it is far more likely that this is the way that Jesus used apocalyptic imagery. He is training our imaginations so that we will be able to participate appropriately in the great salvation drama that is taking place right now — not world events of the future but the presence of the kingdom right now.

How does he convey the sense of absolute urgency, crisis urgency, and still maintain his followers' faithful obedience in their work and worship, with their families and friends? How does he do this without distracting them into speculating about the future or scaring them into a paralysis of hysteria? What he does is use apocalyptic language, but metaphorically. He uses crisis imagery from the well-known stories of Noah and the flood, Lot and Sodom. *That*, that urgency, that comprehensive reordering of the way God is present among us to save, is what is taking place *right now*. Not another flood, not another fire-and-brimstone holocaust, but a radical re-imagining of what it means to follow Jesus and participate with Jesus in the establishment of the kingdom. Apocalyptic is a language strategy for breaking open awareness of the tremendous energies of good and evil contending with one another beneath the apparently benign skin of the ordinary. The language of apocalyptic vision calls the praying imagination into vigorous participation in what God is doing right now.

*　　*　　*

There were many revolutionary movements in Palestine in Jesus' day. Leader after leader appeared with a strategy to get rid of Roman oppression. Apocalyptic language was in the air, most of it understood literally, and virtually all of it assumed violence. The Essenes centered at Qumran also used apocalyptic language literally — a violent end to the present temple regime — but the violence was to be supernaturally deployed.

Jesus was also announcing deliverance from the evil oppression of Rome and corruption of the temple. And he was also working with the common stock of apocalyptic words and images — but he was using that language subversively, metaphorically. This kingdom was powerfully in formation, but not through bloody violence; rather, through sacrifice, suffering, rejection — and persevering, persistent prayer. It is a faith-life, a praying life that participates here and now in God's setting the world right, not waiting for a sign, not looking for an event. Like this widow.

This is another reason why we pray always and do not lose heart. We do it because God is working in a comprehensive kingdom way, and we want to be in on the work.

*　　*　　*

One final observation on Jesus' story of the widow. It is possible to read the story as a command to stick it out no matter what. And some do read it that way: stubbornly praying for a particular healing, staying in an abusive marriage, praying for a dream job. But there are more colors on the palette of persistence in prayer than black and white. The counsel of Evagrius the Solitary, one of our early and enduring prayer masters, is important to keep in mind:

> Often when I have prayed I have asked for what I thought was good, and persisted in my petition, stupidly importuning the will of God, and not leaving it to Him to arrange things as he knows is best for me. But when I have obtained what I asked for, I have been very sorry that I did not ask for the will of God to be done; because the thing turned out not to be as I had thought. . . . Do not be distressed if you do not at once receive from God what you ask. He wishes to give you something better — to make you persevere in your prayer. For what is better than to enjoy the love of God and to be in communion with Him?[2]

Evagrius distinguishes between persisting in "my petition" and persevering in "our prayer." "Persist" and "persevere" can be synonyms. But Evagrius discerningly observes that he had used the same or similar words as a prayer license to be radically disobedient.

Jesus' "pray always" story of the widow immerses perseverance in the ways of God, which are revealed in Israel and Jesus, and engages us in the present apocalyptic urgencies and energies that develop as we follow Jesus through the misunderstandings and muddle of Samaria on our way to Jerusalem. Isolated from those ways and urgencies, persistent prayer soon becomes a cover for nothing other than stubborn willfulness.

2. *The Philokalia*, vol. 1 (London: Faber & Faber, 1979), p. 60.

CHAPTER 11

The Sinners: Luke 18:9-14

If we stop to think about it for two minutes, it becomes obvious that there is far more *inside* a person than there is outside. The visible surface of a body, the skin, is minuscule compared to what is inside but never seen: heart, intestines, veins and arteries, liver, lungs, brain, nerves, blood and bones, gall bladder and kidneys, germs and parasites. A 200-pound man skinned would weigh at least 199 pounds, the skin placed on the scales weighing out to a good deal less than a single pound.

And that of course is just the physical. There is far more that cannot be weighed: thoughts and knowledge, feelings and moods, dreams and visions, words and numbers, prayers and songs, faith and love and hope, habits and memories. Most, in fact, of who and what we are cannot be discovered by cutting us open and examining our guts.

It takes a storyteller[1] to give us access to all that is going on — the swirling maelstrom of sound and silence, visible and invisible, in even the dowdiest of women, the dullest of men.

The same goes for the non-personal world, most of which is hidden from us. Scientists make it their business to find out what's be-

---

1. I am using the term "storyteller" here as representative of all writers and artists — poets and sculptors, painters and musicians, weavers and dancers — who probe the innerness of life.

neath and above: far-flung galaxies in the solar system, the soil and rock and magma under the surface of the earth, the creatures and plants in the oceans, as deep calls to deep. Instead of using the storyteller's imagination of interiority, they use highly sophisticated devices, microscopes and telescopes, radar and sonar, to put together the intricate story of what is going on around, under, and over us — and has been going on for billions of years.

Storytellers activate our imaginations to see and hear beneath the surface of life and involve us in the many dimensions of what is going on behind our backs or just around the corner. It takes a storyteller to reveal the beauty that dazzles like "shining from shook foil" (Gerard Manley Hopkins).

Every time Jesus tells a story, the world of those who listen enlarges, understanding deepens, imaginations are energized. Without stories we end up with stereotypes — a flat earth with flat cardboard figures that have no texture or depth, no *interior*.

*   *   *

Storytellers invite participation. Storytellers make us aware of the way things are, not just aware as spectators but aware so that we can get in on this world of wonders, get our feet walking on its ground, picking a McIntosh apple from a tree and relishing its tartness, diving into a mountain lake and coming up invigorated by the baptism, holding the hand of a child and feeling trust pulse through those fingers.

Jesus does not tell stories in order to illustrate large "truths" about God and salvation, the devil and damnation. There are, of course, truths to know and understand: the truth about God, the truth about right and wrong, the truth about the past. But Jesus doesn't seem to care much about telling us an abstract truth. He intends to get us involved, our feet in the mud and our hands in the bread dough, with the living God who is at work in this world. This is why Jesus tells stories, not to inform or explain or define, but to get us actively in on the ways and will of God in the homes and neighborhoods and workplaces where we spend our time.

Nothing is more rudely dismissive of Jesus than to treat him as a Sunday school teacher who shows up on Sundays to teach us about God and how to stay out of trouble. If that is the role we assign to Jesus, we will badly misunderstand who he is and what he is about. He is calling us to follow and join him in the work of salvation's eternal life being carried out right now on the road through Samaria to Jerusalem.

Here is another of his stories, the story of the sinners.

*   *   *

He told his next story to some who were complacently pleased with themselves over their moral performance and looked down their noses at the common people: "Two men went up to the Temple to pray, one a Pharisee, the other a tax man. The Pharisee posed and prayed like this: 'Oh, God, I thank you that I am not like other people — robbers, crooks, adulterers, or, heaven forbid, like this tax man. I fast twice a week and tithe on all my income.'

"Meanwhile the tax man, slumped in the shadows, his face in his hands, not daring to look up, said, 'God, give mercy. Forgive me, a sinner.'"

Jesus commented, "This tax man, not the other, went home made right with God. If you walk around with your nose in the air, you're going to end up flat on your face, but if you're content to be simply yourself, you will become more than yourself." (Luke 18:9-14 *The Message*)

*   *   *

Jesus sets this story in the place of prayer. Prayer, this universal venture into intimacy with God, so basic and easy to begin but so difficult to sustain. Prayer, this so often suppressed or distracted desire to live a life that is more than skin deep. Prayer, not content to live a merely exterior life of job description, hair color, and complexion. Prayer, a refusal to live as an outsider to my God and my own soul. Prayer, this "best" that is so easily corrupted into the "worst," its rich interior maturity deteriorated into a kitchen midden of pious clichés.

Two contrasting characters, a Pharisee and a tax collector, provide the action of the story. But what catches my attention at the outset is what they have in common: they both go to the same church (the temple), they both pray when they get there, and they are both sinners.

* * *

I am a pastor. Fifty years ago I was given a position of responsibility in a place of prayer. A church congregation is my primary workplace, a place not unlike the temple in which Jesus sets his story. Maybe that is why my pastoral imagination keeps returning to these two men who are in church praying. It is the only story Jesus told that is set in a place of worship. All his other stories take place in nonreligious settings, farms and suppers and weddings, and use mostly a nonreligious vocabulary from the workplace world of non-pastors, the very world in which the men and women to whom I am pastor spend most of their time.

So I take a special interest in these two men, both in church, both praying, and both sinners. I keep returning to them, and I reflect on their similarities and contrasts. I elaborate what I know in a kind of pastoral midrash, a playful engagement with the text that pays as much attention to what is between the lines as to what is in the lines themselves. It is a way of reading the text that medieval Hebrew rabbis delighted in.

I have been pastor to both Pharisees and tax men and still remember many of their names. It isn't always easy to tell them apart. Pharisees for the most part have a pretty good opinion of themselves. They hold responsible jobs, care for their families, keep most of the commandments most of the time, are familiar with the culture of church life, give their offerings week by week in worship, and usually accept positions of leadership when asked. The tax men (and women) are not all that different in appearance but they do not have a very good opinion of themselves. Many carry huge burdens of guilt from the past. Others are troubled by secret sins, addictions, poisoned relationships, and despair. They manage to keep much of this hidden from others, often from their very families. They often attend church by fits and starts. Some of them do very well in their workplaces but may carry a tangle of scars from sexually or spiritually or emotionally (sometimes all three) abusive parents or relatives, pastors or priests, and have a difficult time feeling at home and accepted in a congregation.

I am responsible for encouraging, listening to, conversing with, praying for, preaching to, and teaching these people, leading both Pharisees and tax men in following Jesus. Both show up in the place of prayer where I am a pastor. Both are sinners. I am pastor equally to both. I don't find it easy.

*   *   *

It is not surprising that these two kinds of men, both sinners, are in the same church. Churches are notoriously lax about ordering background checks to identify people with criminal records and installing security systems to screen out people who might use the church as a cover for evil. The consequence is that churches collect a lot of undesirable people, men and women who end up being an embarrassment to the company of people who are honestly trying to worship a holy God, to serve the world in acts of love and justice, repentance and forgiveness, and to follow Jesus every day into their homes and workplaces in sacrificial obedience. If the church had run security checks on the Pharisee and the tax man, neither would have gotten through the door.

A tax man was well known in that society as an unscrupulous crook. Collecting taxes for the Roman government was probably the most exploitative and lucrative job available to a first-century Jew, something like working as a frontman for the Mafia. And the Pharisee? Pharisees in that society were on the whole well respected. They took God and God's law seriously. They were clearly on God's side and made up the moral and spiritual backbone of the society. But this particular Pharisee was a fake Pharisee. He engaged in Pharisee practices that avoided all appearance of evil, but these practices were all external to who he was. It wasn't unheard of that Pharisees, these people who were recognized by the people as on the side of God and the right, might be a little more showy than was necessary and might enjoy a little too obviously the perks of a righteous reputation, but most people seemed to look up to them, or at least to put up with them. Pharisees don't technically do anything obviously bad, after all, and they do a lot of good by upholding the standards of community morality. But neither are they particularly compelling advertisements for a life overflowing with milk and honey.

Tax men are at home in the dog-eat-dog world of money and competition. It is a world where you quickly learn that you are on your own, and anything goes if you can get by with it. Others learn to be wary of tax men. They can't be trusted. They are often up to no good. They live at constant risk and have their eye out for anything they can turn to advantage. They constantly jockey for position between the occupying Romans, who are only interested in using them for their own purposes, and their fellow Jews. Because tax men typically bully and cheat at will, their fellow citizens hate them. But not all of them. Some tax men are surprisingly decent people, keeping the uneasy economy between Roman and Jew working maybe as well as it can. Still, they bear watching, especially by the Pharisees, many of whom are self-appointed watchdogs over the moral behavior of their fellow Jews.

On the day of the story, both men have gone to church to pray. That is what churches are for. People go to church for many of the wrong reasons. The right reason for going to church is to pray. Both Pharisee and tax man have entered a church, and in so doing they have joined a community of men and women who are convinced that cultivating an attentive listening and speaking relation to the God who listens and speaks to them is at the very heart of being human. While there are visible forms and audible words involved in prayer, prayer is mostly an interior act, the most interior act, in fact, that humans can engage in.

No one can tell just by observing whether a person using the forms and words of prayer is actually praying. It doesn't take most of us long to find this out for ourselves, how easy it is to "pray" without actually praying, how easy it is to acquire a reputation as a man or woman who is on good terms with God without bothering to pay attention to God, how easy it is to use the setting of church and the forms and words of prayer to avoid the demanding work of dealing with God, with God's people, with God's Creation. Given the ease of deception, is it any wonder that the place and practice of prayer should be the very best place where we can avoid God without anyone noticing? So it is not surprising that the setting most conducive to the cultivation of interiority should be so often deficient in it. Virtually no one goes to church to pray with the intention of *not* dealing with God, at least early on. But when we find that we can get so effortlessly all the social benefits of being associated with God without having to deal with God, it is hardly remarkable that form without content (our usual word for it is "hypocrisy") is so prevalent in places of prayer.

Nobody that I have ever met started going to church with the intention of cultivating hypocrisy, but when we realize how simple a matter it is to escape detection, before we know it, there we are. Neither have I ever met anyone who is self-aware of hypocrisy. Like high blood pressure, it is a "silent killer," but in these matters it is the interior life of faith and prayer, not the circulatory system, that is damaged. Frequenting a religious place and engaging in a religious practice can get us into a lot of trouble that we aren't even aware we are in. It certainly did for this Pharisee.

Jesus does not use the word "hypocrisy" in telling this story. He uses it at other times and places to expose religious playacting, most famously in Matthew 23, but in this story he puts us in church, between the Pharisee and the tax man, so that we see how it works.

Hypocrisy is a unique sin in that it does not begin in a temptation to do wrong: to dishonor parents, to steal another's money or property, to murder, to be unfaithful to a spouse, to use language to blaspheme or deceive. There is a "forbidden fruit" aspect to the standard sins that makes them attractive, temptations to something desirable, suggestions of excitement, of ecstasy, transcending humdrum mortality, temptations to be "like gods." Hypocrisy is different. Hypocrisy originates in a place of prayer and with people who pray. But there is usually a long pre-hypocrisy incubation period. It usually begins with a genuine attraction to God and righteousness and prayer. But along the way we find out that we can't do it just by fooling around with it in off hours. We would like to be known as a person of prayer with a reputation for righteousness, but when we find out there is more to it than panting like a thirsty deer for fresh water, desire dissipates in distraction. Attentiveness is required. A quiet listening is required. Nothing heroic, mind you, but a non-assertive going to the river and waiting there in a kind of receptive anticipation, like Mary's "Let it be to me . . ." (Luke 1:38 RSV).

Hypocrisy is not the fruit of "bad seed." It is the lazy replacement of a strenuous interior life with God with religious makeup and gossipy god-chatter. Even then it takes a long time for that germ of desire to get completely suppressed. Hypocrisy is slow-growing. In its early stages it is difficult to detect.

And that is why no one is conscious of becoming a hypocrite. The line between that original impulse to be in on what God is doing and the procrastinating indolence of failing to attend to God on God's terms is crossed without awareness. Distraction from intended good ends up as hypocrisy.

All the standard sins are fairly obvious. Those who commit them know what they are doing, however self-deceived they may be about their motives. When you wake up in bed with someone else's spouse you know you are an adulterer. When you pull a trigger and kill a man you know you are a murderer. When you steal a car and drive through a desert blossoming with spring flowers, the beauty of the scenery doesn't wipe out your awareness that you are a thief. But I've never been pastor to a hypocrite who knew he or she was a hypocrite, at least in the early stages.

Both men in Jesus' story are sinners. There is no ambiguity on that score. The tax man is a conspicuous sinner, working in a despicable occupation that exploits others to the point of impoverishment. The Pharisee's status as sinner is not conspicuous. He is a member of a social class that provides him with a role that exempts him from being lumped in with the social stereotype "sinners," the obvious candidates being the thieves, rogues, adulterers, and tax collectors (Luke 18:11), which everyone knows the Pharisee is not. He holds a respectable position in the community. At the same time, it probably would not escape the notice of at least a few of the others in that church that there was considerable religious pomposity in the man, a pomposity that called into question the honesty of his prayers. But pomposity and dishonest prayer are not sins that carry the same social disapproval attached to a thief, rogue, adulterer, and tax man. They are not even designated as sins. But the Pharisee is a sinner all the same.

The tax man knows he is a sinner. The Pharisee hasn't a clue that he is.

Will the story furnish the Pharisee with an imagination adequate to catalyze his mock prayer into real prayer?

*   *   *

What would make my work as a pastor easy would be to stereotype the Pharisee and the tax man. This would simplify things considerably. I wouldn't have to deal with either one as a person with a story. Jesus' story is more often than not de-storied and flattened into a stereotype, an illustration of a moral or an introduction to a theological doctrine. The Pharisee is stereotyped into an incorrigible and loathsome hypocrite. The tax man is stereotyped into a romantic "brand plucked from the burning." The Pharisee is assigned a role as representative of "religion," the tax man as representative of "spirituality."

These are stereotypes that are ripe for demolition: the religious hypocrite versus the spiritual freelancer; institutional religion stiff with the starch of hypocrisy versus spontaneous spirituality keeping company with the birds of the air; religion swaddled in clichés and safe in the arms of Jesus versus spirituality that runs with the wolves and hazards life in the wilderness.

But things are more complex than that. The stereotypes are facile. The pitting of spirituality and religion one against the other is tempting, but it obscures more than it clarifies. Life is more complex than that. A congregation is more complex than that. A mature life of prayer is more complex than that. The fact is that both men are in a place of formal, institutional religion. Both men are there to do the same thing, to pray. Pharisees and tax men rarely show up as either black or white. In actual life they occur in all shades of sepia and gray.

*   *   *

As it has turned out, I find that I like Pharisees. When I began as a pastor, my congregation was made up mostly of Pharisees. Not hypocrites, mind you, but Pharisees. They wanted access to a place of worship where they could clarify the distinctiveness of their baptismal identity over against the muddled superficialities of American culture. They wanted to be part of a congregation where they could nurture that identity. I liked that. I liked being companion to men and women who had an appetite for righteousness and were comfortable with nurturing that appetite into sensitivity and depth within the forms of establishment religion. But knowing how easily hypocrisy breeds in this environment, I also took seriously the work of encouraging attentiveness and receptivity, alert to any evidence of bully activism that so quickly destroys contemplation, the evangelical busyness that reduces prayer to form and formula.

From time to time a tax man, usually out of desperation, would show up in my workplace, my congregation. Their tribe increased through the years. They turned out to be the strongest defense against hypocrisy imaginable. The honesty and freshness and, yes, innocence of a tax man's prayers were a powerful antidote to any incipient hypocrisies that might be developing in the congregation. Their fresh perceptions of grace were quietly infectious among the Pharisees.

*   *   *

Forty-year-old Abigail, a middle-aged hippie, who had spent much of her life dealing with drug addictions and alcoholism in her spouse and children, found her place one Sunday in the back of the church. Always in the back. And then while the last hymn was being sung she would slip out, preserving her anonymity. After about six months she stayed through the benediction. As I greeted her at the door she said, "I feel so lucky. I've never heard these stories before. I never knew there was a place like this on earth. I feel so lucky." It was the first time I had ever heard anyone use the word "lucky" for something that went on in church.

It took another three months before she divulged her name. And then, in bits and pieces, she began telling me her story.

She was not the only one. Every month or so another tax man or woman would show up. And then another. And then another. Not many of them were ever really assimilated into the congregation, never did really "fit" into our Pharisee culture. But early on I realized how important they were to the health of the congregation. I can't recall ever preaching a sermon on hypocrisy. I didn't need to. The tax men and women, sitting in the back of the church, staying as inconspicuous as possible, turned out to be powerful antibodies against hypocrisies of every stripe. In one way or another they conveyed what Abigail named as lucky. These tax men and women salted the congregation with luck, holy luck. Soon many of the rest of us were feeling lucky. Lucky Pharisees. Lucky to have these tax men and women as witnesses (usually nonverbal) to the freshness of grace and the simplicities of prayer. Lucky to have the pre-hypocrite complacencies in ourselves exposed before they hardened into the deadly sin of hypocrisy.

*   *   *

This is the third Samaritan road story in which Jesus invites us into a life of prayer.

The story of the friend (Luke 11:5-13) used the everyday act of going next door at midnight to borrow bread for an unexpected guest as an analogue to prayer. Prayer is not a mystical or esoteric piece of spirituality. It is ordinary. Prayer is not a technique you can learn from a motivational expert on winning friends and influencing people. It is as simple as an act of friendship. Prayer is not something to be used in emergencies and crises, like mouth-to-mouth resuscitation. It is as commonplace as asking for and receiving bread in acts of everyday hospitality. What takes place in our prayers to God is not so very different from what takes place all the time in neighborhoods and in families.

The story of the widow (Luke 18:1-8) helps us to reimagine what we so often designate "unanswered prayers" as something quite different. If we think that the silence of God before our prayers is a matter of calloused indifference, think again. God is the exact opposite of the evil judge in the story, opposite in every detail. Prayer is not begging God to do something for us that he doesn't know about, or begging God to do something for us that he is reluctant to do, or begging God to do something that he hasn't time for. In prayer we persistently, faithfully, trustingly come before God, submitting ourselves to his sovereignty, confident that he is acting, right now, on our behalf. We are his "chosen ones," and don't ever forget it. God is, right now — the word is "quickly" (v. 8) — working his will in your life and circumstances. So keep praying. Don't quit.

And this story of Pharisee and tax man is a vivid exposé of the pretentious silliness of any so-called prayer that is not personal and ordinary, of prayer that is not embedded in the immediate and personal relationships and language of everyday life.

Cumulatively, the three stories assure us that prayer, language used in relation to God, language used to cultivate the vast interiors that make up most of our life, is as natural on any Samaritan road as it is in any temple or church we find ourselves in.

CHAPTER 12

The Minimalist: Luke 19:11-27

Our Hebrew ancestors, finding themselves in Babylonian exile, asked, "How shall we sing the LORD's song in a strange land?" (Ps. 137:4 KJV). Two thousand five hundred years later, the question is poignant still. How do we talk about God while we are immersed in the company of people who have a very different idea of what the word "God" means than we do? How do we talk about the way God works in the world when the people around us don't share the same stories and traditions of the way the world runs that we do? How do we talk about God as we are rubbing shoulders on a daily basis with men and women who practice a way of life that takes for granted a quite different set of ways and means for becoming whole, complete, our true selves, than we do?

How do we "sing the Lord's song," how do we talk about Jesus, in America?

Luke frames the Psalm 137 question around the geographical metaphor of Samaria. In Samaria Jesus is a stranger among strangers. How does he speak with these men and women who do not share a common worship, a common tradition? How do we?

Luke's narration of Jesus' metaphorical journey through Samaria is about to end. Jesus will enter Jerusalem and within a week he will be killed. He set out from Galilee to go to Jerusalem. There he will complete his life of preaching, teaching the arrival of the kingdom of God "on earth as it is in heaven," and recruiting followers along the way. We have to imagine quite a mixed company: committed Galilean disciples, seriously religious Pharisees, corrupt tax men, and, by this time, a considerable number of Samaritans along for the ride.

We have listened to Jesus tell ten stories, the ten Samaritan road stories that are unique to Luke's Gospel, stories that he uses to draw his hearers into an understanding of the kingdom of God. It is characteristic of these stories that they require an imaginative participation by the hearer. With the exception of one story ("The Sinners"), the stories take place in nonreligious settings, with the word "God" occurring only tangentially. These stories are not illustrations of a truth or moral. They are oblique. They come to the hearer on the "slant," slipping past defenses, misunderstandings, hostile preconceptions. Luke has a special interest in pulling outsiders into the company of Jesus, and so he takes these language conditions of Samaria — unfamiliarity with normative Judaism, misunderstanding, uncongeniality — and uses these very conditions to get the attention, and hopefully the participation, of the people who didn't grow up using the language and engaging in the practices of synagogues in Galilee and the temple in Jerusalem.

The final story that Jesus tells on this walk through Samaria is not unique to Luke. It is a reworking of a story that was recorded earlier by Matthew (Matt. 25:14-30). But I want to include this story, for it is an essential transition from the metaphorical journey through Samaria to the actual entrance into Jerusalem and Jesus' final week there, which would be the consummation of his life on Palestinian soil.

*   *   *

While he had their attention, and because they were getting close to Jerusalem by this time and expectation was building that God's kingdom would appear any minute, he told this story:

"There was once a man descended from a royal house who needed to make a long trip back to headquarters to get authorization for his rule and then return. But first he called ten servants together, gave them each a sum of money, and instructed them, 'Operate with this until I return.'

"But the citizens there hated him. So they sent a commission with a signed petition to oppose his rule: 'We don't want this man to rule us.'

"When he came back bringing the authorization of his rule, he called those ten servants to whom he had given the money to find out how they had done.

"The first said, 'Master, I doubled your money.'

"He said, 'Good servant! Great work! Because you've been trustworthy in this small job, I'm making you governor of ten towns.'

"The second said, 'Master, I made a fifty percent profit on your money.'

"He said, 'I'm putting you in charge of five towns.'

"The next servant said, 'Master, here's your money safe and sound. I kept it hidden in the cellar. To tell you the truth, I was a little afraid. I know you have high standards and hate sloppiness, and don't suffer fools gladly.'

"He said, 'You're right that I don't suffer fools gladly — and you've acted the fool! Why didn't you at least invest the money in securities so I would have gotten a little interest on it?'

"Then he said to those standing there. 'Take the money from him and give it to the servant who doubled my stake.'

"They said, 'But Master, he already has double . . .'

"He said, 'That's what I mean: Risk your life and get more than you ever dreamed of. Play it safe and end up holding the bag.

"'As for these enemies of mine who petitioned against my rule, clear them out of here. I don't want to see their faces around here again.'" (Luke 19:11-27 *The Message*)

*   *   *

Luke has prepared us well for this story that introduces us into the "end time" character of Jesus' entrance into Jerusalem and the definitive consummation of his life in crucifixion, resurrection, and ascension.

To begin with, all three Gospel writers record Jesus telling his disciples before he sets out for Jerusalem that that is, in fact, his destination and that he will suffer there, die, and rise again. Luke places the first two predictions just previous to setting out on the trip through Samaria. He places the third one just before arriving at Jericho, the last stop before Jerusalem. The end is near.

He also emphasizes the significance of Jericho as point of entry for "taking the promised land." Joshua (the Hebrew spelling and pronunciation of the name "Jesus"), a thousand years earlier, and now Jesus both use Jericho to provide a visible demonstration of the glory of God and the imminence of salvation (the collapse of the walls for Joshua, giving sight to Bartimaeus for Jesus). And each of them rescues a "lost" soul in Jericho, in turn — Rahab and Zacchaeus.

Luke makes sure we catch the Rahab/Zacchaeus allusion by introducing this final Samaritan story with the words, "while he had their attention (or, in his welcoming words to Zacchaeus, "Today is salvation day in this home!"), and because they were getting close to Jerusalem . . . he told this story."

*　　*　　*

The reason for telling the story is that "they were getting close to Jerusalem . . . and expectation was building that God's kingdom would appear any minute." The story is about a man "descended from a royal house" who made a long trip to get credentials authorizing him to be king. He got what he went for, despite the delegation of citizens who "hated him" and signed a petition stating, "We don't want this man to rule us."

After telling this story, Jesus proceeded from Jericho to Jerusalem, a strenuous seventeen-mile ascent of 3,300 feet. The Palm Sunday parade followed the next day. As Jesus descended the Mount of Olives into Jerusalem he was cheered by a great crowd who recognized him as king and cried out, "Blessed is he who comes, the king in God's name!" (Luke 19:38 *The Message*). Four more times that week in Jerusalem, Jesus is referred to as king, twice at the trial before Pilate (23:2-3) and twice as he was hanging on the cross (23:37-38) — five times altogether, the first time in praising acceptance, followed by four times in murderous rejection. In no uncertain terms they gave their verdict: "We don't want this man to rule us."

*　　*　　*

There is more to this story — we haven't come to the main point yet — but it is perhaps useful to pause and reflect on what Jesus is getting us ready to take in by means of this story: "We don't want this man to rule us." Really? Yes, really.

Jesus' final story on the Samaritan road — it will be echoed a few days later in Jerusalem when Jesus tells the story of the wicked tenants (Luke 20:9-19) — encapsulates a central theme threaded through the entire biblical story.

The thread has two strands: God wants us; we don't want God.

God wants us. Jesus' language is spoken in a world in which God wants us. We are created by God for God. We are estranged from God and God is determined to win us back. God wants us as a lover wants the beloved. God insistently, relentlessly pursues a restored relationship with us. God seeks us. God is and has been seeking us long before we had any idea of seeking God.

Our relation with God begins with God speaking the first word. Before it ever occurs to us to speak to or even think of God, God speaks to us. As he did with Mary. God sent the angel Gabriel to Mary, and Gabriel greeted her with the words, "Hail, O favored one, the Lord is with you!" (Luke 1:28 RSV). Mary had no idea what that meant. She was upset and bewildered, doing her best to understand. How could she know that this was *God* speaking to her, let alone know what was being said? But she didn't have to wait long. The angel elaborated on his greeting, and she learned that God was about to conceive his very own life in her. After a clarifying question and answer, she assented: "Behold, I am the handmaid of the Lord; let it be to me according to your word" (1:38 RSV). God wants us. He intends to conceive new life, *God's life,* in us.

He doesn't wait around for us to come up with the idea that God might be a good idea to consider. God doesn't send us to the library to figure out what men and women have been saying about God and see what we can make of it. God doesn't organize search parties by veteran angels to find out likely places for getting a glimpse, and maybe, if we are lucky, a photograph of God. No. "Our God comes and does not keep silence" (Ps. 50:3). We don't come to God; God comes to us. We don't start the conversation; God starts it.

But — *we don't want God*. The well-documented evidence is that we want to be our own gods. The evidence piles up from every continent and civilization, every century and every religion. It is irrefutable. The evidence is thoroughly and convincingly confirmed in our Scriptures and documented in each and every one of our lives. God is a rival, not an ally, in the god-business. We want to be our own gods. The Snake promised us we could do it — "you will be like God" (Gen. 3:5) — and we have been at it ever since. As it turns out, we are very good at it.

Our ancestor people of God tell us the stories that allow us no wiggle room for escaping the conclusion. After their miraculous provision of food and water in the wilderness, the newly saved Israelites assembled at Mt. Sinai and received God's covenant word in earthquake, smoke, fire, sounding trumpets, and reverberating thunder. The people would never be able to forget that: the Red Sea salvation, wilderness manna and quail, water from the rock, the guiding cloud by day and fire by night, and all of it climaxed in those defining, freedom-giving, personal words of God. But they did forget.

It happened like this. God called Moses to climb back up Sinai for further instructions. The people saw the mountain blaze again with glory. They had to know that something serious was going on. But Moses was gone a long time — forty days and nights — and the people got restless. They got tired of waiting. Their associate pastor, Aaron, provided them with a gold calf-god that they could handle and use, a god without mystery, a god who was there when they needed it. They loved it. They worshiped, ate and drank, and had a grand party.

They made a god, and then they became like the god they made. The Snake's promise turned out to be a lie. They became "like god" all right, but the god they became "like" was dead.

Their gods are metal and wood,
 handmade in a basement shop:
Carved mouths that can't talk,
 painted eyes that can't see,
Tin ears that can't hear,
 molded noses that can't smell,
Hands that can't grasp, feet that can't walk or run,
 throats that never utter a sound.
Those who make them have become just like them,
 have become just like the gods they trust.

(Ps. 115:4-8 The Message)

And we keep doing it over and over and over again. Baal and Asherah and Moloch. The gods of Canaan and Tyre, Egypt and Assyria and Babylon. The gods of Persia and Greece and Rome. The gods of Russia and China. The gods of India and Africa. The gods of England and Australia. And the gods of America. America leads the world at present in golden-calf production.

It is important to observe that the paradigmatic story of our not wanting God is not about pagans who have never heard of the God of "Abraham, Isaac and Jacob." It is about a God-saved people, a "born-again" people if you will, who have been instructed in the full revelation of God and have committed themselves to it. They were all too sincere when they said, "All that the LORD has spoken we will do, and we will be obedient" (Exod. 24:7).

Given the extensive coverage in our Scriptures to the Snake's success in diverting God's people from the living God, the naiveté that assumes that if we just make Jesus more attractive men and women will flock in great numbers to follow him is astonishing. The widespread American assumption that if we can just get the gospel message out loud and clear men and women will sign up on the spot is an illusion of the Snake.

It is an assumption that uses the vocabulary of God's truth disconnected from the truth of God. It is spirituality divorced from the

151

Holy Spirit. It is information about Jesus without participation in the life of Jesus.

*   *   *

But back to Jesus' story of the king who returned to rule a people who "hated him." Before the man left to be made king, he gave ten of his servants identical sums of money and told them, "Operate with this until I come back — put this money to good use, make something of it." In other words, they were to carry on his business while he was gone, continue doing what he himself would have been doing if he had been there, working on his behalf, taking initiative, and using the knowledge and experience that they had acquired in the years of being associated with him as his servants to promote his interests. He would not be on hand to give them specific orders each workday — he was trusting them to figure that out on their own.

The first thing he did on his return was call the servants together and ask them how it went. The first reported that he had doubled what the master had given him. The second said he had increased his stake by fifty percent. The third said that he had done nothing. His excuse was feeble: "I was a little afraid. I know you have high standards and hate sloppiness, and don't suffer fools gladly."

The master — returned now as king — commended the first two servants and, with considerable vehemence, dismissed the third, the play-it-safe, the minimalist.

*   *   *

This is the final story Jesus tells on the Samaritan road. The next thing we know, Jesus and his followers are in Jerusalem. It is a glorious entrance, but the glory is short-lived. Midway through the inaugural parade (the people assume they are welcoming their new king), Jesus is weeping over the city and announcing the city's brutal devastation by enemies, because "you did not recognize the time of your visitation from God" (Luke 19:44). Before the day is over Jesus storms through the

Caiaphas-corrupt temple, throwing out the people who had turned the place into a lucrative marketplace, shamelessly selling religion. He quotes the prophet Isaiah: "My house shall be a house of prayer" (Luke 19:46; see Isa. 56:7) and then uses Jeremiah's words (Jer. 7:11) to convict them of the worst kind of sacrilege, selling "god" to innocent people, robbing people blind while pretending to save their souls.

And that was the end of the king business. Before the week was out the king was dead, hanging on a cross. No kingdom of God.

*   *   *

There can be little doubt, I think, that the crowds cheering Jesus as their new king expected the angelic hosts of heaven to fill the streets that day and take care of the Romans for good. It didn't happen. Meanwhile that story Jesus told on the way up from Jericho to Jerusalem was working its way in the minds and imaginations of some, at least, of Jesus' followers. Maybe they weren't wrong about the kingdom and its king at all. They had supposed that the king and his kingdom would be established by violence — how else would you establish a kingdom? Maybe Jesus all along had been preparing them to understand that the kingdom of God was not present among them in that way at all. Jesus' stories began to fall into place. Maybe they were only wrong in their understanding of the *way* the kingdom was formed and the *way* its king ruled.

These tentative "maybe's" slowly but surely solidified into a firm foundation. Three days after the "failure" of the kingdom and its king, a quiet revolution began to take place, catalyzed in Jesus' resurrection. The king was alive after all — but not in the way they had been expecting. This took some getting used to. How long did it take for all this to sink in? We do not know, but sink in it did. Peter brandishing his sword in Gethsemane, cutting off the ear of Malchus and commanded by Jesus to put his sword away (John 18:10-11), was the last we see or hear of swords in the gospel story. From now on it was stories, not swords, that would form the identity of the followers of Jesus and provide the content and shape of the kingdom in which they were citizens.

153

*　　*　　*

This final Samaritan story slowly began to form a new identity among them. Of course, "We don't want this man to rule us." But he is ruling all the same. Maybe they were now ready to learn the ways he ruled and the ways they could participate in his rule as "servants" entrusted to continue his work: doing what he did; speaking as he spoke; repenting and forgiving; praying and blessing; discovering neighbors in unlikely places; realizing the irreducible personal quality in everything that has to do with God; submitting to the silent energies (manure!) that, like the energies of resurrection, turn death into life; realizing the dangers of "prayer" that is not prayer, how wary we must be of something good, like wealth, becoming a host for something bad, like greed; welcoming a realization of lostness, "the preparing power of chaos," the improbabilities of grace, the apocalyptic urgencies inherent in prayer.

This kingdom of God life is not a matter of waking up each morning with a list of chores or an agenda to be tended to, left on our bedside table by the Holy Spirit for us while we slept. We wake up already immersed in a large story of creation and covenant, of Israel and Jesus, the story of Jesus and the stories that Jesus told. We let ourselves be formed by these formative stories, and especially as we listen to the stories that Jesus tells, get a feel for the way he does it, the way he talks, the way he treats people, the *Jesus way*.

The end of the Jesus story in Jerusalem — his crucifixion, resurrection, and ascension — as it turns out is not the end. Our life with Jesus on the way to Jerusalem continues after Jerusalem. It continues still. The "sums of money" — the stories Jesus told, the life Jesus lived — continue in circulation in the stories we tell and the story we live. The kingdom is here. We are in it. The "sum of money" that we are left with is not something to be guarded, protected, and kept safe, but put to good use.

This final Samaritan story is a sobering word: non-participation is not a casual matter. However timidly or meekly enacted, non-participation is disobedience. (At the same time, it is just as true that there is plenty of room for timid and meek obedience — seven of the servants are not commented on. Not all of us will be as conspicuous in our obedience as the first and second servants.) The story is unrelenting: self-serving minimalism is not an option. There are no non-participants in Jesus' kingdom. This final Samaritan story is an uncompromisingly severe judgment story. The description of the third servant takes up seven out of the seventeen verses in the story. More space is given to the judgment delivered on the play-it-safe, cautious, non-participating, non-servant than the other nine servants, let alone the petitioners against the king's rule, who get only one verse. A timid refusal to obey makes us liable to the same judgment as overt and defiant disobedience. Obediently following Jesus in this already inaugurated kingdom of God is serious business indeed.

II

JESUS IN HIS PRAYERS

CHAPTER 13

Keeping Company with Jesus as He Prays:
Six Prayers

First, Jesus in his stories, stories that grow from metaphors. Metaphor and story characterize Jesus' language. Stories are personal and make us insiders to the place we live in and the people in it. Stories keep us close to the actual ground, alert to the voices around us, present to the silence. There are no formalities, no abstractions, no "big" truths. It's not a language we use to map and decipher the world so that we can always know where we are, not a language that we use to command and control the world and the people in it. Rather, it is a language that provides room for ambiguity and presence, a language that brings us into a conversational participation with one another in this language-created, language-formed, Word-made-flesh world. For those of us who decide to follow Jesus, it only follows that we will not only listen to what he says and attend to what he does, but also learn to use language the way he uses it. We will be on guard against disincarnating our language into formulating ideas or summarizing rules or giving out information.

And now, Jesus in his prayers. Prayer is language that is answeringly attentive to God. Moving from Jesus in his stories to Jesus in his prayers risks leaving the particular, colloquial, local uses of language in which we have been immersed in the Samaritan Travel Narrative and sailing into the wild blue yonder, losing ourselves in grand "spiritual" abstractions. But we must not. And we will not if we keep company with Jesus in his prayers. The stories Jesus tells on the road between Galilee and Jerusalem keep the language he and his friends use on that road local and personal, immediate to the circumstances, present to the conditions. His language is just as local and present and personal with the Father who is in heaven as it is with his companions over meals at the table and while walking on the road.

I want to insist that the language of Jesus in his prayers is neither less nor more himself, soul and body, than in his stories. Prayer is anemic if the language dissipates into mist, into a pious fog of sentimentalities, thinned out to pious clichés. When we keep company with Jesus in his prayers, that doesn't happen.

Story and prayer are the core language of our humanity. We say most truly who we are when we tell stories to one another and pray to our Lord. Story and prayer are also the core language of our Scriptures: God tells us who he is, completely revealed in Jesus, the Word made flesh who completed "the works that the Father has given me to complete" (John 5:36) and all the while is attentively listening and obediently answering, as a Son to his Father — praying. Our Scriptures consist mostly of stories and prayers. We enter most appropriately into that revelation when we listen and tell stories to one another and listen and speak to God in prayer.

And, of course, silence. Silence is indispensable. It is a commonly overlooked element in language, but it must not be. Especially it must not be overlooked in the language of prayer. It is not as if Jesus speaks the revelation of God in his stories and metaphors, and now in prayer we get to say our piece. Silence, which in prayer consists mostly in attentive listening, is nonnegotiable. Listening, which necessarily requires silence on our part, is as much a part of language as words. The colon and the semicolon, the comma and the period — all of which insist on silence as part and parcel of speech — are as essential to language as nouns and verbs. But more often than not, silence gets short shrift in our prayers. Yet if there is no silence, our speech degenerates into babble.

*   *   *

Prayer is our first language. Anybody can pray. And everybody does. We pray even when we don't know we are praying. "Help me" is our first prayer. We don't have it within ourselves to be ourselves. "Thank you" is our last prayer. When everything is said and done, we realize that all that we receive has been gift.

But there is irony here. Prayer, the most natural and authentic substratum of language, is also the easiest form of language to fake. We discover early on that we can pretend to pray, use the words of prayer, practice the forms of prayer, assume postures of prayer, acquire a reputation for prayer, and never pray. Our "prayers," so-called, are a camouflage to cover up a life of non-prayer.

A friend meets me in the parking lot and tells me her troubles. On taking leave I say, "I'll pray for you." I go into the grocery store with my shopping list. The promise to pray is pushed off to the side by assessments on the price of the asparagus, decisions on whether it will be steak or liver for supper, and small talk with the check-out clerk on yesterday's soccer game in which both of our sons played. And so the promised prayer is displaced, or at least considerably watered down, by the urgencies of buying milk and orange juice.

Thankfully we have been given easily accessible protections against the faux prayers and gossipy talk of prayer that cover up the absence of prayer. These are set prayers, prayers provided for us that we can use to keep our praying congruent with the prayers of our ancestors, prayers of others that we can use to stay in touch with the authentic world of prayer revealed in our Scriptures. They are prayers that we can use to distinguish prayer from prayer impostors, fantasy, and magic. They are prayers that don't depend on our own initiative, prayers that don't wax and wane according to the phases of our moods.

In my own family we have a pretty well developed "culture of the table."[1] Meals are a significant element in the way we live. A great deal

---

1. The phrase is from Albert Borgmann. He uses it to great effect in giving us a way of recovering a personal community in the depersonalized wasteland of technology. See his *Technology and the Character of Contemporary Life* (Chicago: The University of Chicago Press, 1984).

of our common life is integrated into preparing meals, considering the tastes and circumstances of those who will be eating the meal, setting the table, eating the meal, cleaning up after the meal. No single meal is quite like another. There are many variables: the kinds of food that make up the meal, which members of the family will be there, guests that we anticipate. We enjoy the work. But occasionally we run out of energy and imagination. When that happens we drive a few miles to a favorite restaurant in order to have someone else do it for us: shop for the food and prepare it, set the table, serve the meal, clear the table, and wash the dishes. A "set" meal: someone else whom we trust does it all for us. All we have to do is pick up the fork that has been set before us, eat the meal that has been set in place, and leave the cleaning up to others.

When we are young children, all our meals are set meals, set before us without thought or preparation on our part. Gradually we learn to do it for ourselves and for others as we grow up. But it is still nice to have someone do it for us when we are tired or without appetite. The analogy to prayer is not exact, but it is close enough in this context.

The classic set prayers for Christians and Jews are the Psalms.[2] And for Christians, the set prayers include the prayers of Jesus.

It is a common and widespread practice in the Christian community to apprentice ourselves to the prayers that Jesus prayed as they are given to us in our Scriptures. We keep conversational company with Jesus as he prays. We get used to the ways he prays so that we can become as honest in our needs, as attentive to the presence of God, as responsive to the Spirit, as wide ranging as Jesus in his participation, and our participation with him, in all the operations of the Trinity.

A young Asian woman in my congregation showed up in my study one day. She had, she said, a gift for me: my Chinese name. She showed it to me. She had written my name in exquisite calligraphic

---

2. In *Answering God: The Psalms as Tools for Prayer* (New York: HarperCollins, 1989), I have written in detail on how the Psalms provide training and discipline in the ways of biblical prayer.

Chinese script. "Here, you write it." My attempt was clumsy. She was patient. After ten minutes or so, I was making an approximate rendering of the Chinese script. "Now say it." She pronounced the syllables slowly. The sounds were unfamiliar; I wasn't used to making these sounds. But, still patient, she coached me. In another ten minutes I was making the right sounds. But she wasn't satisfied. "Very good. You can write your name. You can say your name. But it's not good enough. You have to make your name sing — in Chinese words sing." She gave me a singing lesson. I tried, and tried, but never quite got it right. I'm still an apprentice. Sometimes I think of this when I am praying. I'm saying the words, but are the words singing?

Jesus' prayers provide an accurate and steadfast center for developing a life of mature Christian prayer. We observe Jesus at prayer and follow it up by keeping company with him. We acquire a sense of the historical fact *that* Jesus prayed, and we embrace a continuing apprenticeship in his *way* of prayer.

"Sometimes" — when we aren't trying too hard — "a light surprises" (William Cowper) and we realize that the prayers are singing.

Putting together a life of prayer out of scraps from here and there — "I'll pray for you" clichés, moments of desperation, a burst of praised bliss, a dogged but evanescent resolve to "pray more," pious emotions — never amounts to much. We are after something substantial and whole: said *and* sung, prayer revealed by the Father through the Son by the Holy Spirit.

*   *   *

But Jesus is more than a master to whom we apprentice ourselves: he is even now praying for us. This may be the most important thing to know, not how he prayed, although that is certainly important, but that he is at this very moment praying — *for us*. Jesus is our master in prayer; he is also our companion in prayer. He says to us, "I'll pray for you . . ." — and does it. His promise to pray for us is not lost or overlooked in a vast heavenly clutter of petitions and intercessions, confessions and thanksgivings, ascending in a cloud of incense to his altar. It defeats our imagination to understand how this takes place, but we have it on good authority that it does.

The letter to the Hebrews elaborates this continuously contemporary praying priesthood of the ascended Jesus. The text insists that Jesus did not just pray for us once and leave it at that; instead, "he always lives to make intercession" for us (Heb. 7:25). Jesus prays. He is praying for us right now. He was praying for us yesterday. He will be praying for us tonight as we sleep and tomorrow morning as we wake up. Jesus praying for us is a current event.

You don't think you know how to pray? Yes, there is much to learn; meanwhile Jesus is praying for you. You don't feel like praying? Relax, feelings come and go; meanwhile Jesus is praying for you. You don't have time to pray? Jesus doesn't mind waiting; meanwhile he has plenty of time to pray for you.

*   *   *

Jesus prayed. There are some seventeen references in the Gospels to Christ's active prayer life.[3] Just as Luke has the most frequent citations of Jesus telling stories, Luke also has the most frequent references to Jesus at prayer, nine of them:

He withdrew to the wilderness and prayed. (Luke 5:16 RSV)

During those days he went out to the mountain to pray; and he spent the night in prayer to God. (6:12)

Once when Jesus was praying alone, with only the disciples near him, he asked them. . . . (9:18)

Jesus took with him Peter and John and James, and went up on the mountain to pray. And while he was praying. . . . (9:28)

3. James G. S. S. Thomson, *The Praying Christ* (Vancouver, B.C.: Regent College Reprint, 1995), p. 35.

He was praying in a certain place, and after he had finished, one of his disciples said to him, "Lord, teach us to pray. . . ." (11:1)

"Simon, Simon, listen! Satan has demanded to sift all of you like wheat, but I have prayed for you that your faith may not fail." (22:31)

Then he withdrew from them about a stone's throw, knelt down, and prayed. (22:41)

And being in an agony he prayed more earnestly. (22:44 RSV)

He took bread, blessed and broke it, and gave it to them. (24:30)

*   *   *

Jesus is the one to whom we pray. He is also the one who prays with and for us. Prayer is the language of the Trinity, intimately personal language. When we pray, we embrace the language of Jesus as our language. Nothing happens in this Christian life impersonally, according to blueprint, automatically by code. Every word is personal.

Jesus prayed. When we go to language school with Jesus, we pray.

But we are not left to figure all this out on our own. We have a primer, these set Jesus prayers. If we are shy, unsure of ourselves, we can pray them with the confidence that we are praying after the manner of the Master. We keep company with Jesus and gradually get the hang of what he is doing and how he is doing it.

Here they are, six set prayers that we will explore in the following chapters. Jesus prays with us: "Our Father . . ." (Matt. 6:9-13); Jesus prays in thanksgiving: "I thank you, Father . . ." (Matt. 11:25); Jesus prays in anticipation of the end: ". . . Father, glorify your name" (John 12:27-28); Jesus prays for us: "Father, the hour has come . . ." (John 17:1); Jesus prays "out of the depths" in the agony of Gethsemane: "My Father, if it is possible, let this cup pass from me . . . if this cannot pass unless I drink it, your will be done" (Matt. 26:39, 42); Jesus prays his death from the cross: "My God, my God, why have you forsaken me?" (Matt. 27:46).

Our praying ancestors ask us, Do you want to learn to pray, become proficient in prayer? Do you want to get in on the revelation of God, to become assenting participants in the conversation of the Father and the Son? Start here: keep company with Jesus, the Word made flesh, who completes "the works that the Father has given me to complete" (John 5:36).

CHAPTER 14

Jesus Prays with Us: Matthew 6:9-13

At almost the exact center of Jesus' well-known teaching, the Sermon on the Mount, he takes up the practice of prayer (Matt. 6:9-13). The sermon itself is a scintillating mosaic of metaphors and instruction, warnings and directions, aphorisms and a concluding story that provides a final punch. It is a tour de force of images and words for understanding who we are and what we are doing as we keep company with Jesus. Much of what Jesus says turns a lot of what we think about ourselves and the world around us upside down. There is a lot to take in, a lot to re-learn, a lot to re-imagine.

Prayer is the core of the Sermon on the Mount teaching. It is located at almost the exact center of the Sermon (Matt. 6:9-13). It holds the Sermon together and animates it. A kingdom-of-heaven life consists of things to do and ways to think, but if there is no prayer at the center nothing lives. Prayer is the heart that pumps blood into all the words and acts. Prayer is not just one more thing in an inventory of elements that make up a following-Jesus, kingdom-of-heaven life. Prayer is the heart. If there is no heart doing its work from the center, no matter how precise the words, no matter how perfectly formed the actions, there is only a corpse. It may be a very lovely corpse. The embalmer's art, especially when the embalmer knows his or her Bible, works wonders with appearances. But dead is dead. R.I.P.

This may all be obvious enough. What may not be obvious is that the act of prayer, which is such a gift, is fraught with danger. And so before Jesus takes up the practice of prayer, he posts a warning, *Danger:* "Do not . . ." (Matt. 6:5-8). Three times the danger warning is posted. Don't pray to show off before an audience, to "be seen by others." Prayer is not theater. Don't pray to lobby God with "many words." Prayer is not rhetoric. Don't pray to impress men, women, and, least of all, God.

Prayer is the heart of this kingdom life. But keep this in mind: nobody ever sees a heart when it is working. A heart is not a bumper sticker. When we pray with Jesus we don't wear our heart on our sleeve.

With the well-posted warnings in place, Jesus proceeds: "Pray then in this way."

"Our Father in heaven"

The first word, the pronoun, is significant. Jesus includes himself in the prayer that he is himself teaching us to pray: *"Our . . ."* — you and me. We are in this together. Jesus does not assume an aloof stance of an expert, telling us that this is the only way to pray. Prayer is not concerned with getting the words in the right order. When Jesus includes himself with us, the "our" is an unpretentious puncture in the hot-air balloon of affectation. Jesus does not condescend to those who are apprenticed to him. Jesus doesn't talk much about prayer; he prays. Jesus is not patronizing. He prays with us. And we pray with him.

The "our" continues to be significant. Prayer is always "our." With the "our," Jesus puts himself in our company. With the "our," we place ourselves in the company of Jesus and of all who pray. Prayer is never solitary. We are never alone when we pray. We are with Jesus and all others who follow him.

* * *

In the danger warnings that Jesus posts before he begins to pray, he uses the metaphor "Father" three times for the God to whom we pray.

In the sermon as a whole (Matt. 5–7) Jesus uses the term "Father" fifteen times; in ten of those instances it is expanded to "Father in heaven" or "heavenly Father." "Father" is Jesus' metaphor of choice for God.

Get used to this: *Father.* The oldest and most implacable enemy in the practice of prayer is depersonalization, turning prayer into a technique, using prayer as a device.

Using the metaphor "Father" for God is a language strategy to defend against the subtle but insidious depersonalization of prayer that pervades the human condition. In our technology-saturated culture, we frequently request help by asking, "How do I pray?" or even worse, "How do I pray effectively?" The question distorts what is fundamentally a personal relation into an impersonal technique. God is conceived as an idea or a force or a higher power. Prayer is reduced to an exercise in control: "If I can just get into the right mood and get the right words in the right order, I can get God to do what I want or get what I need."

Two of the danger signs that Jesus posted have to do with eliminating the personal God from the practice of prayer. Warning! Don't depersonalize God and everybody on the street into a faceless audience and put on a religious act. Warning! Don't depersonalize God into an abstraction by using words not as language but as numbers, "heaping up empty phrases," the more the better, never mind what they mean or if they mean anything at all.

The minute we obliterate the personal from prayer, there is no prayer. The heart stops beating. Naming God as Father keeps us alert to the personal in prayer.

"Father" as a metaphor names a person, not an object. Father and son and daughter are not functions. They are unique blood relationships.

*   *   *

Jan and I were waiting in the airline terminal in Frankfurt for our El Al flight to Israel. Passengers from an arriving El Al flight were entering the reception area. A little boy near us, maybe four or five years old, jumped up and ran across the large room shouting, "Abba! Abba! Abba! . . ." and was swept up into the receiving arms of his father.

It was the first time I had ever heard "Abba" in living speech. I had read the word in the Bible. I knew that in Jesus' mother tongue, Aramaic, it was the affectionate word for father, which would be common in family settings. I had read Mark's account of Jesus praying in agony in Gethsemane, naming God "Abba." I had read the way Paul, writing to the Christians in Rome, used the fact that they prayed "Abba" when they addressed God as evidence of the relational nature of their prayers, "the very Spirit bearing witness with our spirit that we are children of God" (Rom. 8:15-16). I had read how Paul had introduced the word when writing to the Christians in Galatia to emphasize to them their basic personal, familial relation to God as children to a father: "God has sent the Spirit of his Son into our hearts, crying 'Abba! Father!'" (Gal. 4:6). I had read what the German scholar Joachim Jeremias had written in his effort to capture the fresh intimacy and spontaneous immediacy conveyed when the word was used to address God. I had heard the word used in sermons by pastors and explained in classrooms by professors. I had heard the word all my life, but always in a "religious" setting.

And now I was hearing it in this depersonalized, technology-dominated airline terminal in Germany, spoken by a child I didn't know to address a man I didn't know. The word didn't tell me anything about the child or the father — but it told me everything I needed to know about their relationship — its immediacy, its intimacy, its joy.

The word came alive — a resurrection. I had long known the meaning; now I saw the meaning lived, incarnated in a father and son running to greet one another in the Frankfurt airport. I heard "father" not in formal address to an anonymous deity but in a child's shouts of recognition. I had encountered "father" often enough in an academic setting around a table strewn with lexicons and exegetical studies. But I had never heard the word used in the living context of a son happily and trustingly greeting his father. I had never heard the word sing. I felt like I was back on that Galilean hillside in the company of Jesus as he prayed with his followers, in the garden with Jesus as he prayed his passion, worshiping with the Roman and Galatian Christians as they found themselves included in Jesus' prayers every time they prayed, *Abba*, "Our Father in heaven. . . ."

*   *   *

Six brief, single-sentence petitions compose this prayer. Each verb is an imperative, a call for action. Prayer is not passive. Prayer is not resignation. God is active. As Jesus prays he enters the action of God. As he prays with us, he implicitly invites us into the action. As we pray with him we volunteer ourselves into the action.

"Hallowed be your name"

God has a name. He reveals himself with a name: Yahweh. The name enters our story and reveals the being of God with us, continuously, as he calls our names — Abraham, Moses, Samuel, Mary, Peter. God is not anonymous. God is not a principle. God has a name.

Prayer is language that is used to address a God who has revealed himself to Moses and in Jesus. Prayer is not a "general delivery" message. It is not a "to whom it may concern" missive.

And this name is holy. Holiness is the distinctive quality of otherness that sets God beyond and apart from — *other than* — us. God is not like us. We are not like God. The first sin, and it continues to be the basic sin, is to presume to "be like God" (Gen. 3:5). We attempt this by bringing God down to our level, reducing him to our image. We attempt it by constructing and then climbing a Babel tower that will bring us up to God's level. Either way is an attempt to obliterate the otherness, to get rid of the Holy. And neither way works.

If we, whether in naïve innocence or in Luciferian hubris, suppose that prayer is a way of bringing God down to our level or raising us to God's level, we are way off track.

*   *   *

I mentioned my delight in hearing "Abba" used as a child's term of affection for his father in the airline terminal in Frankfurt. And I mentioned that the German scholar Joachim Jeremias had tried to provide a fresh appreciation of the childlike spontaneity conveyed by "Abba." Jeremias tried to make a case for "Abba" meaning something on the order of "Daddy." His suggestion was welcomed with enthusiasm by many. The cozy informality of the term found itself used in sermons and teachings everywhere. It was made to order — and under such auspicious scholarly authority, the eminent Jeremias! — for a culture that was uneasy with authority, was anti-hierarchical, and wanted to be on a first-name, even nickname basis with everyone. And now with God.

Then the Oxford scholar James Barr threw cold water on what he discerned was nothing more than sentimentalizing coziness. He convincingly demonstrated that Jeremias was embarrassingly mistaken.[1] But by then it was too late. The horse was out of the barn. The mistake, coziness displacing holiness, keeps showing up in both scholarly and popular writing.

There is, to be sure, a childlike intimacy and delight in the use of "Abba." But the word also continues to carry an element of awe and respect and reverence. I don't cease to be a child in the presence of my father. Otherness is not diminished by affection. Intimacy does not preclude reverence. True intimacy does not eliminate a sacred awe: otherness, Otherness.

The "Daddy" fad that is still sweeping through our churches is a case of premature intimacy. We don't begin by getting cozy with God. We begin with solemn reverence: Holy.

In the first petition, Jesus leads off with a verb that gets us started off on the right foot and places us in a posture of reverent respect, standing in awe — an affectionate awe to be sure, but still awe. "Remove the sandals from your feet, for the place on which you are standing is holy ground" (Exod. 3:5). The first petition protects the third commandment: "You shall not take the name of the LORD your God in

1. James Barr, "Abba Isn't 'Daddy,'" *Journal of Theological Studies* (1988): 28-47.

vain" (Exod. 20:7 NASV); "You shall not make wrongful use of the name of the LORD your God" (NRSV).

*   *   *

For several years I was part of a group in Baltimore called the Jewish-Christian Roundtable. Twenty of us met monthly, ten orthodox rabbis and ten pastors and priests. We basically conducted a Bible study alternating the leadership between Jew and Christian. The rabbis always brought a handout of the Hebrew text that we would study together. And they always collected the pages afterwards — meticulously. I observed that they always counted the pages to make sure they had them all. One day I asked the rabbi in charge what he did with the pages afterwards. He said that he took them home and reverently burned them. He told me that it was a tradition with them. They were not permitted to leave the holy name in the hands of gentiles, lest it be inadvertently used or treated irreverently, or even blasphemously.

My immediate but unspoken reaction was negative. Wasn't this being a bit over-scrupulous? But as time went on I began to feel the weight of their reverence, this hallowing of the name. The experience continues in my memory as an implicit rebuke of the glibness in which the name is often tossed around in the circles I frequent. And it often enters my mind still when I pray "Hallowed be your name."

*   *   *

The word "God" comprises goodness and holiness and glory. But in everyday usage it gets marred with superstition, often unthinkingly. People read into the word "God" fears and ignorance and blasphemy. The name needs constant cleansing and burnishing. When we pray for the hallowing, we are praying to purge the words that name God's presence of any taint of sacrilege, to cleanse the images that fill our minds of any hint of idolatry, to scrape the noun clean of rust and grime until *Jesus* and *Christ* say the clear truth about God.

"Your kingdom come"

As we pray through the six petitions in the company of Jesus, with Jesus praying at our side, we find that the reality of the world, the actual nature of what we deal with in each day's living, is being redefined for us. To begin with, The Holy: God other than us; the God we cannot use for our own purposes; the God we cannot aspire to become so that we can impose our rule on the world.

And now kingdom: the way the world is and the way it works. Kingdom is a metaphor for a world that is ruled by a sovereign, a king. Its usefulness in prayer is its comprehensive inclusiveness: geography (mountains, rivers, oceans, forests, volcanoes, desert sand, and polar icecaps), weather (rain and snow, lightning and hail, sunshine and clouds), seasons (summer and winter, spring and fall), people (races and languages, farmers and bankers), political systems (dictatorships, democracies, socialist states, royal houses), economies (communism, capitalism, barter). Absolutely everything.

When we pray we are deliberately involving ourselves in a reality that is comprehensively created by and under the care of God. The first words out of Jesus' mouth when he launched his public ministry were "The time is fulfilled, and the kingdom of God is at hand" (Mark 1:15 RSV). The term "kingdom" had a long history of use among the Hebrews. Jesus now brings it to fresh focus. What he said in his inaugural gospel text that memorable day in first-century Palestine was, "This kingdom you have been hearing about now for these many centuries is here. Listen to me carefully. Watch me attentively. Join me believingly. I am here to do kingdom work, and I want you to join me in the work. I want you to work alongside me."

Not long after this, in the first prayer he taught his followers he said, in effect, "This is the very work of God that I am doing and I want you in on it body and soul. Not just as spectators or admirers or well-wishers. I want this kingdom life to get inside of you — I want you to *pray* with me the coming of the kingdom."

When we pray "your kingdom come" we internalize and participate in what we see and hear Jesus do and say.

The kingdom of God that Jesus announces as present here and now is not a religious piece of the world pie that God takes a special interest in and enlists us, his followers, to partake of and be filled with, a world that specializes in prayer and worship, giving witness and doing good deeds. No, it comprises Everything and Everyone. There is no other world. There are elements in the world that are in rebellion against the kingdom. There are parts of the world that are ignorant of the kingdom. No matter. What Jesus inaugurates and proclaims is present and comprehensive reality. Nothing takes place outside the kingdom of God.

When we pray, "Your kingdom come," we identify and offer ourselves as participants in this world in which God rules in love and salvation. Implicit in the petition is "My kingdom go. . . ." God has never abdicated his throne. Under conditions in which his rule is frequently denied, challenged daily, often ignored, we pray, "Your kingdom come."

Those of us who grow up under democratic governments commonly count ourselves most fortunate in living under an elected, not imposed, government that best serves the human condition. That might very well be. But it also carries with it the habit of thinking that the best government, including God's government, is run along the lines of a democracy. This is a hard habit to break. God is not president or prime minister of a democracy. God is king. "The LORD reigns. . . . Thy throne is established from old" (Ps. 93:1-2). God is sovereign. That is the assured and frequently expressed witness of Scripture from Genesis to Revelation. But there are no earthly analogies to God's throne and rule. It is not imposed; it is not despotic. All our needs and hungers, our tears and longings, our petitions and praises are assimilated in God's rule. It is a sovereignty that invites our participation. We share his rule, but it is *his* rule.

So when we pray, "Your kingdom come," praying the petition with Jesus praying at our side, we are at the same time implicitly affirming the rule as revealed in Jesus. And we give up second-guessing everything that we can't understand or don't approve of. Many of Jesus' parables provide insights into this kingdom — and we need all the help we can get. For the way that God exercises his sovereignty is hidden. God's sovereignty is seldom obvious. The obscurity is a breeding ground for grudging comments: "If I were God, this is not the way I would do it." But I am not God. Let God be God.

The kingdom we pray for can never be grasped by what we read in the newspapers or in the history books — sometimes even in the books of theology. But it can be discerned by means of our prayers. God rules from heaven, doing his creating, saving, blessing work behind the scenes and from the cross. We acquire a sense of what holds the kingdom together and gives it shape by listening to the stories and praying the prayers that compose the revelation — especially the stories and prayers of Jesus.

If we do not listen carefully to the words of Jesus in the entire context of the story of Israel and of Jesus, the word "kingdom" can easily mislead us. If we permit our culture and politics to define the word, we will think primarily of the newspaper definitions of power and influence and fame. If we even so slightly begin thinking of the kingdom apart from the well-documented Jesus context, we will easily come to think that the kingdom we are praying for is in competition with the kingdoms that are written up in our history books and reported in our current events. Then it isn't long before we are thinking of ways to outmaneuver the kingdom ways that we see operating in business and industry, in government and war, and compete with them on their terms. But the kingdom we are participating in when we pray, "Your kingdom come," is not in competition with the kingdoms of America or IBM or Honda or Microsoft. It is subverting them.

Jesus was as clear as he could be on the subject when he was on trial before Pilate for allegedly leading an insurrection against the Roman empire. What he said was, "My kingdom is not of this world. If my kingdom were of this world, my servants would fight, that I might not be handed over to the Jews; but my kingdom is not from the world" (John 18:36 RSV). Jesus does not repudiate the term "kingdom"; he recontextualizes it. Jesus does not repudiate the title "king"; he subverts it. And it is in this context, this context of thorough immersion in the stories of Jesus and the prayers of Jesus, that we pray, "Your kingdom come."

We must be cautious that we do not isolate the term "kingdom" and the concept of sovereignty from the Jesus who teaches us to pray, "Your kingdom come." Jesus also demonstrates the way God's rule is exercised. And the cross of Jesus provides the focus. For this is not a kingdom imposed on us or anyone else. It is a kingdom that comes into being as we willingly obey and imaginatively pray our participation in the rule. The impatient sovereignty of a dictator does not permit non-participation. The sovereignty of our Father patiently, mercifully waits for worshiping obedience.

Jesus' prepositions are important: his kingdom is not *of* this world. He employs the preposition "of" twice in his conversation with Pilate. His kingdom is not derived from this world or this world's idea of how sovereignty works; it is not up for a vote from this world. But everything we know about Jesus through his stories and prayers tells us that his kingdom has everything, and I emphasize *every thing*, to do *with* this world. Kingdom action and a kingdom life work from a base of God's love for the world and the salvation of the world.

As we pray the second petition in participation with Jesus who is praying it with us, we will not isolate the kingdom we are praying for from the King of this kingdom who is praying with us for its actualization. In Paul's succinct characterization of the kingdom as "righteousness and peace and joy in the Holy Spirit" (Rom. 14:17) there is no repudiation of the world as such but a persistent leaven-salt-light invasion of the world. God rules mightily and eternally "not by might, nor by power, but by [God's] spirit" (Zech. 4:6). Christ is king, truly and literally — but from a cross.

Keeping company with Jesus (but only by keeping company with Jesus) as we pray "Thy kingdom come," we will pray boldly. We know that we are involved in detailed participation in the salvation of the world. This boldness is not arrogance. It is chastened by a thoroughgoing modesty. We don't make up our own strategies and then employ a self-assertive spirit to foment proud visions of a kingdom that uses swords and money and celebrity glamour to beat the principalities and powers at their own game.

"Your will be done"

The third petition is prayed within a larger story of prayers that participate in doing God's will. Thirty years before Jesus gave us this petition, Mary was told that she was going to become pregnant with Jesus. At that time she prayed a prayer similar to the one that Jesus invites us to pray with him here. The angel Gabriel had just appeared to Mary and told her, "you will conceive in your womb and bear a son, and you will call him Jesus" (Luke 1:31). This is the first mention in the Gospel story of Jesus by name. Mary is understandably perplexed. Gabriel allays her confusion. He elaborates his birth announcement by setting the conception of this baby in the large context of God's kingdom: "He [Jesus] will reign over the house of Jacob forever, and of his kingdom there will be no end" (Luke 1:33).

Angel or no angel, Gabriel obviously doesn't know the facts of life. Mary fills him in, telling him that she is a virgin. But Mary doesn't know the facts of the kingdom. Gabriel fills her in: "The Holy Spirit will come upon you. . . ." As sure as she is of the "facts of life," Mary doesn't insist. She opens herself to Gabriel's king and kingdom announcement and prays, in effect, *Thy will be done:* "Behold, I am the handmaid of the Lord . . . let it be to me according to your word" (Luke 1:38 RSV).

Mary's prayer that the will of God be done *is* done: Jesus is conceived and born. And now, thirty years after she prayed it, Jesus, who was the will of God for Mary, prays it with his disciples.

Three years later, Jesus prays the same prayer in Gethsemane: "not my will but yours be done" (Luke 22:42). This prayer is also answered; God's will is done: Jesus is killed and becomes the resurrected King of the kingdom.

*   *   *

I am placing the third petition of the prayer between Annunciation and Gethsemane to insist on a thoroughgoing *Jesus* context for the petition. Praying "Your will be done" cannot be pulled out of the Jesus context, his stories and his prayers, and then used however we want to. We must keep it and ourselves in the story and in the prayers.

All of us live with family and friends and neighbors who ask a lot of questions about the "will of God." I don't keep statistics on such matters, but over a lifetime I dare say that this ranks high on the list of most asked questions by Christians. It is painful to have to say it, but there is an enormous amount of dishonesty and just plain silliness written and spoken about the cause of Christ. Much of it concerns matters lumped under the heading "the will of God."

The phrase "will of God" may well be one of the murkiest set of words in the Christian vocabulary. We live in a time when the air is full of careless comment and commentary on the will of God. Unfortunately, far too many of these comments have neither biblical rootage nor theological integrity. Which is odd, because the Bible could hardly be more clear on the matter. Still, we commonly use "will of God" as nothing more than a cliché drained of content. At other times, severed from Jesus' prayer, it conveys a puzzled plunge into a maelstrom of anxiety. For some it posts a dogmatic No Trespassing sign that shuts off either thinking or praying. For still others, it scrawls a huge question mark over past and future and leaves us floundering in the "holy now" where we do all our actual living.

To use the word "will" in relation to God is not a piece of esoterica. It is not all that different from the way we use the word among ourselves. Will has to with intention, with purpose. Without a will, we live a meandering life. It also has to do with energy. Without a will, we live a listless life.

When we speak of a person who lives with "a will," we don't normally imagine him or her carrying around a blueprint and only doing the things that are specified in the blueprint and then bullying ignorant or rebellious bystanders into compliance. And when we speak of a person who lives willingly, we don't envision someone who does only what is already dictated by a job description. The word does not suggest either compliantly "going along" or reluctantly submitting to coercion.

The biblical and gospel objection to the "blueprint" version of the will of God is that it depersonalizes what is fundamentally a personal relationship — "our Father!" — into something cold and lifeless, without ambiguity, without conversation. "Blueprint" versions of praying for the will of God are a mocking parody of prayer.[2]

The mature, sane, enduring counsel of our best pastors and theologians is this: keep Jesus' prayer, "Your will be done," in the storied and praying context of the Holy Scriptures. Quit speculating about the "will of God" and simply do it — as Mary did, as Jesus did. "Will of God" is never a matter of conjecture. It directs a spotlight on believing obedience.

"On earth as it is in heaven" (An Interlude)

Everything in the life of prayer concerns this life "on earth."[3] Prayer is the most "worldly" thing we do. The first three petitions all have to do with the way we participate in what God is already doing in Christ by the Holy Spirit. God is at work in creation, in salvation, in blessing — on earth. He is at work in our homes and workplaces, in our governments and schools, in our prisons and churches, in ships at sea and automobiles on highways, among the hungry and poor, among the newborn and the dying. Make your own list. Insert your own names. And then pray them.

Heaven is where it all begins. Heaven is where it all ends. Heaven is our metaphor for what is beyond us, beyond our understanding, beyond what we can see and hear and taste and touch, beyond and out of reach of what we can control. Earth is where we play our part, the place where what we don't see and what we do see come together and become creation and salvation and holiness. The polarities of reality, heaven and earth, fuse: "on earth as it in heaven."

The most complete revelation of "on earth as it is in heaven" is Je-

2. Two excellent contemporary writers who effectively counter the blueprint version of the will of God and recover the biblical and gospel original are Jerry Sittser, *The Will of God as a Way of Life* (Grand Rapids: Zondervan, 2004); and Bruce Waltke, *Finding the Will of God: A Pagan Notion?* (Grand Rapids: Eerdmans, 2002).

3. George Herbert, *The Country Parson, The Temple*, ed. John N. Wall Jr. (New York: Paulist Press), p. 284.

sus, the stories of Jesus and the prayers of Jesus. All Jesus' stories and all Jesus' prayers begin in heaven but take place on earth. Our stories and our prayers are our willing, obedient participation in what originates in heaven and takes place on earth. But our stories must be lived and our prayers prayed from *within* the story and prayers of what God does in heaven and earth in Jesus. In the language we learn from the Scriptures and Jesus, heaven and earth are distinct but not separate. Heaven and earth are an organic unity. No iron wall separates them. Everything in heaven — the beauty, the goodness, the hallelujahs, the amens, the holiness, the salvation, the white horse and the twenty-four elders, the slain Lamb and the marriage supper, the four-square city and the river of life — takes place on earth.

"On earth as it is in heaven" expresses the fundamental practicality, the hereness and nowness that is involved in every prayer we pray. Prayer is not an escape from what is going on around us. It is gutsy participation in every earthly detail. Prayer is not a preparatory exercise getting us in shape for heavenly bliss. St. Theresa said, "All the way to heaven is heaven." So, why wait?

"Give us this day our daily bread"

We turn a corner. The first three petitions make us participants in the being and action of God. Jesus prays with us, and as he does so he makes us insiders with him in the work of heaven on earth, companions with him in the hallowing of the name of God, the coming of the kingdom of God, the doing of the will of God. God is in heaven. Heaven is where everything gets started. Jesus starts there. In company with Jesus, we start there. We are not used to this. We have a lifelong habit of starting with a "want list" developed while we are preoccupied with just getting across the street. Indirectly but implicitly, the three petitions renounce want lists: wanting to be "like God," wanting to use God as an assistant as we take control of "our" kingdom, wanting to get access to the so-called secrets of prayer (the blueprints) in order to pursue our own wills, our willfulness.

The three petitions reorient our lives, our imaginations, and our language to the presence and action of God. If we stick to this long enough, make a habit of it, slowly but surely our congenital self-centeredness is radically re-formed into God-centeredness.

*　　*　　*

Now we come upon a significant change of pronouns. The first three petitions are rooted in the heavenly divine "Your": *your* name, *your* kingdom, *your* will. Prayer gets us in on what God is doing. The final three pronouns shift to the earthly human "Us": give *us*, forgive *us*, rescue *us*. Prayer gets God in on what we need to live to his glory.

Prayer involves us deeply and responsibly in all the operations of God. Prayer also involves God deeply and transformatively in all the details of our lives.

*　　*　　*

We start with the body. We are flesh-and-blood creatures. We need bread in order to live. Daily bread. *Fresh* bread. Food. We are souls destined for eternity, but these souls are em*bodied* with digestive systems. If we don't eat we won't pray.

We are human beings created in the image of God, spiritual beings destined for heavenly glory — but the first thing we need to live this glorious life is bread — not "bread alone," true, but bread to start with. Our bodies are not a careless afterthought in the scheme of creation. They complete it. And these bodies, with all the needs associated with keeping them healthy and in good repair, are *God*-created. These bodies need bread, along with the associated basics of shelter and clothing and baths that are involved in having bodies. Regardless of our intelligence, our beauty, our usefulness, our righteousness, and the preciousness of our eternal souls, we need bread. We are not angels.

From time to time cases of "angelism" crop up among us. These occur in people who try to be more spiritual than God in serving God. Bodies, thought to be grossly inferior to souls, are more or less put up

182

with until, as the gospel song has it, we "fly away." Angelism is a distortion of the Christian life much decried by our holy ancestors.

"Give us bread" — and Jesus, remember, is part of that "us" — bans angelism as an option for any life lived on earth. You can't get any more sensual, material, or basic than bread — its yeasty aroma, pumpernickel crust, textured taste.

Praying for bread acknowledges need. We are creatures who are interdependent in this huge and intricate marvel of creation, where everything and everyone is related and in touch with everything and everyone else. When we pray for bread we make a decidedly un-American declaration of dependence. We don't have it within ourselves to be ourselves. We renounce the silly pretentiousness of posing as a self-made person. We humbly take our places in "the great chain of being."

*　　*　　*

The prayer for bread, though, is more than an acknowledgment of need. It is a thankful embrace of a good creation and our place in the created order.

It is not unheard of for us to chafe at our neediness. Having to ask for help is an admission that we can't do this on our own, that we are not in control. There is something in us, call it the Lucifer gene in our DNA, that would prefer never to have to ask for help.

Consumerism is a narcotic that dulls the awareness that we are in need. By buying what we need, we assume control of our lives. We replace a sense of need with a sense of ownership, and our sense of neediness recedes.

Technology is a narcotic. It depersonalizes needs to something that can be handled by a machine or a device. We replace a sense of need by the satisfaction of being in control: "I will manage my own needs, thank you."

Money and machines anaesthetize neediness. They put us in charge, in control. As long as the money holds out and the machines are in good repair, we don't have to pray. But there is a steep price to pay. Narcotics diminish the capacity for personal relationships. Narcotics dull and finally destroy the capacity for living, feeling, loving, enjoying. And praying.

When we choose to live with a diminished sense of the limits imposed by our basic neediness, we falsify our place in the intricate and marvelous goodness of our creation, what the psalmists celebrate as the "land of the living." A refusal to work within limits is a stubborn, rebellious refusal to receive life as a gift. Needs are not limitations that interfere with or reduce or flatten our lives. Needs prepare us for a life of receptivity, a readiness to receive what can only be received as gift. Needs open the door into this vast giving-receiving ecological intricacy of sky and sea, clover and bee, man and wife, horse and carriage. Needs don't reduce us to "mere" creatures; they provide the conditions in which we are able to live in reciprocal relation with wildflowers and woodpeckers, with sons and daughters, with parents and grandparents. The limitations inherent in needs prevent us from illusions of grandeur and the isolations of selfish pride. The limitations of our created state are invitations to live in a generous and receptive dynamic in the creaturely life that teems around us. Limits don't limit us from being fully human. They only limit us from being God.

A violinist does not complain that her violin has only four strings. A poet doesn't rail against the limit of fourteen lines in the sonnet he is writing. Every so-called limit is access to gift, a gift of love, a gift of beauty, all gifts on offer to be received by open hands.

Do we want to live without needs? Then we want to live without God. Our needs are a continuous invitation to live in a reality of gift-giving and gift-receiving. "Ask, and it will be given you; seek, and you will find; knock, and it will be opened to you" (Matt. 7:7 RSV). "The grace of God means something like: Here is your life. You might never have been, but you are because the party wouldn't be complete without you. Here is the world. Beautiful and terrible things will happen. Don't be afraid. I am with you. Nothing can ever separate us. It's for you I created the universe."[4] We live in a grace-filled world. So, "give us . . ."

---

4. Frederick Buechner, *Wishful Thinking: A Theological ABC* (New York: Harper & Row, 1973), p. 34.

"And forgive us our debts, as we forgive our debtors"

God gives. Life is a gift. "God so loved the world that he *gave* . . ." (John 3:16). Giving and receiving is God's creation norm. This is the way the world is. But it is not normative in the human community. There is much amiss among us.

The grace that we are immersed in is continuously obscured by sin, grace's opposite. Sin is anti-gift and anti-personal. Sin ruptures or sabotages a living relationship. Instead of receiving, we take. We decide we don't like the bread given to us on our plate, throw it on the floor, and grab the bowl of ice cream from our sister. The world of grace, which requires personal, open willingness to humbly ask and gratefully receive, is set aside for a depersonalized world of manipulation, violence, efficiency, control. Words are depersonalized into propaganda. Sex is depersonalized into pornography. Politics is depersonalized into oppression. Power is depersonalized into war. We do it a lot. And so we need forgiveness.

Forgive us our debts. Forgive us for our failure to keep honest accounts with our neighbors. Forgive us for refusing the gifts that are given and stealing what is not ours to have. Forgive us for using the gift of language to deceive. Forgive us for using the gift of sexuality to seduce. Forgive us for using the gift of strength to abuse and murder. Forgive us for using the gift of plenty to impoverish another. Paul picks up and repeats the fifth petition: "Just as the Lord has forgiven you, so you also must forgive" (Col. 3:13).

*   *   *

"Sin" is the generic word for what is wrong with us and the world. The extent and inventiveness of humankind in messing up the world, ourselves, and others seems endless. The taxonomy of sin is mercilessly depressing: debts, evil, wickedness, trespass, unrighteousness, guilt, transgression, impiety, disobedience, rebellion, alienation. There are over fifty words for sin in biblical Hebrew.

But exposing and naming sin is not at the center of life lived to the glory of God. Muckraking is not gospel work. Witch-hunting is not gospel work. Shaming the outcast is not gospel work. Forgiving sin *is* gospel work.

As we face the sin mess, Jesus prays with us. He doesn't tell us to get a mop, pail, and scrub brush so he can show us how to scrub sin from our lives, from the lives of our spouses and children, from the lives of our neighbors. He doesn't instruct us on how we can hook up a Holy Ghost power hose to clean up the corruption in the corridors of government, the sacrilege in our churches, the unbelief in our schools. Jesus does not stand aloof from the mess we are in. He joins us where we are, mired in the mud of sin ("became sin for us": see 2 Cor. 5:21). He takes his place alongside us and invites us to pray with him, "Forgive us. . . ."

God does not deal with sin by ridding our lives of it as if it were a germ, or mice in the attic. God does not deal with sin by amputation as if it were a gangrenous leg, leaving us crippled, holiness on a crutch. God deals with sin by forgiving us, and when he forgives us there is more of us, not less.

*　　*　　*

Sin is a refusal or failure to be in personal relation with the living, personal God, and so forgiveness of sin cannot work with some dictionary definition of sin but only in a deeply personal act that restores intimate relationship. The sin that denies the personal can only be dealt with personally.

God is personal, emphatically personal. The Trinity is our most comprehensive, Scripture-saturated way of understanding God's ways of being God as Father, as Son, and as Holy Spirit. All the operations of the Trinity are personal. There is nothing, absolutely nothing, abstract or impersonal in God, the *living* God. And it is his will that there not be an abstract or impersonal bone in the body of Christ, the church.

So if something is going to be done about sin, it is not going to be along the line of laws and rules, codes and regulations. God and every God-created man and woman on earth are inherently personal and can only be engaged in relationships that are personal. Person, image-of-God person, is who we are. Sin is a violation of the essential personal nature of human life with one another and with God. We don't sin against a commandment; we sin against a person. Sin is not an offense against justice; sin is an offense against a living soul. Sin is not sexual impropriety; sin is the debasement of a man, a woman, a child. Sin is not a violation of the law of the land or the rules of a house; sin is a violation of a personal relationship.

And so Jesus comes alongside us and prays with us, "Forgive us. Forgive us our debts, forgive us our trespasses, forgive us our sins." He also trusts us to do the best we can in what he does best of all: "as we forgive our debtors." He can legitimately, genuinely encourage us to forgive because he has already set the stage by extending his forgiveness on such a cosmic scale.

*   *   *

As Jesus prays with us, "Give us bread . . ." he gradually weans us away from the presumption and habit of living independent lives, independent of God, independent creatures who don't want to be simply creatures but want to take charge of the water and air, the trees and land, to say nothing of our children and neighbors and students and employees, to do with as we like. But we are not in charge. We are not in control. We don't have what we need to stay alive.

But God does. God is generous. God gives. Life is a gift. We are gifts. We learn to pray, "Give us . . ." and, with Jesus praying at our side, we begin to get a firsthand feel for what it is like to be on the receiving end of giving, of what it is like to live in a country of grace.

As Jesus takes on the mess of sin and teaches us to face what we are up against each day, he is again at the business of disengaging us from old habits. Did we think that what is wrong with the world is something we can do anything about on our own? We can't. Did we think there are judicial or educational or psychological ways to deal with sin? There aren't. Just as in the world of grace, so in the country of sin, we learn how God does it and we enter into that way of life praying, as Jesus prays with us, "Forgive us our sin."

187

Sin kills. Sin kills relationships. Sin kills the soul-intimacy that is inherent in the image-of-God creature that we are. Sin is deadly, summarized in the "seven deadly sins." Part of us dies when we sin, no longer in a living relation with the living God, the living spouse, the living child, the living neighbor. There is no medicine that can bring the dead to life. There is no machine that can disarm death. Daily we find ourselves walking through this vast sin cemetery of what someone has described as the "undead dead." The only way to deal with sin is by resurrection. Forgiveness is resurrection, life from the dead.

*   *   *

Jesus' death and resurrection form the intricately complex act that accomplishes the forgiveness of sin. How it happens is a deep mystery. *That* it happens, witnessed by our holy Scriptures and confirmed by wise and sane and holy men and women in every place and generation, is a lived and daily reality.

Kurt Vonnegut once remarked that while Einstein's theory of relativity might one day put Earth on the intergalactic map, it will always run a distant second to the Lord's Prayer, whose harnessing of energies in their proper, life-giving direction surpasses even the discovery of fire. The universe-altering phrase he has in mind is "'forgive us our trespasses as we forgive those who trespass against us.' There are no zero-sum relationships in the cosmos. There is no future without forgiveness. World without end. Amen."[5]

"And lead us not into temptation, but deliver us from evil"

This first prayer of Jesus, set before us in our first Gospel, this "Lord's Prayer," is not a score of music written by a master composer that we go off and practice, petition after petition, like musical scales, until we get it "word perfect." Prayer is not that sort of thing. What continues to

---

5. Quoted in David Dark, *The Gospel according to America* (Louisville: Westminster/John Knox Press, 2005), p. 121.

strike me is how companionable this prayer is. Jesus prays with us; we pray with him. Jesus does not teach us about prayer, he prays with us; we do not learn about prayer, we pray with him. There is none of the schoolmaster about Jesus and no condescension. He treats us with immense dignity. Jesus is our Lord, true. But he is also our friend. As we venture into this unaccustomed world of prayer with Jesus at our side, we become personally present and submissive and obedient to God, who is present to us and active in us. Jesus prays what he lives, and we pray with him. And as we do, we find ourselves praying and living what Jesus lives.

*   *   *

Jesus has prayed with us through all the operations of the Trinity: the hallowing of the name, the coming of the kingdom, the accomplishing of the will. He has prayed with us into a life of grace, receiving not getting. He has prayed with us into a life of forgiveness, letting God take care of our sins, not pridefully constructing a moral life that makes us self-sufficient.

We now know that we are deeply engaged in all that God is and does: the holy, the kingdom, and the will. We now know that our hands are open to receive the gifts of creation, are ready to eat from the table where we have been invited: Come and eat. We now know that with our heads bowed and our hearts open we are absolved of sin and are ready to pass the forgiveness on to everyone we meet.

So, what's left? The fact is that we don't know what's left. We have not yet come to the end. "The end is not yet" (Mark 13:7 RSV). We know that we are not yet finished. All the prayers that we have prayed, with Jesus praying with us at our side, are prayers we pray on the way to the cross of Jesus and on to resurrection.

We know that he completed that journey to the cross and resurrection. We know that his death and resurrection are present realities in our lives, "working salvation in the midst of the earth" (Ps 74:12 RSV). We know that we are given the dignity and privilege to live them out in our personal lives. We know that we are even now participating in his death and resurrection (Rom. 6:4). And we know that our leg of the journey is not yet completed.

The five petitions are prayed out of present activity, God's and ours, the circumstances and conditions of our dailiness. But there is more. The sixth petition prepares us for this "more" — reaches into the future and prepares us for what we do not yet know: unanticipated temptations and deceptive evil. We know that temptations will face us along each step of this pilgrim way, but we have no way of knowing what they will be. And we know that evil (or, perhaps more accurately, the Evil One), is "couching at the door" (Gen. 4:7 RSV), ready to pounce on us just as he was ready to pounce on our Lord (Heb. 4:15), to keep us from completing our calling. But we have no way of knowing the deceptive forms it will take. We need help for these times and occasions when we will not be aware that we need help. We pray in preparation for what's next. And we don't know what is coming next.

Jesus joins us with him in a prayer for something that has no identifiable form yet and may easily go unrecognized: "And lead us not into temptation, but deliver us from evil."[6] N. T. Wright translates: "Let us not be brought into the Testing, into the great Tribulation; Deliver us from Evil."[7] Prepare and preserve us from whatever comes next. Later we will come on Jesus' words, "In the world you have tribulation; but be of good cheer; I have overcome the world" (John 16:33 RSV), assuring us that we can count on him to respond to our prayer.

The tribulations will certainly include testings, temptations, and evil. As glorious as the world is, it is also perilous. Dangers that don't have the appearance of dangers are everywhere. Evil that masquerades as an angel of light is commonplace. We need help. And we need help even when we don't know we need help. *Especially* when we don't know we need help.

The sins, the debts, the trespasses, with all their manifestations in

---

6. The Greek words used in the sixth petition contain various shades of meaning: trial, temptation, test, tribulation, evil, Evil One. I have used them all, attempting to give a feel for the variations of emphasis that occur as we pray the petition.

7. N. T. Wright, *The Lord and His Prayer* (Grand Rapids: Eerdmans, 1997), p. 68.

the "seven deadlies," for which we pray "Forgive us," are more or less out in the open. For the most part, we know when we sin, at least in the early stages before excuse-making and rationalizations blunt the conscience. And if we don't know it, our parents and children and neighbors know, and they let us know soon enough. But temptation and trial, testing and evil are in a different class. Temptation and evil almost always appear disguised as good and beautiful. For the most part, they catch us off our guard, take us by surprise.

*　　*　　*

Eve in the garden, dazzled by the Serpent, is tempted to receive as a gift something that she is convinced is altogether good: when she "saw that the tree was good for food, and that it was a delight to the eyes, and that the tree was desired to make one wise, she took of its fruit and ate." She then crowns the goodness with generosity: "she also gave some to her husband, who was with her, and he ate" (Gen. 3:6). Food is a good thing; beauty brings out the best in us; wisdom guides us into living a full life; a shared life doubles the pleasure. The garden temptation is all about participating in an illusory good. On the surface the man and the woman have good reason to suppose that they are participating in a good thing by eating that fruit.

Yet — this is the opening act in a drama that plunged the entire human race into temptation and evil, playing to a full house ever since. Some of us are cast in bit parts, others in starring roles, but we are all in it.

Jesus in the desert is tempted by the Devil to do three things that are only possible for him to do because he is the Son of God: turn stones into bread, display his miraculous powers by leaping off the temple roof without so much as spraining an ankle, rule all the kingdoms of the world. Making bread is a good thing, performing miracles is a good thing, ruling the world is a good thing. The desert temptations are all about doing good (Matt. 4:1-11).

Jesus does not take the bait. He does what the man and woman in the garden don't do. He refuses to do the seemingly good that is put before him. That refusal is a major element in delivering the children of Adam and Eve from evil. And we are those children.

*   *   *

Sin, by whatever name it is called, is still sin. But by separating the temptation-and-evil sin out from the debt-and-trespasses sin and giving it its own petition, Jesus gives us insight into a form of sin that doesn't arrive at our doorstep labeled "sin."

It is evident — empirically verified in every family, school, business, and nation — that all of us have a basic bias toward sin sometimes referred to as original sin, sin previous to us, sin that we pick up without intending or even knowing what we are doing. We are born into a life of fundamental "fallenness." Nobody escapes involvement, "no, not one" (Ps. 14:3). The damage of sin is partially mitigated by teaching and training in moral behavior that keeps some of the wrongdoing in check. But not all. Society provides backup protection with disciplinary sanctions, police forces, and armies to keep things under control and stave off moral anarchy. But all these, necessary as they are, are impersonal and are not able to deal with the relational separation that is sin. Forgiveness is the only known way of restoring the relationship, the personal dimensions of intimacy with God and one another that are at the core of our humanity.

Alongside this bent toward sin that all of us experience, there is also a paradoxical goodness, an innate capacity to act with generosity and joy and care, to worship and love, quite apart from any stimulus of threat, reward, or advantage. We smile and laugh and serve and are kind spontaneously, quite apart from being taught or trained. This field of goodness, even innocence, is where temptation sets its snares and evil practices its deceptions. We are not prepared for this. It doesn't occur to us that this innate capacity for good is subject to temptation and frequently develops into evil. Who could have dreamed that an artless goodness that brings the best that is within us into words and acts is corruptible?

We are warned and given guidelines to keep us from the many

and various sins that hurt and destroy and diminish the people around us, that deface the goodness and beauty of the world, that blaspheme God, that contribute to the general mess of humankind. But we are caught off-guard when what we feel deep within us as unadulterated good turns bad. The temptations that use the raw material of good for evil can continue unrecognized for a long time without awareness, sometimes until it is too late and the resultant evil is in full spate. "Lilies that fester smell far worse than weeds" (Shakespeare).

We have little or no imagination for comprehending the evil that originates in our desire to do good, to serve God, to help our neighbors, to make the world a better place. The stories of Eve in the garden and Jesus in the desert are strategically placed to supply a powerful antidote to our naiveté. They are unforgettable.

The story of Eve in the garden tells us that a person in a completely unspoiled, attractive, and beautifully idyllic place, with everything anyone could ever want or even dream of, can be deceived into making good into evil.

The story of Jesus in the desert tells us that a perfectly prepared person (in this case the Son of God), fully aware of the uniqueness and will-of-God blessing on his life, ready to step across the threshold and set in motion the words and acts that will accomplish the most glorious work imaginable, the salvation of the world, is still seriously at risk.

A good person in a good place is no proof against temptation.

A good person with good work to do is no proof against temptation.

*　　*　　*

I have oversimplified. It is not as if either Eve or Jesus was totally unprepared for the temptation that used the good as a bait to sin. Eve had the tree-of-good-and-evil command etched deeply in her soul and, with Adam, a well-developed life of prayerful companionship with God through all those evenings in the garden. And Jesus had the preaching of the prophets, the songs of the psalmists — nearly two thousand years of salvation storytelling — alive and working in his life.

Still, we can't underestimate how often the energy of experienced goodness is used to fuel temptation to sin. We can't underestimate the frequency with which a good life is perverted into evil.

I have been a pastor for most of my adult life. My job involves dealing daily with sinners of every sort. Also many saints, most of whom don't know they are saints. My sense is that the debts and trespasses that get their start in our innate propensity to sin, the sins that we ask forgiveness for in the fifth petition, are much more easily discerned and dealt with than the temptations and evil that get their start in our desire and capacity for good, and for which we pray for deliverance in the sixth petition.

I am no longer surprised that great evil finds its formation in places where people come to worship God yet are seduced into the pleasures of playing God. I am no longer surprised to recognize great evil in places of power, in business and government, for instance, where people have access to enormous resources to do good and yet are seduced into using the power to be powerful themselves. I am no longer surprised to come across great evil in families and marriages, where the opportunities for intimacy and affection are most accessible, and find that those opportunities have been squandered into seductions of depersonalized manipulation and control. Far more evil takes root in the places where goodness abounds than in desperate slums and the criminal underworld. Why should that surprise us? It got its start, after all, in Eden.

*   *   *

Fifth-petition sins, for which we ask forgiveness, are far easier to notice and take responsibility for than sixth-petition temptations — the temptation that seduced Eve, the temptations that Jesus rejected — temptations carefully crafted to deceive us into using good to do evil.

And so, because of the heightened peril involved in these temptations, Jesus gives us this petition of prevention: "Be our companion-guide on this perilous path so that when we come upon a temptation that doesn't look like a temptation, a temptation with a halo and fluttering angel wings, we won't be seduced as Eve was, that we will be as discerning as Jesus was: 'Let us not be brought into temptation.'

"We know that the danger is great. We know that all of us are vulnerable to the stratagems of the Devil, the cunning half-truths of the Serpent, the siftings of Satan. We need a prepared imagination well-versed in the wiles of the Evil One. We are out of our depth. Save us, help us, rescue us: 'Deliver us from evil.'"

An extensive vocabulary for asking God to do for us what we cannot do for ourselves permeates our Scriptures. Deliverance is the bottom line in the country of salvation.

We never know when or in what form we will face temptation, be brought to trial, or find ourselves enmeshed in evil. Jesus underlines the urgency of preparation for what is coming next by giving the sixth petition in the form of a double imperative: "Lead us not. . . . Deliver us. . . ."

*   *   *

Charles Williams refers to the Lord's Prayer as an "august ritual of intercession."[8] Yes: "august ritual" indeed. It permeates the Christian praying imagination. "The shortest memory may retain it, and the busiest life may utter it" (Alexander Whyte).

"For yours is the kingdom, and the power, and the glory, for ever. Amen."

That's it. Prayer succinct and bold. With Jesus at our side, praying with us, we know where we stand. We are ready to follow Jesus. No hemming and hawing. No shuffling of feet, uncertain what to do next. No nervous small talk, like a guest not knowing how to say goodbye and leave.

We step back and trust God to do with our prayers whatever, however, and whenever he chooses. The leave-taking, using familiar

8. Charles Williams, *Many Dimensions* (London: Faber and Faber, Ltd., 1931), p. 216.

words of David in 1 Chronicles,[9] puts us outside the prayer itself in a kind of holy detachment. All our intentions, our experience, our energy are now in the prayer. All now is in our Father's hands. Julian Green in his diary wrote, "all prayers are granted, sooner or later, but one has to reach the age of fifty to discover this, with the necessary perspective. Youth does not know it."[10]

*   *   *

I was visiting a woman in her mid-forties. She had been widowed for several years, children grown, and feeling at loose ends. Nobody needed her; she had no need for employment. For a few months she had been worshiping, but erratically, in the congregation that I served as pastor. I was sitting in her living room, listening to this familiar rehearsal of mid-life meandering, a soul adrift. The conversation, like her life, didn't seem to be going anywhere. There didn't seem to be any place for me to get a foothold.

She had a piece of needlework in her lap, stretched across an embroidery hoop. Then, with just a faint note of vibrancy in her voice, she said, "Do you know what I need? I need something to give tautness, shape to my life. I need an embroidery hoop for my soul. I'm a limp piece of cloth — you can't do fine needlework on a limp piece of cloth."

She had given me my foothold. I said, "I've got just the hoop for you. The Lord's Prayer is exactly that sort of device for your soul: a frame across which to stretch your soul taut with attention in the presence of God." We spent the next hour or so in conversation on prayer, and savored together the simple, practical, accessible structure for prayer that has been used as a frame for people just like her and me — and you — for two thousand years.

9. The actual words: "Yours, O Lord, are the greatness, the power, the glory, the victory, and the majesty; for all that is in the heavens and on the earth is yours; yours is the kingdom" (1 Chron. 29:11).

10. Julian Green, *Diary 1928-1957* (New York: Carroll & Graf Publishers, 1964), p. 262.

CHAPTER 15

Jesus Prays in Thanksgiving:
Matthew 11:25-26

Matthew places Jesus' prayer of thanksgiving in the context of John the Baptist's misunderstanding and the villagers' rejection. Misunderstanding and rejection don't seem to be promising stuff for producing thanksgiving. But in Jesus they do. Here's the prayer:

> "I thank you, Father, Lord of heaven and earth, because you have hidden these things from the wise and the intelligent and have revealed them to infants; yes, Father, for such was your gracious will."

This is a prayer I like very much: unprovoked, spontaneous, exuberant thanksgiving. The circumstances in which the thanksgiving erupts, artesian-like, into the Jesus story are grim, hardly conducive to thanksgiving. The grim conditions consist of a misunderstanding by the person most deeply involved in launching Jesus on his way as Messiah, and then, compounding the misunderstanding, a rejection by the people in the villages in which Jesus spent most of his early ministry, the men and women who had seen Jesus in action and listened to him talk.

*   *   *

Here's the misunderstanding: Jesus has just been approached by John's disciples asking him "Are you the one who is to come, or are we to wait for another?" (Matt. 11:3). John is locked up in Machaerus, a high-security prison as notorious in first-century Palestine as Sing Sing is among us. Herod the Great built it. His son, Herod Antipas, has put John there for the "political" crime of calling him on the carpet for his adultery with Herodias, his brother Philip's wife. John's powerful prophetic voice is no longer heard in the land. It will soon be silenced for good at a gruesome birthday party, at which, rather than a cake with candles, John's head is served up still dripping with blood, on a platter.

John was the Isaianic voice that introduced Jesus as the long anticipated Messiah to the people of Palestine. His preaching prepared the way for Jesus to be received as "the one who is to come," inaugurating the kingdom of heaven.

As John prepared "the way of the Lord" he captured the attention of the entire country. The day he baptized Jesus, his preaching was confirmed from heaven by the descent of the dove, a sign of the Holy Spirit, and immediately ratified by the voice from heaven, "This is my Son, the Beloved, with whom I am well pleased" (Matt. 3:17).

With that, John's work is done. His Isaianic "voice in the wilderness" presents Jesus to the nation. He then slips off to the sidelines so as not to get in the way of the Way: "He must increase, but I must decrease" (John 3:30; see John 3:27-36). Jesus moves into the center: those "sidelines" for John turn out to be the Machaerus prison. John is content to "decrease," but, understandably, he is waiting for news reporting on Jesus and his "increase." Reports were apparently sparse. Jesus isn't capturing headlines. Restless to know what is going on, John sends his disciples to ask Jesus for an accounting. "Are you the one who is to come, or are we to wait for another?" (Matt. 11:3). Is John feeling, as so many feel today, that Messiah Jesus is not sufficiently messianic? The Messiah has arrived, the kingdom of heaven is at hand: What's taking so long? Nothing seems to have changed: John is in prison and Herod is carrying on as dissolutely arrogant as ever.

Jesus reassured John's disciples, "Yes, I am the Messiah. Yes, I am doing the messianic work as defined in the Isaiah text that John preached. But maybe not in quite the way John is expecting it."

John and Jesus were different in the ways they went about their work. John preached in thunder to popular acclaim; Jesus told stories over meals and with friends on the road. John was a public figure confronting the high-profile sin of Herod Antipas in the public square; Jesus worked for the most part inconspicuously in the small villages in Galilee. John was an ascetic in diet and clothing; Jesus enjoyed a glass of wine, even at times in the company of disreputable outsiders. It is understandable that John would wonder what exactly was going on. It is understandable that John might be offended at Jesus' ways of going about his messianic work. Where is the "increase" that John was expecting? Where are the swelling crowds, the dramatic confrontations with the dissolute powers that be?

Jesus reassures John in his perplexity, "Yes, John, I am doing exactly what you prophesied so well about me. But let me do it my way. Do you recall these words from the Isaiah scroll that you know so well, '. . . my thoughts are not your thoughts, nor are your ways my ways . . .'? (Isa. 55:8). Let me bless you in your prison cell even as you bless me in 'my ways' as I carry out the messianic work into which you launched me — 'blessed is anyone who takes no offense at me'" (Matt. 11:6).[1]

*   *   *

And the people in the villages with whom Jesus lived? They essentially ignored him. If John the Baptist's misunderstanding was a disappointment to Jesus, the indifference of the people was more like a slap in the face.

Most of Jesus' early kingdom of heaven, messianic work was done in three small villages — Bethsaida and Capernaum on the north shore of Lake Galilee, and inland, about an hour's walk away,

---

1. F. Dale Bruner translates this verse, "God bless you, John, if you do not throw the whole thing over because I am different." *The Christbook, Matthew 1–12* (Waco, Tex.: Word Books, 1987), p. 413.

Chorazin. The villages form what we sometimes refer to as the "evangelical triangle." Most of Jesus' "mighty works" took place in these villages (Matt. 11:20): healings of a blind man, a paralytic, a Roman centurion's dying son, and a demoniac among others. Most of Jesus' disciples came from these villages. Bethsaida was hometown to Philip and Andrew. It was also where Jesus fed the five thousand. Peter and his wife made their home in Capernaum, as well as Peter's brother Andrew. Jesus moved from Nazareth and made his home in Capernaum, taught in the synagogue there, and used the village as home base for his kingdom of heaven work until he went to his cross in Jerusalem.

All of these villages were within walking distance of each other. They were all small villages, villages in which virtually everyone would be known and recognized. No one in a small town is anonymous. No one would have been ignorant of Jesus. All would know the stories of his healings. Many would have heard him preach and teach.

Many — perhaps most — ignored him. Turned a deaf ear. Dismissed Jesus as irrelevant to their lives. Jesus compares the three small villages to three large, prosperous, infamously evil cities of ancient times: Tyre, Sidon, and Sodom. "You think those pagan hotbeds of evil were bad? You are worse. Do you think that just because you don't live in sexual squalor and godless immorality and filth you are a cut above the rest of the world? You are teetering on the brink of hell. Willful indifference to God is the worst thing. A steely refusal to repent, to stubbornly persist in a complacent, self-satisfied life, is a doomed life. God is present among you and you are saying with your lives that you aren't interested."

There is evil that doesn't look like evil. The evil rampant in the villages of the evangelical triangle was not conspicuous. It was not flagrant and arrogant like the evil that stalked the corridors of the House of Herod, that was running wild in Rome. Conspicuous sin does not flourish in small villages.

There is no suggestion in Jesus' confrontation with his neighbors that they were bad in any conspicuously moral or criminal sense. Jesus' reproach is an exposure of their active indifference to God, their refusal to leave the ruts of conventional ordinariness. They are mired in a colorless banality, an inconspicuous evil that makes no headlines but outdoes Sodom, Tyre, and Sidon in its consequences. They recognize God as God, yet deliberately snub him. Jesus generously offers them a participating life in the kingdom of heaven, and they shrug their shoulders.

*   *   *

The person who understood Jesus best misunderstood him — misunderstood Jesus' failure to get him out of prison, misunderstood Jesus' avoidance of public charisma as being non-messianic. The people who knew Jesus best in his and their dailiness didn't know him — didn't embrace his presence among them as savior and healer, friend of sinners, and bread of the world.

These are the conditions in which Jesus was immersed the day he broke into this most exuberant thanksgiving:

> "I thank you, Father, Lord of heaven and earth, because you have hidden these things from the wise and the intelligent and have revealed them to infants."

*   *   *

The reason I am extravagant in my liking of this prayer of thanksgiving is because there is nothing in the "conditions" to account for it. The conditions — John's misunderstanding of Jesus' messianic ways and the villagers' mulish indifference to his messianic presence — are depressing. The conditions would seem to face Jesus with a serious reassessment of the way he has been going about being Messiah. If John didn't get it and his neighbors didn't get it, maybe he had better try something different.

So how do we account for the thanksgiving? Only, I think, by realizing that John's misunderstanding and the villagers' indifference — conditions that called into question the effectiveness of Jesus — is nothing more than a parched crust on the surface of the kingdom. Beneath that heavily trafficked hardpan the kingdom of heaven is coming into being in God's way. Jesus knows that God's way is to work his gracious will with the childlike, the simple, those who haven't fallen into the habit of thinking they are "like gods" and don't need God, those who haven't let inattentive familiarity with synagogue worship anesthetize them into supposing that they know exactly how God works.

"Wise" and "prudent" are ironic in the prayer. I would suggest "sophisticates and know-it-alls" to catch the tone in which Jesus speaks the words. It doesn't thwart Jesus that the man who knows more about Messiah than anyone else and has attracted great crowds by his preaching now misunderstands what is now taking place. It doesn't throw Jesus that all these good villagers, their eyes glazed over and ears dulled by the complacencies of a self-satisfied religion, don't see and hear God at work right before them.

Misunderstanding and indifference are, like the poor, "always with us." They are not reliable indicators of the presence of the kingdom. Pollsters, who love to inform the world on the statistical status of God, have no prophetic credibility in kingdom matters. Jesus does not put out his messianic strategy for a referendum every couple of years.

And so the conditions that so often induce hand-wringing and gnashing of teeth among so many of us are relativized by Jesus' prayer of thanksgiving. Hidden kingdom energies surge just beneath the surface all around us. Huge subterranean rivers of prayer — faith and obedience and praise, intercession and forgiveness and deliverance, holiness and grace — flow freely underground. And in virtually every nook and cranny on earth, obscure in the shadows, overlooked in the crowds, are the "infants." These are the "babes and infants" that God has always used as a bulwark to "still the enemy and the avenger" (Ps. 8:2).

Jesus does not minimize the "conditions." He takes them very seriously indeed. He confronts and rebukes. He exposes pretension and weeps over hardened hearts. But he doesn't despair. He doesn't second-guess the Father. He doesn't dilute his holy resolve with something less than holy.

And so — thanksgiving. Not just for the wildflowers and butter-flies, for the moonlight on a blanket of snow, for athletic grace and symphonic sound. Thanksgiving is certainly appropriate for all that gives witness to goodness and truth and beauty, and so it doesn't surprise us when it is given under these favorable conditions. But Jesus' thanksgiving surprises us. Jesus' geyser of thanksgiving is honey in the rock (Deut. 32:13 and Ps. 81:16).

CHAPTER 16

Jesus Prays in Anticipation of the End:
John 12:27-28

At almost the exact center of the Jesus story as John tells it, there is a brief prayer of four words: "Father, glorify your name" (John 12:28). For the first eleven chapters John has immersed us in the action of Jesus, "the Word made flesh," Jesus alive. Jesus works his way through Galilee and Jerusalem, meeting men and women, named and unnamed, calling disciples, having conversations with individuals, healing the lame, raising the dead, feeding the hungry, giving sight to the blind, giving lengthy discourses on the kingdom of God that he is bringing into being. John anchors Jesus in real history, in actual towns, talking in the language of ordinary people, eating meals with them. John means us to take "made flesh" seriously. All of life, human life, is sacramental, a container for and revelation of the holy: the Word. Jesus is human, very human, thoroughly human, emphatically human: "made flesh."

One of the literary features of Jesus' language is his use of metaphor to reveal who he is, the famous "I am" sayings. Prominent among these metaphors are the seven *I am*'s of Jesus that John assembles:

"I am the bread of life." (6:35)

"I am the light of the world." (8:12)

"I am the gate for the sheep." (10:7)

"I am the good shepherd." (10:11 and 14)

"I am the resurrection and the life." (11:25)

"I am the true vine." (15:1)

"I am the way, and the truth, and the life." (14:6)

All these metaphors use words that are familiar in our common everyday usage to give the life of the Spirit in Jesus concrete immediacy. Metaphors are to be taken seriously and not reduced to a "meaning" or a "truth." They keep our feet on the ground, connected to what is all around us, praying out of our common humanity. Maxine Kumin, a most perceptive poet, writes, "Metaphor is not smaller than life. It mediates between awesome truths. It leaps up from instinctual feeling bearing forth the workable image. Thus in a sense the metaphor is truer than the actual fact."[1]

The concluding ten chapters in John's Gospel take us detail by detail into the story of Jesus' death. The last week of Jesus' life is the story of his death. It opens with Jesus at dinner hosted by his friends, Lazarus, Martha, and Mary, during which Mary anoints Jesus' feet with perfume, an anointing that Jesus interprets as "for the day of my burial" (John 12:7). The next day the Palm Sunday entrance into Jerusalem places Jesus in place of prominence at the Passover Festival. The crowd of hosanna-singing people thought they were participating in the coronation of their king. It did look exactly like what their prophet Zechariah had prophesied (Zech. 9:9).

This was not the first time that Jesus was identified as king. Nathanael, after a brief conversation on first meeting Jesus, exclaimed, "Rabbi, you are the Son of God! You are the King of Israel!" (John 1:49).

---

1. Maxine Kumin, *To Make a Prairie* (Ann Arbor: University of Michigan Press, 1979), p. 117.

Sometime later, Jesus fed five thousand with bread and fish. The people realized that they had just been served a miracle meal and decided to make Jesus king on the spot. But Jesus eluded their attempt by slipping away alone to a mountain (6:15).

And then at his Palm Sunday entrance Jesus is acclaimed "King of Israel" (John 12:13). "King" is pretty heady stuff. Jesus has to entirely reorient their expectations. The disciples have been listening to king talk and Messiah talk ever since they started following Jesus. Momentum is gathering. It looks like it is going to happen. And sooner rather than later.

He throws cold water on all this overheated king talk by talking about his death (John 12:23-36). He is their King, yes; he is their Messiah, truly. But not in the way they are thinking about it. In a very short time, they are going to hear him, a dying man, deliver his inaugural address as king from a cross.

Jesus has his work cut out for him. He gets his disciples off by themselves and has a long, leisurely conversation with them (John 13–17). He starts out by washing their feet. He follows it up by going over, again and again and again, the ways in which he is king and Messiah, and the ways in which they are going to experience and serve him as king and Messiah. Unhurried and patient, he completely revises their expectations. He is preparing them for his death. He then gathers the conversation all up in a closing prayer.

The next day he is crucified.

*　　*　　*

The prayers of Jesus can never be isolated from the life of Jesus. Prayer is not a subject on its own. Prayer is not a specialist activity. In a symphony orchestra some play the clarinet, some play the oboe, some play the violin, and some play the trombone. But in the Christian life it is not that way: we don't have some who visit the sick, some who sing the hymns, some who read Scripture, some who give money, and some who pray. In the Christian life we do not choose aspects, get some instruction and training, and then specialize in what we like or feel we are good at (or avoid because we have no aptitude for it).

Prayer is not something we pull out of the web of revelation and incarnation and then sign on to be "prayer warriors." It is more along the analogy of breathing: if we are to live, we all have to do it. Although there are illnesses connected with breathing, there are no excellences. We don't single out individuals and say, "She (or he) is a great breather."

Prayer is woven into the fabric of life. Prayer is woven into the fabric of Jesus' life. The notices of Jesus at prayer are part of everything else he does. None of his praying and none of his prayers can be taken out of context and studied on its own.

*   *   *

The link between the two parts of John's storytelling, Jesus' life and Jesus' death, is Jesus' prayer: "Father, glorify your name."

"Glory," both as noun and verb, is one of the large, horizon-filling words in Scripture. But a dictionary is of minimal help in getting a sense of the compacted energy radiating from its syllables. We need the entire story of Jesus as given to us by our four master Gospel storytellers. And then we need that story backed up and filled in with the entire story of creation and covenant in Torah and Prophets, in Psalms and Proverbs, in Epistles and Apocalypse. We can't comprehend glory in bits and pieces; we need the Story from Beginning to Ending, from Birth to Death and Beyond.

I acquired a feel for the many dimensions contained in glory from my pastor when I was about ten years old. He conveyed it in his voice, or maybe I should write, his *Voice*. He was Welsh. His voice from the pulpit reverberated in a full Welsh timbre and tonality through the sanctuary. When Pastor Jones spoke the word, it began low and rumbling, like the sixteen-foot pipes in an organ. It gathered volume and resonance until it filled the sanctuary, the sound filling not only our ears but our hearts. Most people articulate the word in two syllables, "glo-ry." In Pastor Jones it was multi-syllabled, "glo-o-o-o-o-o-o-ry," on an ascending scale of decibels and pitch.

I loved to hear the word and still do. Paul Jones, roaring the word into the lives of his congregation, made it truly Johannine. It was years before I learned the dictionary meaning of the word, more years yet before I learned the foundational place it held in the biblical languages, but I knew its meaning: it means that something magnificent is going on, is coming together, something that has to do with God and us in that congregation even as we listened to Pastor Jones say the word, something transforming, enlivening, and wonderful. It is a word that gathers to a greatness all the bits and pieces of our lives into the wholeness and completion of Jesus' life. A resurrection word.

It hardly mattered what the subject of the sermon was in our little church in our little Montana town, there was hardly a Sunday in which glory did not erupt. Whether it arrived in context or out, I never knew: hellfire sermons, hope of heaven sermons, sermons on repentance, sermons on love — glory. Glory was half exclamation, half witness. Whenever it occurred in a sentence there was an explosive burst of beauty and vitality.

*   *   *

But however wonderful and accurate my early learning of glory, it was quite without rootage in my life. And it is rootage I am after: rootage as I go to worship and to work, rootage as I read the newspapers and talk with my friends, rootage as I vote in elections and buy tires for my car, rootage as I get cancer and have surgery and convalesce, rootage as I accumulate birthdays and anniversaries, rootage as I write letters and read books.

The rootage I look for is described in lines just preceding the prayer, "Father, glorify your name." Here are the lines: "The hour has come for the Son of Man to be glorified. Very truly, I tell you, unless a grain of wheat falls into the earth and dies, it remains just a single grain; but if it dies, it bears much fruit" (John 12:23-24). I like the way Maxine Kumin said it: "I put down roots and I put up leaf."[2] That is what I am after.

Jesus anticipates his imminent death. As I take in his words, I real-

2. Kumin, *To Make a Prairie*, p. 7.

ize that roots of glory are in death and burial. This is going to take some re-learning. It looks as if glory involves more than what I heard in the thunder that came from Pastor Jones's pulpit. It looks as if I am going to have to let go of what I expected and enter a mystery.

But as with all gospel mysteries, it is not a total mystery. We are given hints and guesses. All gardeners know something of this. The flowers and vegetables that grow so wonderfully in their gardens are the consequence of seeds they planted in the ground.

Glory is what I am after. As it turns out, I am a slow learner. Glory is not just more of what I already have, or the perfection of what I already see. Do I suppose that the Christian life is my biological, intellectual, moral life raised a few degrees above the common stock? Do I think that prayer is a kind of mechanism, like a car jack, that I use to lever myself to a higher plane where I have better access to God?

The language of Jesus tells me something quite different: I become less. Instead of grasping what I value more tightly, I let it go. "Blessed are the poor in spirit" (Matt. 5:3) is one way Jesus said it. "Those who want to save their life will lose it: and those who lose their life for my sake will find it" (Matt. 16:25) is yet another way.

*   *   *

Gradually, going over these images and metaphors again and again, I begin to get it. I have a lot of unlearning to do. But I am not alone in this. I have friends with whom I am unlearning and relearning. And here is a wonderful thing that begins to come into focus: we don't have to wait until we die before we die. We don't have to wait until after our funerals to get in on the glory. As St. Teresa, one of our most irreverent and audacious saints, used to say, "The pay starts in this life."

*   *   *

It helps me to be patient in my slow learning to observe that it wasn't exactly a piece of cake for Jesus either. He introduces his brief prayer not in readiness but in resistance: "Now my soul is troubled. And what should I say — 'Father, save me from this hour'?" (John 12:27).

It wasn't easy for Jesus to redefine glory so that it included loss, rejection, and death. It gives me some breathing space in my prayers to know that it at least occurred to Jesus *not* to pray for this kind of glory but to pray for rescue from it. He considered praying, "Father, save me from this hour." But having got it out on the table, he doesn't pray it. He no sooner considered it than he rejected the possibility. To pray for rescue would be to reject his basic identity, his life as gift for others, his life sacrificed in love so that all could live saved. It would be a prayer that violates the very nature of prayer.

The prayer that Jesus did not pray is as important as the prayer he did pray. That Jesus, who "in every respect has been tempted as we are" (Heb. 4:15), did *not* pray, "Father, save me from this hour," makes it possible for me also *not* to pray it, to reject the me-first prayer, to reject the self-serving prayer, to refuse to use prayer as a way to avoid God.

First the No, and only then the Yes.

"Save me from this hour?" *No.*

"Father, glorify your name"? *Yes.*

*   *   *

Maybe it takes a lifetime to learn to pray this with a pure heart. But as we pray, and learn as we pray, it becomes increasingly clear that we must let Jesus daily redefine the word "glory" or we will miss it entirely.

The Greeks missed it. John tells us that there were some Greeks in Jerusalem the day that Jesus prayed this prayer. They wanted to see Jesus. They were tourists in the Holy City, there to see him. They had heard about Jesus, heard about the glory, and wanted to see it for themselves. Cameras at the ready, guidebooks in hand, they approached Andrew and Philip and tried to hire them as tour guides (John 12:20-22).

When Andrew and Philip told this to Jesus, he, in effect, dismissed them. Instead of posing for a photograph for the Greeks, he talked about his death. The glory that Jesus had been revealing in word and deed all his life is now to be displayed fully: "The hour has come for the

Son of Man to be glorified" (John 12:23). "Hour" means *time to die:* it's time for the Son of Man to die so that the Son of Man may be glorified.

Andrew and Philip have to go and tell the Greeks to go back home and take pictures of the Parthenon. Jesus will only disappoint them. The glory with which Jesus is glorified is not inspirational. It does not promote emulation. It is not conspicuous. It is not glamorous. It is not the sort of glory that is featured in glossy magazines and travel posters advertising sun and sand on the Greek islands. You can't take a picture of it.

*   *   *

We pray in the company of Jesus in order to learn this, to re-learn the meaning of words that have been corrupted by our culture and debased by our sin. Jesus is the dictionary in which we look up the meaning of words. We look up "glory" and what do we find? Obscurity, rejection, a sacrificial life, an obedient death. And through and in and around all of that, the bright presence of God backlights what the world despises and ignores — what *we* so often despise and ignore. Jesus' life and death come to focus in this prayer and illuminate life — all of life — so convincingly that we drop to our knees and say, "Glory — that is the kind of life I want. Father, glorify your name."

*   *   *

This is the only prayer of Jesus in which we hear the Father speak. The striking thing is that Jesus and the Father are on, as we say, "the same page." Jesus prays that the Father's name will be glorified; the Father answers Jesus: "I have glorified it, and I will glorify it again" (John 12:28). All three tenses are comprehended in the prayer. Glory in the past, glory in the present, glory in the future. The anticipation of glory ends up as participation in glory.

CHAPTER 17

Jesus Prays for Us: John 17

"I am praying for them. . . .

"I do not pray for these only, but also for those who believe in me through their word." (John 17:9, 20 RSV)

Jesus has only a few hours to live. He will soon be a corpse hanging from a cross. He has just had supper with his disciples in Jerusalem, his last supper with them, as it turns out. After supper, Jesus washes the feet of his disciples from a basin of water and wipes their feet with a towel. Peter protests. He thinks his Lord is demeaning himself.

A few days earlier Jesus and his disciples had supper in the village of Bethany, slightly less than two miles east of Jerusalem. This supper was at the home of the sisters Mary and Martha and their brother Lazarus. Martha served the meal. There was a foot washing. At this supper it was Mary who washed Jesus' feet, but with an expensive perfume — more like an anointing than a washing. And she used her hair, not a towel, to wipe his feet. Judas Iscariot protested this foot washing as Peter was to do a week later, but on different grounds. Judas raised claims of social justice — the money should have been used for the poor. Jesus defended Mary's extravagance (John 12:1-8).

Both foot washings prepare for coronations. The foot washing in Bethany prepares for the jubilant "Hosanna! Hosanna!" shouts of the

Passover crowd as they anticipate the coronation of Jesus, "King of Israel." The foot washing in Jerusalem prepares for the "Crucify him!
Crucify him!" demands of Jesus' priest-incited enemies, who hang Jesus on a cross placarded "King of the Jews." Both foot washings are met
by protests, the first by Judas because he understands all too well how
he can turn that perfume into ready cash, the second by Peter because
he completely misunderstands the way in which Jesus is Lord.

Jesus is near the end of his public ministry. The best and the worst
of his disciples still don't get it: for Judas, Jesus is a way to get something for himself; for Peter, Jesus is a way to get in on something that is
more than himself. They are both wrong. There is certainly a great deal
of "getting" involved in following Jesus. He gives and gives and gives.
We get and get and get. But it is not a kind of "getting" that either Judas
or Peter imagines it to be.

*   *   *

Jesus has his work cut out for him. Those closest to him continue to
misunderstand from the best of motives (Peter) and from the worst (Judas). Jesus doesn't panic. He doesn't raise his voice. He doesn't chastise
them for their obtuseness. He chooses to spend his last hours with
them in an extensive, rather meandering conversation that concludes
in a long prayer, the longest recorded prayer of Jesus that we have.

The Conversation

The conversation (John 13–16) is leisurely and repetitive. God cannot
be rushed into human hearts. A life of love and obedience can't be
rushed into human hearts. Even though his disciples don't yet know it,
Jesus knows that his life is in crisis and that the crisis is about to break.
But his tone is reassuring, intimate. Throughout the conversation the
disciples ask seven questions and interject one comment that betray
their incomprehension. This is not a conversation that models lucid
communication. But it is a model conversation for revealing the mind

of Christ and providing insights into the difficulties of "getting it" — getting the hang of the indirections inherent in revelation and the unforced intimacies of love.

Peter asks the first question. It is provoked by Jesus washing his disciples' feet with a basin of water and a towel. When Jesus comes to Peter, Peter protests with a rhetorical question: "Lord, are you going to wash my feet?" Of course Jesus is not going to wash his feet. Jesus is Lord; Peter is his disciple. The Lord washing the feet of a disciple turns things upside down. But is there also this? Is Peter as the leader, always named first in the listings of the disciples, already aware of his preeminence? And is the position already beginning to go to his head? If Jesus washes his feet, doesn't that undercut the deference and respect that is due to him from the other disciples? Jesus on his knees at Peter's feet dramatically reverses any pretensions by Jesus' followers, let alone Peter, to the privileges of leadership. Jesus dismisses Peter's question (John 13:3-20).

Jesus tells them that one of their number will betray him. They are bewildered. Betrayal? Impossible! Who could it be? The "beloved" disciple, presumably John, is seated next to Jesus. He asks the next question, "Lord, who is it?" Without naming him, Jesus gives a sign that it is Judas, but nobody catches the significance of the sign. In that setting of intimacy, betrayal isn't conceivable — Satan entering into one of their number while they are in the very presence of Jesus? Hardly (John 13:21-30).

Jesus then tells them that he will be with them "only a little longer." Peter asks, "Lord, where are you going?" But Jesus does not give a direct answer. He knows that Peter hasn't the wherewithal to understand. So he answers by indirection (John 13:31-38).

Now it is Thomas's turn. Jesus tells his friends that he is going to prepare a place for them in his "Father's house" and that they already know the way. Thomas thinks that Jesus must be talking of the way to some town or other, like Bethany or Jericho, and asks, "How can we know the way [if you don't name the town you are headed for]?" Jesus' answer, "I am the way . . . ," is cryptic. It is going to take them years to assimilate this one (John 14:1-7).

Philip is the fifth to speak. Not a question this time, but a request. He is confused by Jesus' use of the term "Father" and asks Jesus to "show us the Father." Jesus answers his implied question with another question: "How can you say, 'Show us the Father'?" Philip apparently, even after all this time, has no idea that Jesus is talking about God. But Jesus is patient. He goes over the old ground once more (John 14:8-14).

Jesus introduces the person of the Holy Spirit and what they can expect from him. Judas (not Iscariot — Judas Iscariot left the room before this conversation got well under way) asks for a clarification. This is now the sixth question. Things are getting tangled up. He asks, "Lord, how is it that you will reveal yourself to us, and not to the world?" Jesus' answer is another non-answer. At least it seems that way on first hearing. But the disciples are being prepared to listen in a deeper, more inward way to Jesus' words. He tells Judas, in effect, to relax, not to be overeager. There will be plenty of time for assimilation and comprehension. The Holy Spirit "will teach you everything, and remind you of all that I have said to you" (John 14:15-31).

When Jesus again says, "A little while, and you will no longer see me, and again a little while, and you will see me," some of his disciples (none are named this time) are again confused. "What does he mean by saying this 'a little while'? We do not know what he is talking about." This is the same question Peter had asked earlier without getting a satisfactory answer. Neither does Jesus answer the question this time, but he does reassure them that he is taking them, if not their questions, seriously: "On that day you will ask nothing of me." No more questions. But there is something besides questions that they will ask: "Very truly I tell you, if you ask anything of the Father in my name, he will give it you. Until now you have not asked for anything in my name. Ask and you will receive, that your joy may be complete" (John 16:16-24).

"Until now you have not asked for anything in my name." Really? That's all that they have been doing, asking questions. They want information and ask for it. They want facts, and ask for them. They want to pin things down and they ask for that. Jesus doesn't give them what they ask for; instead, he uses their questions to take them into uncharted territory, lead them on into a trust and relationship that they don't yet know how to ask for. They think they need to know who and when and where. Jesus is hinting and suggesting intimacy and Spirit.

He is quite up front in what he is doing and yet not doing; he is not being coy with them: "I still have many things to say to you, but you cannot bear them now." You are not ready now, but you will be. There is suffering and sorrow and disappointment ahead. Along the way you will develop eyes and ears to take in what you are blind and deaf to at present. You are obsessed with facts; you will acquire a taste for truth: "When the Spirit of truth comes, he will guide you into all the truth" (John 16:12-13).

The last words from the disciples in this conversation are a little embarrassing to those of us who hold these men in such high esteem. They think they know so much, and they understand so little: "Yes, now you are speaking plainly, not in any figure of speech! Now we know that you know all things, and do not need to have anyone question you." No more questions? Jesus tells them not to be so sure. They think they finally have it together, but they don't: "you will be scattered, every one to his home, and you will leave me alone." They have a long way to go, but they are on the way (John 16:25-30).

*   *   *

It is all right to ask questions. But question-and-answer sessions are perhaps not the best way to carry on a conversation in the style of Jesus. Questions can serve to clear the air. But it is futile to worry the questions, like a dog with a bone. We seldom know enough to ask the right questions. In the company of Jesus we learn not to insist on answers to our questions — we learn to let Jesus carry the conversation where he wills.

Jesus wills to carry the conversation into prayer. In one sense the conversation continues, but Jesus is no longer talking to his disciples. He is talking to his Father (and the disciples' Father); he is talking to God.

It is time to pray. The disciples are still in the room, but they are no longer asking questions and making comments; they are listening to Jesus speak with the Father. As Jesus' followers, we are most definitely included as listening participants.

The Prayer

We cross the threshold of John 17 and find ourselves in a room of quiet listening. It is the same room. Everything is the same, but nothing is the same. The basin and towel are on the table where Jesus left them. Judas is still absent. The eleven disciples who have been following and listening and talking to Jesus are the same eleven. Jesus is the same as he has always been with them, the one they have been following and listening to. And those of us who through the centuries have come to believe in Jesus through the witness of these eleven and are now reading this text are the same.

But Jesus is no longer talking to us. Jesus is talking to the Father. Jesus is praying. He prays a long time. This is holy ground. We find ourselves embraced in a holy listening. We are in a place of prayer, a praying presence. Our mouths are stopped. We are quiet: be still my soul.

We are not used to this. We are not used to being quiet. We talk a lot. We talk about Jesus and God. We talk to Jesus and God. We witness, we give counsel and advice, we preach and teach, we gossip and discuss, we sing and pray. But we are now in the room that is John Seventeen, in the prayerful presence of Jesus who is praying — praying, as we will soon find out, for us. Yes, *for us.*

Being prayed for is also an element in the life of prayer — a very large part, but often largely underappreciated. When it is Jesus who is praying for us, being prayed for may well be the largest part of prayer.

We remember where we are: we are in the John Seventeen Prayer Meeting. Jesus is praying. We have John's Gospel open before us. The eleven are quiet, but not passive. They are being prayed for. We also are quiet, but not passive. We are actively listening. We want to be in on what Jesus wills for us, just as we were organically tied into the conversation. We will to be prayerfully present to the praying Presence. We have nothing to say. Jesus, the Word made flesh, is speaking to the Father. He is including us in his prayer.

In the John Seventeen Prayer Meeting any lingering guilt we are carrying for having been unfaithful in prayer slips away. Any inadequacy that dogs us in prayer disappears. Wallflower bashfulness and fearful cringing evaporate. The world of prayer expands exponentially. We are no longer preoccupied with what we know or don't know, asking questions, looking for answers. We are just ourselves as ourselves, spaciously free in the expansive presence of Jesus, who is praying. We are in the presence of Jesus praying for us. We "let ourselves be gripped by this primary truth, namely, that the whole compact mass of created being and essence and the everyday world we are so familiar with sails like a ship over the fathomless depths of a wholly different element, the only one that is absolute and determining, the boundless love of the Father."[1]

*   *   *

Jesus prays. The text says, "After he had spoken these words, he looked up to heaven and said, 'Father, the hour has come; glorify your Son so that your Son may glorify you" (John 17:1).

The prayer of Jesus is in continuity with the immediately preceding conversation of Jesus. Jesus doesn't shift gears in either tone or content when he moves from conversation to prayer. He talks the same way to the Father as he does with his friends, the same way with his friends as he does with his Father.

The conversation began with the words, the "hour has come" (John 13:1). Jesus ends it with the same term, "the hour is coming, indeed it has come" (16:32). By now we know what this sentence means: "It's time to die."

Jesus' death, his "hour," sets the context for the conversation; it continues as the context for the prayer. But glory supplies the action. Death and glory do not seem to be natural bedfellows. But in Jesus they are.

1. Hans Urs von Balthasar, *Prayer* (London: Geoffrey Chapman, 1963), p. 36.

*   *   *

Readers of John's Gospel are already well acquainted with "glory" and "glorify." On the first page of John's Gospel he selected "glory" as the single word that would characterize the revelation of Jesus as Son of God and Messiah: "we have seen his glory, the glory as of a father's only son" (John 1:14). "Glory," whether as verb or noun, is used four-teen times as the story unfolds in the first half of the Gospel (chapters 1–11), concluding with Jesus' statement to Martha, just previous to the raising of Lazarus: "Did I not tell you that if you believed, you would see the glory of God?" (11:40).

Immediately following the triumphant Hosanna Parade, as Pass-over Week gets under way, the vocabulary of "glory" and "glorify" ac-celerates. The words will be used another nineteen times as the story of the next five days, Jesus' passion and death, is told.

Jesus used the anchoring verb "glorify" in his brief prayer in John 12 as he anticipated his crucifixion: "Glorify your name." This prayer, this *verb*, marks the beginning of the transition from the story of Jesus' life, his God-revealing, eternal (3:16) and abundant (10:10) life, told in chapters 1-11, to the story of Jesus' death, his willingly sacrificial, salvation-working death told in chapters 12–19.

As we read the story, John's pen steadily yet unobtrusively re-shapes our imaginations item by item through Jesus' prayer, so that we are able to recognize glory in a deepening, interior way. If we let this prayer of Jesus have its way with us, we will recognize glory in Jesus' death. As Jesus walks and talks on country roads and city streets, on Gal-ilean hillsides and in the Jerusalem temple courts, our imaginations gradually expand to take in new dimensions of glory, glory that is not re-stricted to the splendor of Solomon's temple and the Queen of Sheba's spice- and gold-laden camels. Glory is not only what dazzles the eye but what illuminates the believing heart. Glory expands inward. It compre-hends a revealed reality that works invisibly from beneath, infusing life from below, where seeds sprout and trees take root and springs rise si-lently from aquifers deep in the rocks. It reaches into the deep interior that volcanoes tap for the fire and lava that make mountains.

Jesus develops these inward dimensions of glory as he prays his John 17 prayer: "Glorify your Son so that your Son may glorify you." This is glory that does not look like glory, glory that to all appearances is unrecognizable as glory — not brightness but night, not celebrity but mockery. A few hours after Jesus prays this prayer, the prayer is answered: Jesus is dead and buried.

The noun "glory" (three times) and the verb "glorify" (seven times) dominate the prayer. The prayer brings these seemingly self-canceling opposites, glory and death, together, making them polar elements in the same event. In the act of dying, God glorifies Jesus. In the act of dying, the Son glorifies the Father. Jesus prays for glory. Glory takes place. Glory as death and death as glory is not an easy or comfortable truth to take in. But for those of us who follow Jesus, it is absolutely central for first understanding and then participating in the glory that is our salvation and the salvation of the world.

*   *   *

The juxtaposition of death and glory, glory and death, in the conversation and prayer is dramatic, but quietly dramatic. The realities are intertwined in ways that seem almost natural, as if they have always belonged together, which, in fact, they have — "from the foundation of the world" (John 17:24). There is no argumentative language here, nothing didactic. And certainly no pulling of emotional heartstrings. We discern truth in this language; we detect urgencies. But there is no manipulation. It is personal language, relational language, what Martin Buber has so excellently explored as I-Thou language.

This is important. There is nothing quite as destructive to the gospel of Jesus Christ as the use of language that dismisses the way Jesus talks and prays and takes up instead the rhetoric of smiling salesmanship or vicious invective. If, in the name of Jesus, truth is eviscerated into facts, salvation depersonalized into a strategy, or love abstracted into a slogan or principle, the gospel is blasphemed.

*   *   *

The language of the prayer, in continuity with the conversation, is permeated by the personal. Jesus addresses God as Father, a metaphor that insists on personal relation, six times, and by second-person pronouns ("you" and "yours") forty-three times. Jesus refers to himself by name once (Jesus Christ), by the personal metaphor Son once, and by first-person pronouns ("I," "me," "mine," "my") fifty-seven times. Prayer is personal language used between persons. Jesus is not "a truth" abstracted from the immediate and particular personal.

Supplementing these personal names and pronouns, there are forty-five references ("they," "these," "their," "them," "those") to the eleven disciples who are in the room with Jesus as he prays for them. Some of these pronouns reach out across the centuries to the yet-to-become-disciples that include us. Jesus gathers them and us into his prayer in this embracing act of intercession. We are being prayed for. By actively listening in the presence of the praying Jesus, we participate in the prayer.

The intimately personal use of language that is prayer is further emphasized by the use of the involving, participatory preposition "in" nineteen times. Prayer is not a distancing operation. Prayer is not a religious exercise that "puts things in perspective" or "puts people in their place." It is involving. Jesus involves himself in the work of the Father. Jesus involves himself in the life of his disciples. Jesus involves us in what God is involved in.

In the context, Jesus' suffering and death only hours away, the prayer and the suffering make up the stuff of intercession. "I wonder whether you realize a deep, great fact? That souls — all human souls — are deeply interconnected? That, I mean, we can not only pray for each other, but *suffer* for each other."[2]

Jesus' prayer is not about ideas or projects; it is personal involvement in all the operations of the Trinity. By virtue of Jesus' prayer we are involved in everything that the Father does and the Son says and the Spirit incarnates in us. The long conversation in which Jesus and

2. Baron Friedrich von Hügel, *Letters from Baron Friedrich to a Niece*, ed. and with an introduction by Gwendolen Greene (London: J. M. Dent & Sons, Ltd., 1958), p. 25.

his disciples have just been engaged is now gathered up in the intimacies of prayer, in which they find themselves participants in the relation of Father and Son and Holy Spirit.

*   *   *

Jesus prays many things for us. We can well imagine that these intercessions include virtually everything involved in making us and healing us, our salvation and our sanctification, our bodies and souls. In the John Seventeen prayer he prays for the Father to give us eternal life (vv. 2-3); he prays that we might have his "joy made complete" in us (v. 13); he prays for the Father to keep us safe, to protect us from the evil one (vv. 6-15); he prays that the Father will sanctify us in the truth (vv. 17-19).

There is one final named intercession: Jesus prays that we will be included, even as Jesus is himself included, in all the operations of the Trinity — that we will be full participants in all that God is and says and does, in all the ways that God is and says and does. When we consider all that this means in terms both comprehensive and intimate, this is nothing less than astonishing — participants in the godhead, insiders with God. But Jesus means it. He makes sure we understand that this is no offhand, casual, last-minute addendum, one more item to add to the prayer. This final intercession is deeply inclusive, all-embracing. He makes sure we pay full attention to it by repeating it six times:

> "Holy Father, protect them . . . that they may be one, even as we are one." (v. 11 RSV)

> "I ask . . . that they may all be one." (vv. 20-21)

> "As you, Father, are in me and I am in you, may they also be one in us." (v. 21)

> ". . . so that they may be one, as we are one." (v. 22)

> "I in them and you in me, that they may become completely one." (v. 23)

"... so that the love with which you have loved me may be in them, and I in them." (v. 26)

Personal and participatory language characterizes the entire prayer. But the sixfold repetition here — *that they may be one, as we are one* — puts this intercession in bold print. Don't miss this: Father, Son, and every last one of us by the prayer and the cross of Jesus and the work of the Holy Spirit are made one. Just as glory and death juxtaposed in the life of Jesus catalyze into resurrection, so here intimacy and inclusivity are integrated by the prayer of Jesus into the community of Jesus' followers soon to be formed by the Holy Spirit: the church.

*   *   *

The prominence that John gives to this prayer as he draws us into the final pages of the story of Jesus, and the likelihood that Jesus continues to pray it as he intercedes for us ("always lives to make intercession ..." — Heb. 7:25), requires that we deliberately take our places in the John Seventeen Prayer Meeting, entering into and submitting to the prayer that Jesus continues to pray for all of us who follow Jesus, that *we may be one* even as Jesus is one with the Father.

*   *   *

A major difficulty in taking this prayer to heart is that it doesn't seem to have made much difference for twenty centuries now, and certainly doesn't seem to be having much of an impact on Christians at present. The Christian church is famous worldwide for being contentious and mean-spirited, for using the words of Moses and Jesus as weapons to exclude and condemn. One of the identifying marks that Jesus gave his disciples is that "you have love for one another" (John 13:35). But not many centuries had passed before outsiders were saying, "Look how they vilify one another!" We kill with verbs and nouns, swords and guns, "Christians" marching under the banner of the cross of Christ.

Given the accumulation of carnage across the centuries — wrecked churches, wrecked families, wrecked souls — it is hard to stay in the John Seventeen Prayer Meeting with the eleven, quietly submitting ourselves to Jesus' prayer to the Father that "they may be one, even as we are one."

*   *   *

It is understandable that many survey this sorry track record and decide to leave the room where Jesus is praying and take matters into their own hands. Many Christians, impatient with what they perceive as the inefficiency of Jesus' prayer, attempt to solve the problem by the imposition of unity, unity by coercion — that is, authority depersonalized into an institution. The style is hierarchical. The methods are bureaucratic. Any person or congregation who refuses to conform is excluded: anathematized, excommunicated, or shunned. Unity is preserved by enforcing an institutional definition.

Other Christians, also impatient with Jesus' prayer, solve the problem by schism. They reduce the scale of unity to what can be managed by gathering men and women of like mind and temperament. Often there is a strong and charismatic leader who shows up to define the reduced parameters of the so-called unity. If persons or groups find that they no longer fit into the theological or worship or behavioral style that defines the unity, another schism is always an option — simply split off with others of like mind and spirit. Unity is preserved by personal preference.

The repetitive urgency with which Jesus prays that we be one, just as he is one with the Father, throws deliberate acts of schism into sharp relief as acts of insurrection, an eruption of violent willfulness in the very presence of the one who is interceding for our relational unity with one another according to the unity of the Trinity. The frequency of this violence done to the body of Christ, a violence justified by rationalizations without end, is nothing less than astonishing. Defying Jesus in the cause of Jesus. A huge scandal.

The saving fact is that the defiance doesn't prevent Jesus' prayers from doing their work — slowly, incrementally, marvelously. But that doesn't mean that the scandal of defying Jesus in the name of Jesus is any less of a scandal. The scandal is often boastfully vaunted as necessary to preserve the church. But whatever the language used, whatever slogans are placed on the banners, it is pretty clear that the schismatics at some point walked out of the John Seventeen Prayer Meeting.

I grew up being taught to hate Catholics. Later in life I acquired a condescending, snobbish distaste for schismatics. All the while I was doing violence to the people of God. It took me a while — it takes most of us a while — to submit to the prayer of Jesus and find myself being formed into the unity that Jesus is constantly bringing into being. I now find brothers and sisters in Christ, a lot of them, all across the spectrum of church and churches.

Wherever we happen to find ourselves along this spectrum, ranging from a comprehensive unity imposed from above to fragments of unity maintained by schism, it is important to know that there are many, many stalwart and mature and obedient followers of Jesus all along the spectrum, from the pope in the Vatican to a coterie of snake handlers in the Appalachian hills.

If we stay in the room with Jesus as he prays for us, we will acquire a readiness to embrace all the baptized as brothers and sisters. It may be slow in coming, but Jesus' prayer will have its way with us. We will no longer define other Christians as competitors or rivals. Jesus does not evaluate or grade his followers as he prays. He does not lay out plans to settle the controversies that he knows will arise. He is praying us into an easy camaraderie. The longer we stay in Jesus' praying presence the more we will understand that our impulses toward schism and sectarianism, our rivalries and denunciations, have no place in the room while Jesus is praying for us "to be one."

When Peter discovered a man of faith in the secularized city of Caesarea in the unlikely person of a Roman soldier, Cornelius, he said, "I perceive that God is no respecter of persons" (Acts 10:34 KJV). Is it permissible to add to Peter's sentence "or of churches"? I think so.

The Trinity

There is another, and far more satisfying, way to understand and assess Jesus' prayer than impatiently dismissing it as ineffective, the leading entry on the list we keep of "unanswered prayers," and then taking matters into our own hands. It is the way Christians have learned to understand the One and the Many, Unity married to Particularity, as Trinity.

The "one" that Jesus is praying us into is the One who is the Trinity. This "one" is truly one, but it is a one that gathers all particularities into a relational unity. Everything contributes to the being of everything else, enabling everything to be what it distinctively is. Every thing has to do with every other thing. Every person has to do with every other person. Nothing is forced. There is nothing mathematical about this. All are, whether they know it or not, involved, whether in submission or resistance, in all the operations of Father, Son, and Holy Spirit.

Holy Baptism is the sacrament that preaches the enactment of this Trinitarian foundation that is basic to all existence. We are baptized in the name of Father, Son, and Holy Spirit. We become our true selves by entering the waters of baptism, our particular identity affirmed and clarified in a personal name and in a personal relationship with all the ways, the modalities, in which God is God. We are not autonomous. We are not ourselves by ourselves.

Sin is an isolating act. It separates us relationally from God, from God's creation, and from God's community. Reestablishing the complexity of relationships into which we are created cannot be accomplished by fiat, by decree. A personal, relational intimacy cannot be achieved impersonally. We name forced sexual intimacies as rape, certainly one of the most violent degradations of a person. God does not engage in rape.

There is a conversation in a Charles Williams novel in which the characters discuss why God does not take care of holy things better, and why it is never appropriate to do for God what he does not seem to be doing for himself. These words are spoken: "God only gives, and He has only Himself to give, and He, even He, can give it only in those conditions which are Himself."[3] God cannot work in ways that are not in tune with himself. God is personal and free. And so whatever takes place in prayer is personal, freely given and freely received. Prayer is not a supernatural technique for coercion. Prayer does not lump sinners and saints into separated piles of anonymities, one pile assigned to damnation, one assigned to salvation. Prayer takes each particular person and thing, and everything that is particular about that person and thing, with absolute seriousness and simultaneously preserves absolute freedom. We cannot become one with one another or with God apart from freedom.

And that is why it takes so long for these men and women for whom Jesus is praying (namely, *us*) to become "one, even as we are one," why it cannot be forced or rushed. It is why no matter how many are shaped by Jesus' prayers into this Trinitarian unity, the Unity itself is always in process as new followers enter the shaping process in which there are no shortcuts. No assembly-line efficiencies permitted. Automobiles can be made that way, but not saints. The work of sanctification (another word for this becoming "one, even as we are one") is never a finished product that any single congregation can test drive and, if satisfied, sign up for. The Unity is not a model to be copied; it is a Trinitarian relationship — Father, Son, Holy Spirit — of reciprocity to be entered.

Trinity is comprehensive and intricate, fusing the One and the Many. To understand and participate in all the operations of the Trinitarian God requires a lifetime of sacrificial adoration (weaning ourselves from ourselves) and patient submission to the patient prayers of Jesus that all shall be one. The church, which provides visibility through the lives of particular men and women, in particular places, at particular times, is not an idea. Nor is it an ideal. It is a historical reality existing in time. It is constantly in formation. Like a piece of music, it takes time to become what it is. All the notes must be played by all the instruments assigned to play them before it is what it is. If we willfully refuse to be part of the orchestra, if we insist on everyone playing the

---

3. Charles Williams, *War in Heaven* (Grand Rapids: Eerdmans, 1974), p. 251 (original edition, 1930).

same note over and over, or if we find a single melody or chord of the music that we particularly like and play that, the results are not likely to be anything like what either the composer of the music or the conductor of the music will be satisfied with.

Being the church is intricately complex and demanding, but no more difficult in kind than anything else that is worthwhile being. The church is the large, healthy, Trinitarian gathering ground where we let God be God the way he wills to be God and let Jesus pray us into participation into the dynamic unity revealed between Father and Son and Spirit that is, precisely, glory. The church is the primary arena in which we learn that glory does not consist in what we do for God but in what God does for us. It is the pruning field where we submit ourselves to death and dying, Jesus dying on the cross and our daily dying. It necessarily involves refusing to take charge of the people around us and refusing to force them, whether by parental intimidation or military force or political manipulation, to do it our way. And it necessarily involves refusing to go off and dissipate life in a round of one-night stands with glamorous people or in adrenaline-fueled causes, satisfying our ambitions and indulging our whims "in the name of Jesus."

*   *   *

One of the oldest metaphysical questions has to do with the basic nature of reality, a question that Christians who spend any time in the John Seventeen Prayer Meeting deal with. Is life in the community of Jesus one or many, singularity or multiplicity? The Greeks pondered this extensively. Parmenides was the champion of "the one." Heraclitus championed "the many." Christians, much influenced by the conversation and prayer of Jesus, early on began to reformulate the discussion in terms of Trinity: "No sooner do I conceive the One than I am illumined by the splendour of the Three: no sooner do I distinguish them than I am carried back to the One" (Gregory of Nanzianzus).[4]

4. Quoted by Colin E. Gunton, The One, the Three and the Many (Cambridge: Cambridge University Press, 1993), p. 149.

*　　*　　*

It is worth noting, I think, that Jesus takes full responsibility for our unity, "that they may be one, even as we are one." He prays. It is significant that Jesus' intention that "they be one" is expressed in prayer to the Father and not in a command or exhortation to the disciples "to be one." Being a community of faith in Christ is a complex business. We have neither the knowledge nor the competence to pull it off.

As we submit to Jesus as he prays for our unity, we must also submit to the way he chooses to achieve it, the way of glory, glory that embraces suffering and death. This is the way, the only way, that allows us the freedom and dignity of participation. The unity for which Jesus prays is articulated exclusively in the language of personal relationship and willing participation. An imposed unity is no part of Jesus' prayer. A schismatic reduction is no part of Jesus' prayer. All of us today who are baptized and named Christian are being prayed by Jesus into maturity in the company of "the one, holy, catholic, and apostolic church."

*　　*　　*

Six pages on (in my English Bible) and about forty days on in the story as it is told (Luke having picked up where John left off), we find these same disciples, still in Jerusalem and still praying. Meanwhile, Jesus' crucifixion, resurrection, and ascension have been accomplished. But the praying disciples don't know what comes next. Jesus' mother and brothers have joined the eleven, still praying in continuity with the John Seventeen Prayer Meeting. The prayer meeting grows in size — 120 are counted at one point. They continue to pray as they take care of the matter of replacing Judas Iscariot. As they pray, they are given Matthias as a replacement to join them as a "witness . . . to the resurrection" (Acts 1:22).

They are still at prayer — it has now been fifty days since the Resurrection and ten since the Ascension. It is the Jewish Feast of Pentecost. And then it happens. The promised Holy Spirit is among them, as Jesus had reassured them earlier in his conversation. And Jesus' prayer for them "to be one" receives confirmation, visibly in the fire, audibly in the languages — one fire, sixteen languages. The unity is accomplished even as the particularity is preserved.

The Acts Two Prayer Meeting is the firstfruits of roots formed by the prayers of Jesus in the soil of the John Seventeen Prayer Meeting fifty days earlier. Those roots, intercessory roots, continue to send out shoots of Trinitarian wholeness, drawing people and nations into its embrace.

CHAPTER 18

Jesus Prays the Agony of Gethsemane: Matthew 26:39, 42

"My Father, if it is possible, let this cup pass from me; yet not what I want but what you want. . . .

"My Father, if this cannot pass unless I drink it, your will be done."

A few hours before Jesus is hanging on the cross in agony, he is in agony praying in Gethsemane. The two agonies are the same Agony. The agony is given a name: "this cup." A cup holds a liquid that is drunk. The peculiar property of the cup is that we hold it with our hands, put it to our lips, tip it into our mouths, and swallow the contents. It requires a coordinated, willing spirit, accepting and receiving. It requires taking the contents into our entire digestive system, distributing them throughout the muscles and bones, red blood cells and nerve ganglia. The cup is a container from which we take something that is not us into our lives so that it becomes us, enters into our living.

The cup that Jesus holds in his hand in Gethsemane that night is God's will — God's will to save the world in a final act of sacrificial love. The cup that Jesus drinks is a sacrificial death in which Jesus freely takes sin and evil into himself, absorbs it in his soul, and makes salvation out of it — drinks it down as if from a cup. Jesus' name is, translated into English, "Yahweh saves." As Jesus drinks the cup, he becomes his name.

This is, of course, sheer and unfathomable mystery. It is a mystery unexplained, but it is not an obscure mystery. It has many witnesses: poets and farmers, singers and parents who give witness that the willingness to die is an act of acceptance and an embrace of life.

*   *   *

Previous to his final week, Jesus spent most of his years in the small towns and on the country roads of Galilee. These years were get-acquainted time. There was leisure for conversation, opportunities to ask questions and listen to Jesus teach. People were able to observe Jesus as he moved into their neighborhood and healed the sick, broke through the taboos that kept lepers and Samaritans and Gentiles at a distance and women in their place. In a religious atmosphere that was stagnant with the bad breath of nitpicking moralism, Jesus was a fresh breeze. Under a Roman occupation that was brutal and oppressive, Jesus was undiminished and unintimidated.

He walked among the people with an unostentatious grace that let people know that there is another way to live, a way to live freely, fully alive. Word got around. People talked. Terms like "Son of God," "Son of Man," and "Messiah" were mentioned. People found themselves coming alive in Jesus' presence in unexpected ways. Many became convinced that God was doing something in Jesus that was unprecedented, and so they became followers. They committed themselves to the way of life that Jesus himself was living.

When this had gone on for roughly three years, something like a critical mass was achieved. Recognition came into focus. Peter was the first to articulate it: "You are the Messiah, the Son of the living God" (Matt. 16:16) — God personally present and at work among them, Eternal Life, Real Life, the Salvation of the World, Christ.

Then Jesus did an odd thing: he started talking about death, his own death and the death of all who followed him. He left Galilee for Jerusalem. There had been earlier pilgrimages to Jerusalem, but they had been, precisely, pilgrimages — they always returned home to Galilee. Now Jesus has started talking of Jerusalem as his destination and his death. For three years in Jesus' presence they had been immersed in life talk. The subject has now changed radically: death.

Will Jesus be able to keep his followers as he changes the subject from life to death? Will the four Gospel writers be able to keep our attention and command our loyalty as they change the subject from life to death?

*   *   *

We have a transcript of just six of the many prayers that Jesus offered throughout his lifetime to the Father. The first two are prayed in Galilee as he draws his followers into his abundant life. The remaining four are prayed in Jerusalem the last week of his life as he anticipates his salvation death. The prayer in Gethsemane is the third in this quartet of passion prayers.

All of our Gospel writers immerse us in the details of Jesus' final days, his rejection, suffering, and death. These final four prayers are a strong defense against the persistent satanic illusions that seduce us with promises that if only we follow Jesus' life we will be trouble free, pain free, boredom free, anxiety free. The four prayers make sure we have ample access to prayers that embrace with our entire being — our emotions, our understanding, our imagination — the realization that following Jesus means following him step by step through the valley of the shadow of death and the cross.

*   *   *

In Gethsemane Jesus knows that he will soon die a violent death. He also knows that he doesn't have to. He is free to accept or refuse this death. His death is not a necessity, not an impersonal doom. It is not the *anankē* invoked by the Greeks, not the *fate* of the Romans, not the *karma* that the Buddhists use to make sense of the cosmos. Jesus knows, and lets us know, that his death is a free act of obedience.

233

Jesus prays his way into and through this death. In the praying, death acquires an unguessed dimension: no longer a dead end but a harbinger of resurrection, no longer a terminus but a beginning: "The end is where we start from" (T. S. Eliot). As we pray Jesus' passion prayers, his "death prayers," we find that death also changes meaning for us.

The first of this quartet of passion prayers, "Father, glorify your name" (John 12:28), anticipates this death. The prayer "Father, the hour has come . . ." (John 17:1) prepares us for this death. The final prayer, prayed as Jesus dies on the cross, beginning with "My God, my God, why have you forsaken me?" (Matt. 27:46), prays the death itself. In this third prayer, "My Father, if it is possible, let this cup pass from me . . ." (Luke 22:42), he is entering the throes of death itself and includes us in his agony.

*   *   *

The Gethsemane prayer is bracketed by the Supper, at which the disciples sacramentally ate and drank Jesus' body and blood, and the cross, on which they would see that body broken and that blood poured out.

The setting is a garden named Gethsemane, meaning "Oil Press." It was at the base of the Mount of Olives, which had orchards of olive trees. The oil press was located there to harvest olive oil, a staple in Middle Eastern food culture. Jesus and his disciples "often met" (John 18:2) here. It was a little way off the beaten track, the road from Bethany at the top of the mountain, the home of Jesus' friends Mary, Martha, and Lazarus, down and through the Kidron Valley, and then into Jerusalem. The "often met" suggests that it was a place that Jesus and his disciples found convenient and congenial for prayer when they came on feast-day pilgrimages to Jerusalem. The prayers at the Oil Press fused what Jesus said at the Supper with what Jesus did on the cross.

The timing is Thursday evening of Holy Week. After Jesus and his disciples ate the Last Supper in Jerusalem, they sang a hymn and walked to Gethsemane to pray. Judas, who knew the place well, having prayed there often with Jesus, in an act of betrayal led soldiers there to find and arrest Jesus. Two criminal trials followed in succession, one beginning in the middle of the night at the house of Caiaphas, the high priest, the second, as morning dawned, before Pilate the Roman governor. The unholy alliance of religion and politics collaborated in finding Jesus guilty. He was sentenced to death. A few hours later he was a corpse, hanging from a cross.

The first of Jesus' prayers that we have in writing, the Lord's Prayer, the prayer that Jesus used to teach us the essential rudiments of prayer, has two sets of imperatives, three in each set. In the first set, we learn to pray ourselves into participation in the presence and work of God. In the second set we learn to pray for what we need from God so that we will be able to participate believingly and faithfully in this presence. In each set of three, we can discern a progression in intensity. The third petition in each set releases the accumulated energies gathered in the two preceding petitions and sends them on their way.

In his Gethsemane prayer, the final prayer before he is nailed to his death on the cross, Jesus selects the third petition from each set of three in the Lord's Prayer. The agony of Gethsemane completes and fills out what Jesus introduced to us back in those early days in Galilee as he was teaching us to pray. From the first set he selects the imperative addressed to the Father, "Your will be done." From the second set, he selects the word "temptation" and inserts it into an imperative addressed to us.

"Your will be done"

God's intention for Jesus, God's way of accomplishing salvation, God's way of delivering us from the Evil One. This is the concluding and summarizing petition of the first three incisive, God-orienting, reality-defining imperatives in the Lord's Prayer that lay a strong foundation for a life of believing obedience to keep us awake, alert, and present in the way of Jesus: *Hallowed be your name. . . . Your kingdom come. . . . Your will be done.* Each successive imperative gathers energy and increases in intensity, the way a spring is coiled tighter and tighter until it is released by a trigger. The triggering words are, *On earth as it is in heaven.*

With that, the three imperatives are fused into an obedience that leads Jesus willingly to the death that will change everything into resurrection.

"Watch and pray that you may not enter into temptation"

It is crisis time. The stakes have never been higher than in this Gethsemane prayer meeting. What Jesus is facing, we also are facing: "Watch and pray that you may not enter into temptation" (Matt. 26:41 RSV).

Jesus picks up "temptation" from the third petition in the second set of three in the Lord's Prayer: *Give us bread. . . . Forgive us our sins. . . . Lead us not into temptation, but deliver us from evil.* These are the imperatives in which we ask for what we need to do in order to be obedient participants in the hallowing of God's name, the coming of God's kingdom, and the doing of God's will. This petition for help in the time of trial, temptation, and deliverance from evil is also the third in a series of increasing intensity. Lifted from the Lord's Prayer and placed in the Gethsemane prayer, the petition articulates Jesus' concern that we be awake and present and obedient to this life of salvation, that we accept the trial and undergo the testing, that we say no to the temptation to defect and abandon the Jerusalem dimension of our calling, that we refuse to turn our backs on the cross and go back to the familiar and far less demanding world of Galilee and settle into a conventional religious life of teaching the truth about Jesus and doing good works in imitation of Jesus.

*   *   *

Jesus prayed this prayer in the company of his disciples. He wanted them to pray with and for him. They were in the garden together to pray together. But they didn't do it. He took the three, Peter, James, and John, apart with him and told them, "I am deeply grieved, even to death; remain here, and stay awake with me" (Matt. 26:38). Then he went on and prayed his agonizing Gethsemane prayer: "My Father, if it is possible, let this cup pass from me; yet not what I want but what you want." He came back to his disciples and found them asleep. He reprimanded them: "Could you not stay awake with me one hour? Stay awake and pray that you may not come into the time of trial; the spirit indeed is willing, but the flesh is weak" (Matt. 26:40-41). That scene is repeated two more times. Three times Jesus asks his disciples to pray with him. Three times they fall asleep on him.

And then the prayer meeting is over. Jesus is prepared for everything that is facing them through the night and morning. He is prepared for the two trials, prepared to die, prepared for the cross. The disciples are not prepared. Within the hour "all the disciples deserted him and fled" (Matt. 26:56).

*   *   *

Luke adds this detail to the Gethsemane scene: "In his anguish he prayed more earnestly, and his sweat became like great drops of blood falling down on the ground" (Luke 22:44). The agony of the cross would not have been possible without the agony of this prayer. Prayer accomplishes within us, within our spirits, deep within our souls, what is later lived out in the circumstances and conditions of our obedience. A stiff upper lip won't do it. A fierce resolve won't do it. An exemplary life won't do it.

Every thing and every person has an interior. Prayer goes beneath the surface and penetrates to the heart of the matter. Unlike mere action, prayer is not subject to immediate evaluation or verification. If we are addicted to "results" we will quickly lose interest in prayer. When we pray we willingly participate in what God is doing, without knowing precisely what God is doing, how God is doing it, or when we will know what is going on — if ever.

*   *   *

An essential element in what took place on the cross that next day, as the Nicene Creed has it, "for us . . . and for our salvation," was formed by the prayers Jesus prayed that night. Action without prayer thins out into something merely exterior. A prayerless life can result in effective action and accomplish magnificent things, but if there is no developed interiority, the action never enters into the depth and intricacy of relationships where the stuff of creation is formed, where salvation is worked, where men and women find themselves present and at home with the ways of God — Father, Son, and Holy Spirit — as his name is being hallowed, as he brings his kingdom into being, as his will is being done.

CHAPTER 19

Jesus Prays from the Cross:
The Seven Last Words

"Christ is in agony until the end of the world."

CHARLES PÉGUY

Death is the defining act ("reason") of Jesus' life: "it is for this *reason* that I have come to this hour" (John 12:27). The dying took three hours — from noon to three o'clock in the afternoon on a Friday just outside Jerusalem. As Jesus was dying he prayed. He prayed seven one-sentence prayers. None of the Gospel writers gives us all seven: Matthew and Mark give us one (Matt. 27:46; Mark 15:33); Luke gives another three (Luke 23:34, 43, 46); John writes down the final three (John 19:26-27, 28, 30).

The seven "words from the cross" have commonly been read or sung in various liturgies in what is intended as a chronological sequence. I have chosen to take them in the order in which they appear in our four canonical Gospels, not in a causal chain but simultaneously present to one another in a kind of mosaic or collage. Each prayer stands on its own, but none is in isolation from the others. The seven sentences develop, as they are prayed, an inward coherence. Instead of a sequential list, the seven become one in rhythm and harmony.

The praying community of the church has prayed these last

words of our dying Savior to practice the presence of Jesus. We sink our souls into this mystery, these "depths" (Ps. 130) in which our salvation is forged. We want our death to be congruent with his death — congruent with his sacrificial life, a willed offering of all that we are, and a witness to the resurrection.

*   *   *

Jesus' death is a real death. His death is historical fact. Nothing in Jesus' life is as meticulously documented as his dying and death: "dead and buried," as our Apostles' Creed has it, a death every bit as physical as each of ours will be. His heart stopped, his breathing stopped, his brain stopped. There was a precipitous drop in body temperature. Dead. But there was more, far more, to Jesus' death than the cessation of vital signs. Salvation was accomplished. A divine event was enacted in the death of Jesus. His death, a willed and sacrificial death, was an offering for the death-dealing sins of the world, a death that conquered death. It was the death of death.

This is a great mystery, the greatest mystery in the cosmos, in heaven and earth, and, strictly speaking, unfathomable. Not that some of our best minds haven't tried. Their thinking and praying are not without use. They turn up insights and glimpses into the profound and eternal workings of the Trinity that prevent us from being complete outsiders to this salvation mystery in which our lives are radically and comprehensively re-created — "ransomed, healed, restored, forgiven," as we so robustly sing. But when all is said and done, we realize that we will never get much beyond "the outskirts of his ways" in comprehending the inner workings of the cross and our salvation.

This mystery shapes the way Christians live and die, believe and love, forgive and are forgiven. It is a mystery that we inhabit, not just stand before and ask questions out of curiosity.

*   *   *

The death of Jesus on the cross can be understood and accounted for easily enough on a physical and historical level. But the salvation that

Jesus accomplished on the cross cannot be. And it is this accomplished salvation, not a coroner's autopsy of the death, that brings us back to the cross over and over again. Revisiting Jesus' death is different from visits we make to a cemetery bringing flowers, keeping the memory of our beloved dead in focus. We are not at the cross to remember or do homage. We are here to probe the meaning of our daily dying in the company of Jesus' dying for us.

St. Paul gives us the vocabulary for doing this, praying our own daily dying as participation in these eternal dimensions of Jesus' death. When Paul writes, "I have been crucified with Christ" (Gal. 2:19), he probes the salvation dimensions of Jesus' death as he experienced them. When he writes, "I die every day!" (1 Cor. 15:31), he is giving witness to the sacrificial offering of his life he makes every day of his life as he follows the way of Jesus to the cross. When he writes to his brother and sister Christians, "you have died, and your life is hidden with Christ in God" (Col. 3:3), he is drawing them into participation in the salvation workings of Jesus' death. When he writes from a prison cell, himself condemned to a Roman execution, that Jesus "became obedient to the point of death — even death on a cross," he urges his readers, "Let the same mind be in you that was in Christ Jesus" (Phil. 2:5-8).

*   *   *

Christians die twice. The first death is when we set out to follow Jesus, deny self, take up his cross, and choose to live obediently and believingly in his sacrificial company and not pridefully isolated in our own.

We pray in company with Jesus as he prays his death. As we do this, our death gets included in his death. It is a way of prayer that brings us into an embrace and acceptance of the death we die as we are baptized into Christ and become witnesses to a resurrection into which we, having died, are raised with Christ (Rom. 6:5-11).

Before Jesus prayed his death on the cross, he commanded us to die even as he himself would die: "If any want to become my followers, let them deny themselves and take up their cross and follow me" (Matt. 16:24). Which is to say, ". . . follow me to my death on the cross."

Death is a nonnegotiable element in being a human creature. It is also nonnegotiable in being a follower of Jesus. One of the ways to assimilate what that involves (not the only one, but too good to pass up) is to pray these seven single sentences in company with Jesus as he prayed them in his dying.

*   *   *

But *caveat orator:* Let the pray-er beware. Meditating and praying with Jesus as he dies on the cross is not an invitation to morbidity. There have been times in the community of Christ that Christians have attempted to experience and appropriate the suffering of Jesus on the cross by indulging in practices of mortification: extremes of fasting, deliberate sleep deprivation, wearing hair shirts, self-flagellation (the medieval "discipline"). There is a story I like very much of a monk who imposed on himself the discipline of not smiling — how could he even think of smiling when Jesus was suffering? A sacrilege! A fellow monk in exasperation told him, "Go ahead, make yourself miserable. But do it on your own time. Don't make everyone around you miserable, too."

As ascetically heroic as such practices may seem to be, there is something suspiciously like arrogance involved, a presumption that our self-imposed pain, deprivation, and suffering can add or contribute to what Jesus accomplished on the cross, who "died for sins once for all, the righteous for the unrighteous" (1 Pet. 3:18 RSV), making a "full, perfect, and sufficient sacrifice for the sins of the whole world."[1]

*   *   *

We begin all our prayers, and most emphatically these prayers from the cross, at the empty tomb, the place of resurrection. We start from

---

1. From the "Order for the Celebration of the Lord's Supper," *The Book of Common Worship* (Philadelphia: The Presbyterian Church in the United States of America, 1946), p. 162.

resurrection. Jesus' death (and ours) cannot be understood or participated in apart from resurrection. Cross and resurrection are the south and north poles, true gospel polarities, of a single, undivided, salvation world. Remove either pole and you gut salvation. We would not be praying these prayers from the cross of Jesus if there were no resurrection from the tomb of Jesus. This suffering and this death are the stuff of atonement. Cross is absorbed and transformed in resurrection. Resurrection comprises crucifixion — it is not an addendum to it. Morbidity (a neurotic obsession with suffering) and masochism (self-imposed suffering) have no place in the work of saving atonement. Our basic approach to the cross is gratitude.

The fact, whether historical or theological, is that we would not be praying this prayer from the cross if there were no resurrection. The agony of Jesus on the cross is the beginning of resurrection. Citing Matthew 27:51-52, Hans Urs von Balthasar is bold: "The splitting of the earth opens hell, and the upturned graves liberate their bodies to resurrection."[2]

The seven prayers of Jesus from the cross are metaphor, but no less real for being metaphor, that we can pray with him in our daily dying.

1. "Eli, Eli, lema sabachthani . . . My God, my God, why have you forsaken me?" (Matt. 27:46; Mark 15:34)

Death cuts us off from our moorings. It is the final dismissal. It is also the ultimate incomprehensibility. I no longer belong. I no longer fit. And I am not given an explanation. These metaphorical mini-deaths as we follow Jesus on our way to the cross anticipate and prepare us for what many Christians make a habit of praying for: "a good death." These mini-deaths (and some of them are not so "mini") — dead ends, rejections, bewilderments, snubs, abandonments, unanswered questions, wrong turns — each "death" in its turn is a shadow of death. We die ten thousand deaths before we are buried.

2. Hans Urs von Balthasar, *Prayer* (London: Geoffrey Chapman, 1963), p. 243.

Faith in God is not an escape from reality. Faith in God is a plunge into reality in all its dimensions, and not the least of these realities is death. There is much to be said of the comfort and strength that come from believing in and following Jesus as he reveals God to us: "Blessed be the Lord, who daily bears us up" (Ps. 68:19); "your rod and your staff — they comfort me" (Ps. 23:4); "Comfort, O comfort my people, says your God" (Isa. 40:1); "Blessed be the God and Father of our Lord Jesus Christ, the Father of mercies and the God of all consolation, who consoles us in all our affliction, so that we may be able to console those who are in any affliction with the consolation with which we ourselves are consoled by God" (2 Cor. 1:3-4); "Do not let your hearts be troubled, and do not let them be afraid" (John 14:27).

But there is also this: when we follow Jesus in the way of the cross (it's the only way available to us!) we also find ourselves in circumstances that we absolutely abhor, dealing with people with whom we experience revulsion, discovering things in ourselves that are shameful and embarrassing. We look for a detour, a shortcut. We want to change the subject. We want to find an alternate route to salvation, bypassing all interim death and dying. But even Dorothy on the yellow brick road didn't have an easy time of it, nor did her companions make things any easier.

Jesus' way of dealing with sin and evil and death ("the last enemy") — all that is wrong with and in the world — is to walk into the midst of it and work salvation right there. And he wants us with him as he does it.

It is not easy. Nobody (at least among our ancestors in the faith) said it would be easy. It wasn't easy for Jesus.

The first prayer from the cross reveals the very worst that comes to us in a life of belief in God: the experience of absolute abandonment by God. Death, not as completion, a satisfying arrival at heaven's gate, a "welcome home" greeting from God. No: death as nothing, nada, night.

Nobody is exempt. Even Jesus is not exempt. Especially Jesus.

*   *   *

One of the surprises that inevitably come to Christians who follow Jesus in the way of salvation is the vast number of people, both living and dead, who experience and cry out their despair at being abandoned, whether by God or spouse or child or friend, asking "Why?" We hear Jesus' cry of dereliction repeated, echoing down the corridors of the centuries, ricocheting off the walls of our churches and homes.

And however long or attentively we listen, we never get an answer to the "Why?"

Does it help to find ourselves in the company of Jesus as he prays his "Why?" I think it does.

Does it help to find Jesus in our company as we pray our "Why?" I think it does.

Does it help to realize that as Jesus prays his sense of God-abandonment he is praying a prayer that he learned as a child? It is the first line of Psalm 22. It is a psalm that expresses excruciating isolation, emotional devastation, physical pain. It is also a psalm that ends up in a congregation, "the great congregation" (v. 25) of men and women among whom he is able to give witness that God "did not hide his face from me, but heard when I cried to him" (v. 24). Does it help to know that this psalm ends differently than it begins? I think it does.

And does it help to observe that this is the first single-sentence prayer from the cross — but not the last? Jesus keeps praying. Fragments of prayer torn out of childhood innocence, broken shards of prayer from broken lives, have a way of coming together again in the company of Jesus. Jesus is not done praying. And neither are we.

2. *"Father, forgive them; for they know not what they do."* (Luke 23:34 RSV)

It is worth recollecting the identity of the "them" and the "they" — these people who are killing Jesus. We know some of their names: Caiaphas, the presiding high priest at the religious trial on a charge of blasphemy; Pontius Pilate, the Roman governor presiding over the political trial on a charge of sedition; Judas, who betrayed Jesus "into the hands of sinners" (Matt. 26:45); the eleven disciples, who at his arrest "deserted him and fled" (Matt. 26:56); Peter, who compounded their collective cowardice with his denial of Jesus in the high priest's court-yard; the young man who escaped being implicated in Jesus' arrest by leaving his clothes in the hands of the soldiers and running away like a scared rabbit, naked. And maybe also Barabbas, who was pardoned instead of Jesus? Although he may have been only an innocent by-stander. Others are nameless: the mocking soldiers who taunted the dying Jesus, exacerbating their mockery by offering sour wine to slake his thirst; the criminal on the neighboring cross deriding him.

Did they not know what they were doing? If arraigned in a court-room, any one of them, the named and the unnamed, would have needed a mighty clever lawyer to prove his innocence.

Jesus, on trial on trumped-up charges. The religious court and the secular court, collaborating in his condemnation and death sentence. Onlookers and friends alike, scattering like rats from a sinking ship. And what does Jesus do? He absolves them from guilt on the grounds that they don't know what they are doing. He prays to his Father for their forgiveness.

*   *   *

For those of us who choose to pray this prayer of Jesus, this is sobering indeed. Do we not have a duty to insist that justice is served? Are we not responsible for seeing that the laws of the land are preserved? Are we not compelled to make sure that immorality and crime are expunged from society and nation by whatever is required — by legislation, by force, by imprisonment, by war, by execution, by preaching?

And to bring the question home at a personal, everyday, neighbor-hood, and family level, when wronged do we just lie down and take it? Do we cultivate a doormat persona and passively let mean and bullying, rude and conniving people, whether they are parents or spouses, employers or neighbors, children or friends, take advantage of us, violate us, defraud us, and then respond with a mousy "Father, forgive them"?

These questions are usually rhetorical, intended to evoke the answer, "Of course not! I have my rights! Nobody is going to push *me* around." As such, the questions effectively remove forgiveness from our personal agendas, at least when our interests are involved. If they succeed in doing that, removing Jesus' forgiveness prayer, they are questions insinuated into our lives by the Devil.

Justice is a complex matter. The world of law and the courts, determining guilt and innocence, preventing criminal behavior and protecting the weak and the luckless, has always been a foundation pillar of every political and social system, including the Jewish and Christian. There is much, very much accumulated wisdom gathered from all over the world and from every century under the heading "justice." We could not function without it. Men and women who administer justice are essential to our safety and sanity. Biblical prophets and apostles speak some of the strongest and most compelling words on the subject.

All the same, justice is not the last word. In all matters of wrongdoing, in all matters of sin, in all that has to do with what is wrong with the world and with us, what is wrong with our enemies and our friends, forgiveness is the last word.

I have no interest in eliminating the tension between justice and forgiveness by taking justice off the table. Given the subtleties of sin and the persistence of evil, we would soon be living in moral anarchy and political chaos if there were no provision for justice. But I am interested in reintroducing the priority of this Jesus-prayed forgiveness into our lives. In matters of sin and injustice and evil, the last prayer of Jesus is not for justice but for forgiveness. The act of forgiveness does not eliminate concerns for justice, but it does introduce a personal dimension into those concerns that gives witness to the gospel.

Praying Jesus' forgiveness prayer trains our spirits in compassion, not revenge; in understanding, not irritation; in acceptance of a brother or sister sinner, not rejection of a neutered alien. It also makes room for the possibility that "they know not what they do." More specifically that they do not know that they are hurting or defiling an image of God, that they do not know that they are defrauding or maiming "one of the least of these who are members of my family" (Matt. 25:40).

We live in a world seething in sin and awash in violence. We daily read and see the news of it in the media. We also come up against it, even though unreported in the police logs, many times a day in our homes and workplaces and neighborhoods. What I am contending for as a consequence of praying Jesus' prayer from the cross is that forgiveness should become our first response to every person who demeans and hurts and takes our life. There certainly will be matters of justice for society to deal with along the way, and it may be important for us to participate in them. There are judges and prosecuting attorneys, police and juries, and there are many of us who pursue and uphold the cause of justice who are counted among them. But who else is there to say "Father, forgive them" but Christians who know how to pray that prayer with Jesus? However important justice is — and it *is* important — forgiveness is more important. The Christian at prayer, even as Jesus at prayer, is not first of all an impersonal agent of justice but a personal conveyer of forgiveness and a witness to the resurrection.

Such forgiveness is not soft sentimentality. It is hard-edged gospel. Such forgiveness is not a moral shrug of the shoulders. It is a white-hot flame of resurrection love forged in the furnace of the cross.

Assuming that the criminal crucified next to Jesus was receiving a just death sentence (he said as much himself), the sentence was not revoked in Jesus' prayer. The criminal died for his crime. But forgiveness trumped justice. It always does.

3. "Then he [one of the condemned criminals being crucified alongside Jesus] said, 'Jesus, remember me when you come into your kingdom.' He replied, 'Truly I tell you, today you will be with me in Paradise.'"
(Luke 23:42-43)

The next fragment from the prayer mosaic from the cross is an answer to the prayer of a criminal. It is Jesus' personal response to his next-door neighbor in crucifixion, a criminal who had just heard Jesus forgive all of those responsible for Jesus' condemnation and death sentence. The prayer of the criminal is, "Remember me . . ." Jesus' answer to his prayer is an immediate, unqualified, no-strings-attached, "Truly." And "Today."

*　　*　　*

Life after death is a perennial concern of the human race: "What's next? Is there more? And if there is more, what is it? — strolling Jerusalem's golden streets . . . the fire and brimstone of hell . . . penance in purgatory . . . a shadowy life serving the beck and call of mediums and 'channelers' . . . transmigration into a cow or a giraffe?"

But in the twenty-first century fewer people seem to be asking that question. In my own experience as an American pastor for over fifty years, it is one of the least asked questions I get. And the frequency of the question is diminishing. We live in an age — at least in the affluent West — when lavish consumer comforts and astonishing technological prowess steadily contribute to a sense of deferred death — among some, perhaps, even illusions of immortality. If we can put it off long enough, just maybe, who knows, it won't happen.

I have been an active believer and participant in the Christian faith all my conscious life, and, quite frankly, I am bored with most, if not quite all, of the "heaven and hell" talk I overhear. It seems to bring together infant fantasies and adolescent selfishness, projections of what we imagine would give us an eternity of self-indulgence for ourselves and a satisfying comeuppance for the vermin who have made life, as we imagine it was meant to be, unlivable.

Jesus' answer to his neighbor on Golgotha both focuses and simplifies "life after death" concerns.

Frederick Buechner, a novelist I like very much, writes in his memoirs of a conversation with his mother. She asks him if he really believes that "anything *happens* after you die." Because of her deafness, his answer is a shouted "YES!" In a letter in which he elaborates on his answer, the son testifies to his mother that his faith is based on "a hunch": "if the victims and the victimizers, the wise and the foolish, the good-hearted and the heartless, all end up alike in the grave and that is the end of it, then life would be like a black comedy." He goes on to tell his mother that life "feels like a mystery. It feels as though, at the innermost heart of it, there is 'Holiness.'"[3]

3. Frederick Buechner, *The Eyes of the Heart* (San Francisco: HarperSanFrancisco, 1999), pp. 14-16.

Set alongside Jesus' answered-prayer-fragment to the criminal on the cross, that seems to me just right. Jesus promises his companionship "today" in paradise, that is, heaven. And he leaves it at that. No speculation. No conjecture over what is involved other than Jesus himself. Isn't that enough? Clear, unequivocal affirmation ("Truly" — equivalent to a shouted YES!) and the blessed assurance, "with me."

I find it significant that it is a crucified criminal who is the first to recognize that Jesus on the cross is his savior and, with no moral or righteous qualifications, is saved. And at the very moment of his prayer, "remember me," his salvation is accomplished — "today."[4]

There is more to understand about life after death, but what more do we *need* to know besides this: that something *happens* after we die, and that Jesus will be there?[5] Eternity is not perpetual future but perpetual presence.

4. "Father, into your hands I commend my spirit." (Luke 23:46)

On a Friday just outside Jerusalem, Roman soldiers erected a cross on the crest of the hill Golgotha, "Skull Hill." Nobody had any idea at the time that it marked a major intersection between heaven and hell. But between the hours of twelve and three on a Friday it was the site of a cosmic crash, the effects of which have continued to reverberate for two thousand years throughout the world. When the wreckage was removed, it became clear that something completely unexpected and unintended had taken place, at least by the men and women who had a hand in it. It was nothing less than the harrowing of hell and the salvation of the world.

On that Golgotha intersection, signposted by that Roman cross, the hates and fears of all the years collided with the flesh and blood, the spirit and soul, of Jesus. Random, free-floating, unattached fragments

---

4. See the exegetical comments of Joel Green, *The Gospel of Luke*, New International Commentary on the New Testament (Grand Rapids: Eerdmans, 1997), p. 823.

5. I have tried to gather together the extensive witness of St. John on heaven in my book *Reversed Thunder* (San Francisco: HarperCollins, 1988), pp. 168-85.

of evil — the hysterical mob shouts of "Crucify! Crucify!," the odious hypocrisy of Caiaphas, the smug cynicism of Pilate, the brutality of the mocking soldiers, the calculating treachery of Judas — were pulled into the vortex of the hill's cross-shaped center, where Jesus, his body ravaged by nails and thorns and thirst, prayed.

One of the prayers, a single-sentence prayer like the others, was unlike the others he prayed from that cross. It was a prayer seemingly completely out of the context of that cross, a prayer of childlike simplicity: "Father, into your hands I commend my spirit." It was a prayer of unquestioning trust, the kind that we associate with the bedtime prayers that many of us prayed in our childhood:

Now I lay me down to sleep
I pray the Lord my soul to keep;
If I should die before I wake,
I pray the Lord my soul to take.

Uncalculating trust. A no-questions-asked readiness to leave everything in the hands of the Father. A prayer that comes out of a deep sense of well-being, security, safety, protection, with hands of blessing touching us and a reassuring voice of affection tucking us into a dreamless sleep in the company of holy angels.

But the circumstances in which Jesus prayed this child-prayer were anything but secure and safe. Jesus hanging naked on that cross was exposed to assault and ignominy, curses and mockery. Every detail that we imagine might go into praying "Father, into your hands I commend my spirit" is unimaginable in the bloody carnage that is Golgotha.

But if we are to pray this prayer in company with Jesus, we must imagine it. If we fail to do this we will dilute Jesus' prayer into a faithless prayer of resignation — a final giving up and giving in to what we can no longer do anything about, "throwing in the towel."

Jesus was not giving up; he was entering in — entering into the work of salvation in which everything he experienced was being put to the uses of salvation. And he was most certainly *not* praying in the physical and emotional embrace of a child being comforted into a relaxed sleep.

Paul wrote to the Corinthian Christians that he himself was "always carrying in the body [that is, *his* body] the death of Jesus, so that the life of Jesus may also be made visible in our bodies" (2 Cor. 4:10). One of the ways in which Christians do what Paul did is to pray Jesus' prayers from the cross in the context of the cross. This fourth in the mosaic of Jesus' prayers from the cross is particularly difficult to keep in its crucifixion context and still pray it. A childlike relaxation into the arms of Jesus when everything is going well and we are surrounded by those we love and trust, yes. But a deliberate, trusting committal into the hands of the Father when we have been blindsided on a Golgotha intersection and our life has been totaled? Lovely as Jesus' prayer is, it is not likely to come spontaneously from our lips in such circumstances.

In the first of Jesus' prayers, the Lord's Prayer, Jesus taught us to pray with him, "deliver us from evil." In this final mosaic prayer we find ourselves, as we daily die with Jesus, committing ourselves to the Father's care in the thick of evil. Both prayers are Jesus' prayers. If we want to stay in the company of Jesus, we can't pick and choose. We want to be fluent in the language of both prayers: "deliver us," and "I commend my spirit."

This is difficult, but not impossible. Many of our spiritual ancestors have long counseled us to cultivate a "child mind." They tell us that it is essential that we not let our emotional or physical circumstances dictate the language of our prayers. They tell us that Jesus in both his living and dying is the primary context in which we live. They tell us that the Holy Spirit is our teacher in prayer. They tell us to nurture a childlike simplicity that trusts God's providence and grace in what is actually present to us. Jesus said as much himself: "unless you change and become like children, you will never enter the kingdom of heaven" (Matt. 18:3), and "you have hidden these things from the wise and the intelligent and have revealed them to infants" (Matt. 11:25).

One of the wisest and most passionate among our praying ancestors is a French priest, Father Jean-Pierre de Caussade. His phrase "abandonment to divine providence" parallels Jesus' "into your hands I commend my spirit." He elaborates the lived implications of commitment/abandonment across the entire spectrum of human experience in his short and intense book *Abandonment to Divine Providence*. He writes of "the sacrament of the present moment." A key sentence in Caussade is: "If we have abandoned ourselves to God, there is only one rule for us: the duty of the present moment." His writing, backed up by a "crowd of witnesses," weans our imaginations away from God as we want him to be to wanting God just as he is, revealed in Jesus in the here and now, praying, "Father, into your hands I commend my spirit."[6]

This is not a prayer we hold in reserve for our deathbed, a prayer of reluctant relinquishment as we give up the ghost. We pray it when we get out of bed each morning, alive yet another day, ready to go to work painting a house, teaching a class of kindergartners, surgically removing a cancerous breast, writing a check for college tuition, planting a field of barley: "Father, into your hands I commend my spirit."

5. *"Woman, here is your son. . . . Here is your mother." (John 19:26-27)*

Jesus prays from the cross. Each time he opens his mouth, he reveals another detail of what is involved in accomplishing the grand and holy work of salvation that shatters the gates of hell and opens the gates of heaven: the cry of dereliction that is the epitaph of the death of God; the Savior's no-strings-attached absolution of those who are killing him; the promise of heaven to a criminal; Jesus' offering of himself as a sacrifice to accomplish the way of salvation for the world that God loves. And with more to come.

The prayers that come together on that cross define our lives.

---

6. One statement that is particularly apt in the context of praying from the cross: "In this state of self-abandonment, in this path of simple faith, everything that happens to our soul and body, all that occurs in all the affairs of life, has the aspect of death. This should not surprise us. What do we expect? It is natural to this condition." Jean-Pierre de Caussade, *Abandonment to Divine Providence*, trans. John Beevers (New York: Image Books/Doubleday, 1975), p. 95.

They provide a definitive witness to the way that God brings good out of evil, enacting the impenetrable mystery that reverses "lost" into "found." They introduce the word "gospel" into our language in such a comprehensive way that no one is consigned to live or die without hope.

In almost every way, it is too much to take in. It is not unlike the experience many of us have had at the scene of an automobile accident at night where there is a death and serious suffering. The darkness is broken by the beams of headlights, the scream of sirens, sobs and cries of pain, paramedics pulling bodies from the wreckage, all against a confused backdrop of a milling, anonymous crowd. It is surreal. The crisis disorients. The sudden reality of death and suffering forces us to deal with what we keep at the edge of our lives, from which routines of meals and work, schedules and sleep insulate us. It all seems unreal. A dream — or a nightmare.

This is not unlike what we are faced with at the cross of Jesus, only in a more acute degree. The actions we perceive and the words we hear during the three hours are so heavy with meaning that we are overwhelmed. We are not used to living in crisis. There is too much to take in. Poets and novelists, theologians and musicians ponder and probe and pray this death endlessly and find layer after layer of meaning. The event of death, which philosophy and Scripture tell us is definitive in giving meaning to life, is experienced as something less than real. Small details — household details and domestic habits — feel more substantial.

*　　*　　*

Four soldiers are gambling at the foot of Jesus' cross. They have just finished doing their assigned work of crucifixion. Now they are throwing dice to see who gets Jesus' clothes. Jesus looks past them and sees four sorrowing women — his mother, his aunt, Mary the wife of Clopas, and Mary Magdalene — while John, "the disciple Jesus loved," stands nearby. The soldiers are preoccupied with getting something for nothing, oblivious to the eternal life hanging above them. The women are present out of sheer love, quietly reverent, giving dignity to this desolating death.

But now we hear a very different word from the cross, a word that puts our feet back on the firm and familiar ground of the ordinary: "Here is your son. . . . Here is your mother."

The words are a relief in a way. Jesus returns us to our familiar surroundings: domesticity and family relations. If Jesus' prayer from the cross can be heard, so to speak, on home ground, the danger that we will stand year after year before the cross as spectators is considerably diminished.

With these words, Jesus made his mother and his disciple mutually participants in all that is involved in his death: abandonment, forgiveness, the hope of heaven, atonement, sacrifice, pain, salvation. And, it goes without saying, resurrection. These are no longer primarily items for discussion or Bible study. They are no longer privileged material for making great art and music. All Jesus' words and actions, from this moment, enter the arena of everyday domesticity to be worked out and practiced precisely there: "Mother, here is your son. John, here is your mother. . . . From now on, as you speak and serve, respect and love one another, for you are doing it to me."

If we miss these words, "here is your son . . . here is your mother . . . ," we risk walking away from the cross with nothing more substantial than a powerful emotion that can be renewed under the right conditions, or a sacred truth that we can carry as a talisman. But if we listen, really listen, we will hear something like, "Take a good look at the one standing next to you. Get to know her, get to know him, as I, Jesus, know and am known by them, as a mother knows her son, as a son knows his mother."

W. H. Auden in his poem "Nones," a prayed meditation on Jesus dying on the cross, wrote,

> . . . its meaning
> Waits for our lives.[7]

---

7. W. H. Auden, *The Shield of Achilles* (New York: Random House, 1955), p. 75.

6. "I thirst." (John 19:28 RSV)

This one-word prayer (in Greek, *dipsō*) is unique in the mosaic of prayer fragments from the cross. It is the only prayer in which Jesus expresses physical agony. Think of it: seven prayers prayed across those three hours on the cross and only one of them out of physical pain. There is more to death than what happens to the body. There is the sense of abandonment, there is forgiveness, there is the hope of heaven, there is responsibility for the people who are left behind, there is a sense of summing up (the final prayer fragment). And there is pain: the body shutting down, lungs failing, heart failing, kidneys failing. In Jesus' death this leave-taking of his body was experienced as excruciating thirst: "I thirst."

It is not likely, given the wide range of the particular details that the four Gospel writers give us, that believers and followers of Jesus will fail to realize the wounds and suffering, the alienation and the pain concentrated in Jesus' body through those three hours of his dying. By and large Christians do not distance themselves from it. We keep in touch with Jesus' pain-racked body suspended from that cross. We meditate and fast, we pray and sing hymns, we go on pilgrimages and hold crucifixes.

We can hardly avoid facing and dealing with the plain, incontrovertible fact that Jesus had a body and that he totally inhabited that body until the last vestige of life was drained from it. "I thirst" is the sacred witness that there was no "spring of water gushing up to eternal life" (John 4:14) left in him.

In spite of this hard-edged, indisputable historical data — Jesus in his dying prayer for water, literal not metaphorical water — there are an astonishing number of people who somehow manage to think of and treat Jesus apart from his body: Jesus as a spiritual presence, Jesus as a theological dogma, Jesus as a moral example, Jesus as a "higher power," Jesus as a poetic truth.[8]

8. This is a mistake about Jesus (or, more insidiously, a false teaching) that has bedeviled the community of Jesus from the beginning and shows no sign of slacking off: namely, that Jesus' body was not "really" Jesus, but just a form he used and then

Clearly, Jesus, as he prayed from the cross, did not fail to include his physical condition, his pain expressed in his thirst. What I am interested in right now is that the reality of our bodies in our daily dying must also be included in our prayers — and not just as an afterthought. Nothing in Jesus' body was excluded from his act of atoning sacrifice on the cross. And nothing in our bodies, including the pain, is excluded. Paul put it well: "Take your everyday, ordinary life — your sleeping, eating, going-to-work, and walking-around life — and place it before God as an offering" (Rom. 12:1 *The Message*).

One other aspect of Jesus' "I thirst" prayer in the completed mosaic needs mentioning. If some people delete, or at least minimize, Jesus' dying pain from the prayer in a pious attempt to make him more "spiritual" than he really is, there are others who isolate the physical pain from the other six elements of his prayer from the cross and feature it to the exclusion of all else. Jesus' physical suffering and dying take over and dominate. Relationships (with God, the criminal, the mother of Jesus, the disciple of Jesus), the definitive act of forgiveness, the hope of heaven, the final verdict are pushed off into the shadows as the spotlight focuses on every detail of the crucified body.

The effect of isolating the pain of Jesus from all the relationships, present and eternal, that are present in the prayer mosaic of Jesus has the effect of dehumanizing and depersonalizing Jesus' pain. It becomes a thing, an object to be pitied or admired, or a truth to be preached and taught. It is a form of spiritual pornography. Sexual pornography is sex without relationship, the intimacy of sexuality reduced and debased into an object to be looked at or used. Spiritual pornography is prayer and faith without relationship, intimacy with Jesus reduced and debased into an idea or cause to be argued and used.[9]

Our Gospel writers don't do this. And neither does Paul as he de-

---

slipped out of while on the cross. This denial or avoidance of the reality of Jesus' body and his death keeps cropping up century after century and goes under the name of "gnosticism." The gnostic lie is epidemic in our postmodern world.

9. The Mel Gibson movie, "The Passion of the Christ," was a conspicuous instance of this on the American scene in 2004.

velops our praying and obedient participation in the dying and death of Jesus. All the parts of Jesus' prayer from the cross are embedded in the grand story that includes all the operations of the Trinity.

7. "It is finished." (John 19:30)

The Genesis story of the first week of creation concludes with this: God, having spoken creation into existence, rests from his creation work and blesses the day. The verb "finish" is used twice: ". . . the heavens and the earth were *finished*. . . . God *finished* the work that he had done, and he rested . . ." (Gen. 2:1-2). A good creation, complete — nothing left to do.

In deliberate parallel to the opening pages of Genesis, John in his Gospel presents Jesus as speaking salvation into existence. As he tells the story of the last week of Jesus' life, the completion of the work of salvation, he concludes with the double use of the Genesis verb "finish": ". . . when Jesus knew that all was now *finished* . . . when Jesus had received the wine, he said, 'It is *finished*'" (John 19:28, 30). A good salvation, complete — nothing left to do.

This is a good note to end on. It is the note on which Jesus ended his prayer from the cross. It is not unlike the emphatic "Amen" affirmation that we commonly use to conclude our prayers. Without something like this, prayer peters out, like a departing guest who can't seem to get out the door but shuffles his way through an endless eddy of postscripts, addendums, and footnotes.

This seventh and final piece in the prayer that Jesus prayed from the cross is an unqualified, definitive "It is finished." (Like the sixth prayer fragment that precedes it, it also is a single word in Greek, *tetelestai*). "It is finished" is a summing-up prayer. But the Greek verb does not mean finish in the sense of "this is the end" or "that's all there is," as we might say of a race that is over or a book that we have finished reading. It conveys a sense of completion, an accomplished wholeness.

The same verb is used in Jesus' prayer in John 17:4 when he prayed to the Father, "I glorified you on earth by *finishing* the work that you gave me to do." It does not mean that Jesus' life has simply come to an end but that everything Jesus came to do is now complete, no loose ends, nothing left hanging. We get a sense of the comprehensive fulfillment that Paul conveyed to the congregation in Rome: "We know that all things work together for good for those who love God" (Rom. 8:28). And is there an echo of Jesus' "It is finished" in the "It is done!" in Revelation 16:17, spoken from the throne of God and the Lamb when the final bowl of God's wrath was poured out by the seventh angel? God's decree, accomplished "on earth as it is in heaven."

*   *   *

In the extended reflection in the letter to the Hebrews on the "once for all" (Heb. 9:26) completion of the work of salvation, salvation's many dimensions now catalyzed in the death of Jesus, we read that "when Christ had offered for all time a single sacrifice for sins, 'he *sat down* . . .'" (Heb. 10:12).

As we read between the lines in Hebrews, we get the sense that there were Christians around who honored the centrality of the crucified Jesus in their lives but weren't content to leave it at that. Jesus sat down. But not them. They had important things to do. They became a congregation of religious busybodies. What Jesus did was central, of course, but they kept finding things that would round out salvation in a more satisfactory way — angels, for instance, and Moses, and more and more priests to help Jesus out. Any number of religious "add-ons" they took it upon themselves to supply.

It happens a lot still. We "get religion." Soon we become impatiently self-important and decide to improve matters with our two-cents worth. We add on; we supplement; we embellish. But instead of improving on the purity and simplicity of Jesus, we dilute the purity, clutter the simplicity. We become fussily religious, or anxiously religious. We get in the way.

No Christian congregation is free of "Jesus-and-" Christians. In the Hebrews text it is Jesus-and-angels, Jesus-and-Moses, Jesus-and-priesthood. Through the centuries these Jesus hyphenations have proliferated into Jesus-and-politics, Jesus-and-education, Jesus-and-business, or even Jesus-and-Buddha. Not that politics and education and business and Buddha do not require attention. But they are not the action that Jesus prayed into our lives on the cross.

"It is finished" deletes the hyphens. The focus of prayer becomes clear and sharp again: God's completed salvation action in Jesus. We are set free for the act of obedient faith, the one human action in which we don't get *in* the way but are *on* the way.

Raymond Brown, always magisterial in his study of Jesus on the cross, offers an intriguing insight that deepens the sense of completion but at the same time gathers our prayers to a substantial finish. He observes that as Jesus concluded his prayer "he bowed his head and gave up his spirit" (John 19:30). Brown suggests that it is at least plausible that Jesus handed over the (Holy) Spirit to those at the foot of the cross, in particular to his mother and the beloved disciple.[10] What could be more appropriate? In this way these men and women could not only see and hear the completion of Jesus' salvation work but also find themselves included and participant in it. Just as we continue to do to this day.

10. ". . . while going to the Father, Jesus gives his spirit to those who are standing near the cross. In Jn. 7:37-39 Jesus promised that when he was glorified, those who believed in him were to receive the Spirit. What more fitting than that those believers who did not go away when Jesus was arrested but assembled near the cross, should be the first to receive it?" Raymond E. Brown, *The Death of the Messiah*, vol. 2 (New York: Doubleday, 1993), p. 1082.

CHAPTER 20

Praying in Jesus' Name:
Acorns into Oak Trees

When I was young and vulnerable to every "wind of doctrine" that gusted through our Montana valley and rattled the windows in our small congregation, one itinerant preacher with a reputation of being a "prayer warrior," an acknowledged expert in all the ways of prayer, captured my adolescent attention. One of his dogmatisms was that all prayers had to conclude with the phrase "in Jesus' name," or "in the name of Jesus." "In Jesus' name" was a kind of imprimatur that validated whatever preceded it, regardless of its content. Without the correct address, who knows where the prayer might end up? The phrase was a defense against the Devil or one of his angels beating Jesus to the punch and using my prayer for evil and the damnation of my soul. The preacher rescued me from the eddying ambiguities of adolescence and gave me a clearly defined, black-and-white framework into which I could fit all my prayers. He warned that one can't be too careful in these matters. And I was careful.

It took me a few months to recognize the silliness of his dogmatically formulated ignorance. But silly as it was, it ended up doing me good — it activated my imagination to think about the import and consequences of praying "in Jesus' name." Eventually it sent me to the "in the name" occurrences in St. John's Gospel and the entire conversational context with his disciples in which Jesus spoke to them on his last night with them. Five times he used the phrase: "I will do whatever you ask *in my name* . . ." (John 14:13); "if *in my name* you ask me for anything, I will do it" (14:14); ". . . the Father will give you whatever you ask him *in my name*" (15:16); ". . . if you ask anything of the Father *in my name,* he will give it to you" (16:23); "Until now you have not asked for anything *in my name*" (16:26). Was Jesus giving us a magical "Open sesame" that would get us anything we wanted? Hardly. He was inviting us into his entire life, a life of intimate personal relationship in which his words "became flesh" — not in general, but in a local and present and particular way in all the various circumstances that make up everyday living.

It didn't take me long, with some help from my parents and friends, to understand that "in the name of Jesus" was not a verbal formula, like a magic spell, that had the power of making something happen simply by getting the words right and in the right order. "Name" is an entrance into the entire world that is inhabited by and realized in a named person, in a named place. A name is not an impersonal password, interchangeable with a Social Security Number, but a personal recollective, gathering relationships and ancestors, work and words, geography and soul — all the insides and outsides of a person's life fused in a name, the way it is in the often sung hymn:

> At the name of Jesus every knee shall bow,
> every tongue confess Him King of Glory now;
> 'Tis the Father's pleasure we should call Him Lord,
> who from the beginning was the mighty Word.[1]

After a year or so I had escaped the snare of certitude that I welcomed so avidly at first ("the snare is broken, and we have escaped" — Ps. 124:7) and entered, via the name of Jesus, into the wide and comprehensive company of Jesus: Jesus the Word made flesh, Jesus telling stories rich in associations with the generations of stories descended from his Moses and Elijah and Daniel ancestors, Jesus praying in con-

---

1. Words by Caroline Maria Noel (1870), *The Hymnbook* (Philadelphia: United Presbyterian Church USA, 1955), p. 143.

tinuity with David's variously pain-soaked and exuberant Psalms and his mother's magnificent Magnificat.

*   *   *

The first two pages of our Scriptures immerse us in bravura demonstration of language at work — God using language to create everything that is. But no sooner have we read the story of the glorious Word-formed cosmos than we turn the page and come upon language being used to corrupt what has just been created.

It takes us by surprise. Things are going along so well. God creates: everything he makes is good, good, good, good, good, good — and then a resounding seventh *very good*. God plants a garden with delicious trees and gives it to the man and woman as their home. There is good work to do. There are marvelous animals to enjoy. A great river flows out of the garden and waters the whole earth. The man and woman are the crowning touch. A world of beauty and intimacy and innocence, made out of words.

And then something goes wrong, disastrously wrong. How could anything go wrong when everything is going so *right*? But it does. The disaster is triggered in a conversation between the Snake and a not-yet-named woman. An exchange of words, many of the same words that were just used in the glorious making of the world and everything in it. Sin and evil arrive on the wings of words, and the creation is desecrated. Not out-of-control emotions, not insubordinate genitals, not bullying arrogance, not shooting guns and bombs bursting in air, but words. Sacred words defiled and the word-created holy creation desolated. The general mess in which we now find ourselves originates in a misuse of language. The man and woman use fig leaves to cover up their loss of innocence and intimacy with makeshift aprons.

Two sentences frame the conversation that tells the story. First, "the man and his wife were both naked, and were not ashamed" (Gen. 2:25). Then, seven verses later, "the eyes of both were opened, and they knew that they were naked; and they sewed fig leaves together and made themselves aprons" (3:7 RSV).

The man and woman started out so well. They were designed by God himself and alive with the very breath of God. They were in a good place with good work to do — poets working with words, gardeners working with soil and plants — all their needs met, open and intimate with one another, open and intimate with God. They woke each morning to a world of beauty and abundance in which they had dignity and purpose and use.

"Naked and not ashamed": completely at ease, completely at home, nothing to hide, nothing to fear, open to one another, open to the animals and weather and earth, open to God. And then, after a brief conversation with the Snake, we find them desperately sewing fig leaves together to cover up what can't be covered up. The fig leaves signpost a language catastrophe. Words are no longer a means of intimacy, of revelation. They're fig-leaf words. The man and woman who speak them are no longer open to one another, free in the garden, lost in wonder, delighted in what had been given to them. No longer open to God. When asked about it, the man says, "I was afraid, because I was naked; and I hid myself" (Gen. 3:10). Fig-leaf language deals with God but in a way that subtly avoids God ("the serpent was more subtle than any other wild beast . . ." — Gen. 3:1 RSV). Fig leaves cover what is there to be revealed. The fig-leaf words seem so harmless — they get their start, after all, in a sacred place: the Holy Garden of Eden. They continue to flourish in sanctuaries and chapels all over the world. The devastation is widespread.

Given the glory and ubiquity of language in everything that has to do with life, life in its most inclusive sense — the life of God, the life of man and woman, the life of animals and trees and oceans — it is more than dismaying to find that language so easily and frequently is used to adulterate, defile, and cheapen life, and the God of life.

*　　*　　*

Language is sacred. All words are holy. But when they are torn out of the story that God speaks into being and then used apart from God, language is desecrated: words become non-personal, words become non-relational. It isn't long before the holy creation is desecrated. The words used by the Snake and the woman retain their dictionary meaning. But without the syntax of the God story they are fig leaves, without connection, without voiced relationship with the Lord of language, with the Word made flesh, with the Spirit who gives us "utterance" as we tell "in our own tongues the mighty works of God" (Acts 2:11 RSV).

*   *   *

The six prayers that we pray with Jesus after the manner that he prayed them, these "set prayers," give us a feel for the world in which Jesus prayed, the expansive world of intimacy and trust created by colloquy with Jesus as he prays with and for us. Praying these six prayers also provides us with an apprenticeship in the life of prayer, prevents self-absorption, with our attention more on ourselves (am I doing this right?), and mitigates self-consciousness (what are people going to think of me?). They give us an inconspicuous but secure place in company with the cloud of witnesses who pray and with Jesus as he prays.

There is a prevailing bias among many American Christians against rote prayers, repeated prayers, "book" prayers — even when they are lifted directly from the "Jesus book." This is a mistake. Spontaneities offer one kind of pleasure and taste of sanctity, repetitions another, equally pleasurable and holy. We don't have to choose between them. We *must not* choose between them. They are the polarities of prayer. The repetitions of our Lord's prayers (and David's) give us firm groundings for the spontaneities, the flights, the explorations, the meditations, the sighs, and the groans that go into the "prayer without ceasing" (1 Thess. 5:17 KJV) toward which Paul urges us.

*   *   *

It is the nature of prayer to offer a way of assent to the Word of God that is incarnate in Jesus, the Word of God written in our Holy Scriptures, the Word of God made present to us by the Holy Spirit. It is a way of language that is congruent with the language in which we listen to, receive, and respond to the Word.

We learn the language of prayer by immersing ourselves in the language that God uses to reveal himself to us, the Jesus-language world. We pray in the context of Jesus at prayer. Our prayers are no longer shaped by our culture. We are well warned against religious Snake language. Our prayers are rescued from being conditioned by our psyche. We acquire a prayer language adequate for listening and speaking in the large world of the Trinity, revealed in Jesus by the Father through the Holy Spirit. Prayer is personal speech, Father and Son speech, God and daughter speech. It is language put to the uses of relationship. It is conversation. God listens to us; we listen to God. God speaks to us; we speak to God. It would be too much to say that it is a conversation between equals, but at least both parties are speaking the same language, a language of revelation, a deeply relational language, not an informational language, not a manipulative language.

Father: prayer is not an alien act, not outsider stuff. We are praying within the family. We are praying out of our natural affinity with God.

Son: we are not praying in the dark, groping and guessing. The Son reveals the Father. We don't know everything but we know something. We know God as Savior, Giver, Lover, Listener.

Holy Spirit: we are not praying "on our own." Prayer is not gathering up our spiritual energies to make a statement or launch a cause. Even though prayer involves our words, our meditations, our actions, there is far more to our prayer than *us*. Mostly it is the Holy Spirit making God known and initiating *in us* responses of praise, petition, and obedience: "the Spirit helps us in our weakness; for we do not know how to pray as we ought, but that very Spirit intercedes with sighs too deep for words" (Rom. 8:26).

*   *   *

Prayer renounces language that manipulates God (the way of magic). Prayer rejects language that reduces God to my control (the way of idols). Prayer is vigilant against language that depersonalizes God into an idea or a force or a feeling (the way of pious introspection). Prayer is wary of the influence of spiritual technologists with professed expertise for using prayer to "make something happen," a technology for coercing God or other people to insure that *our* will be done. Prayer is alert to tendencies within ourselves that privatize prayer and insulate us from the company of the communion of saints. And prayer is certainly not a spiritual cover for taking a vacation from the world and its problems and responsibilities.

Prayer is a way of language practiced in the presence of God in which we become more than ourselves while remaining ourselves. In the practice of prayer God honors our freedom, God gives us dignity. Balthasar speaks of our lives as "a sustained utterance of prayer. . . . Man only needs to know, in some degree, what he really is, to break spontaneously into prayer."[2]

For the most part we do not become fluent in the language of prayer on our own, or by reading a book, or by signing up for a course. We become fluent in prayer by keeping company with Jesus. We learn to pray "in Jesus' name."

*   *   *

I want to eliminate the bilingualism that we either grow up with or acquire along the way of growing up: one language for talking about God and the things of God, salvation, and Jesus, singing hymns and going to church; another language we become proficient in as we attend school, get jobs, play ball, go to dances, and buy potatoes and blue jeans. One language for religion and another for everything else, each with its own vocabulary and tone of voice. I want to break down the walls of partition that separate matters of God and prayer from matters of getting food on the table and making a living.

I am interested in recovering the common speech of the Bible, language not split into distinct dialects, one for work and domestic af-

---

2. Hans Urs von Balthasar, *Prayer* (London: Geoffrey Chapman, 1963), p. 36 (first published in German in 1957).

fairs, another for what we think of in stereotypes as "spiritual" — one dialect for the street, another for church.

I want to knock down the fences that keep prayer confined to religious settings and religious subjects. I want to enlarge the field of prayer — exponentially if I am able — to take in the entire creation and the whole of history, our entire lives gathered in intention before God, leaving nothing and no one out. I want my prayers, and the prayers of my friends, to ricochet off the rock faces of mountains, reverberate down the corridors of shopping malls, sound ocean deeps, water arid deserts, find a foothold in fetid swamps, encounter poets as they search for the accurate word, mingle their fragrance with wildflowers in alpine meadows, sing with the loons on Canadian lakes. I will continue, of course, to pray in sanctuaries and prayer closets and at deathbeds. But I want far more. I want to participate in prayers that don't sound like prayers. Prayers that in the praying aren't identified as prayers. Prayers without ceasing.

I don't mean to say that all our words and silences are, in themselves, prayer, only that they can be.

Jesus, equally at home in heaven and on earth, equally at home in his "Father's house" and in Joseph and Mary's house, used the same language — personal, metaphorical, particular, relational, local — wherever he happened to be, whether in the synagogue or out on the street, and with whomever he was talking to, whether a Samaritan or God. He didn't debase the holy into the secular; he infused the secular with the holy. As we keep company with Jesus in matters of language, language itself becomes sacramental. We do not cultivate an insider language for discourse on things and ideas predefined as "spiritual." We do not permit the unbelieving world to suck the transcendence out of words and reduce them to chaff. We let Jesus shape our speech and prayers, speaking and praying the common language of the tribe, alert to each word imbued with revelation, each sentence redolent with grace. We practice a listening and a praying that is on the lookout for Jesus speaking and praying, unwilling to miss even a whisper or syllable of the Word made flesh.

When Moses was instructed by God to build a structure for worship, the wilderness tabernacle, the center was designated the "most holy" place, or the "Holy of Holies," the place where the focused action between God and humans took place. It was protected from both curious spiritual voyeurism and pagan sacrilege, whether inadvertent or deliberate, by a finely wrought curtain or veil. No one was permitted into the Holy of Holies except the High Priest, and then only once a year. The holy and the profane were strictly separated.

God's holy presence was guarded from desecration by either prayerless curiosity or blasphemous idolatry. God must not be used.

The tabernacle, a portable shrine in the wilderness, and the temple in Jerusalem that later replaced it trained God's people for nearly two thousand years in reverence before The Holy in tabernacle and temple, a holy reverence that became "fear of the Lord" in life outside the holy place. A people of God are always in need of thoroughgoing training in holiness. We, sinners all, have a deep-seated habit of wanting to use God for our purposes, to reduce God to an object we can control. We cannot. The veil protecting the Holy of Holies tells us we cannot.

The centuries of worship training in the inviolability of God's holiness are deeply ingrained in our understanding of that heavily veiled Holy at the center of the place of worship. The veil protected it from prying eyes and busybody hands. And so the shock is nothing less than seismic to be told that the first thing that happened when Jesus died on the cross was that "the curtain of the temple was torn in two, from top to bottom" (Matt. 27:51; Mark 15:38; Luke 23:45).

What happened? The Holy Place is now Every Place. The Holy One of God is contemporary With Us. His time is our time. There is no more separation between there and here, then and now, sacred and secular. The letter to the Hebrews makes a big thing of this, helping us to see the death of Jesus on the cross opening up "a new and living way" by which we can live an integrated life (see especially Hebrews 9–10).

Paul also uses this imagery, but in a slightly different way, when he speaks of the death of Jesus as having "broken down the dividing wall" between Jew (the religious insiders) and Gentile (the religious outsiders), bringing us together as one people (Eph. 2:14).

There and here fused, then and now fused, sacred and secular fused, us and them fused. The veil ripped in two. The walls broken down. The partitions smashed.

And language? Yes, language. All language is available for giving witness to the holy, to name the holy, wherever and whenever, just as Jesus used and uses language. The prayers of Jesus are foundational to and continuing within our prayers.

*   *   *

Ludwig Wittgenstein, one of our most accurate philosophers of language, tells how he came across the sentence, "A whole world is contained in these words." It struck him as not quite right. He made this comment: *"These words?* How *can* it be contained in them? — It is bound up with them. The words are like an acorn from which an *oak tree* can grow."[3]

When I read his words, they seemed apt for what is involved when we pray "in Jesus' name." Jesus' prayers do not contain all prayer. They are acorns from which a praying life grows in us, becoming deep-rooted, heaven-reaching oak trees.

3. Ludwig Wittgenstein, *Culture and Value,* trans. Peter Winch (Chicago: University of Chicago Press, 1980), p. 52; my emphasis.

Some Writers Who Honor
the Sacred Inherent in Language

It is no small thing that the Christian community has men and women
who pay close and continuous attention to the way it uses words. The
sacrilege of language is epidemic in our culture. We live in a language
wasteland. The care of words is urgent Christian work. Our assignment is clear: keep them personal, preserve their place in the cre-
ation/salvation story, maintain congruence between our conversations and our prayers. The major way we do this is by keeping
company with Jesus in his stories and in his prayers. I also find it useful
to keep up conversations with men and women who do this well.
Some of them write books. When they write well I read their books.
Here are seven writers that I like very much.

N. T. Wright, *The New Testament and the People of God; Jesus and the Victory of God; The Resurrection of the Son of God*
Better than anyone else I know in my generation, Tom Wright, with
immense patience, has given painstaking attention to the words of Jesus, the actions of Jesus, the world-encompassing story at which Jesus
is the center. Wright is a historian. He takes place seriously. He takes
time seriously. He takes words seriously. And he writes seriously, accurately, and well.

For a hundred and fifty years many well-intentioned men and

women (and some not so well-intentioned) have been busy disentangling Jesus from his roots in history and giving us his words, his ideas, his example on a platter free from the limitations of history, cut loose from the everyday. We are then free to insert them wherever we find ourselves and however we fancy. But left to ourselves that way, we tend to drift off into pious, or not so pious, wool gathering. Wright won't have it. He gives us the texture and taste of Jesus lived on real ground in actual time, Jesus who became our salvation on real ground and in actual time. The three volumes that I recommend are immense, but immensely readable. Plan to spend a year reading each one of them. They are that good. (Minneapolis: Fortress Press, 1992, 1996, 2003)

Eugen Rosenstock-Huessy, *Speech and Reality*
Language originates in a living voice. In its purest form it is spoken and heard, not written and read. Mouth and ears, not pen and ink, are the prerequisites of language. After many years of schooling and living in a culture that assumes literacy, we tend to think of books and newspapers and libraries as having a monopoly on language, especially on language taken seriously. Rosenstock-Huessy recovers for us what is so easily obscured: language is basically *speech voiced* not *words written.* Language is inherently revelational and relational, a spoken exchange of lived reality between named persons, not an impersonal transfer of ideas or facts that can more conveniently and accurately be made with a book. The implications that proliferate from the "speech thinking" of this German who immigrated to America, this Jew who converted to Christianity, are enormous. (Norwich, Vt.: Argo Books, 1970)

William Stafford, *Stories That Could Be True: New and Collected Poems*
Stafford is a poet who uses words with uncommon reverence. He is a pacifist, a Christian who spent the four years of World War II in camps for conscientious objectors in Arkansas and California. The way he used words eventually made me a pacifist. But my conversion started not with his views on violence and war but with the way he used words in the making of poems. Like this: ". . . let the presence be like smoke . . . not hold on to what cannot be held onto." His poems give me a feel for

the inherent sacred core of words and a sense that I had better trust them — not use them to make others do anything, but to reveal what is there before us, the word-created life that we all have in common. (New York: Harper & Row, 1977).

Francis de Sales and Jane de Chantal, *Letters of Spiritual Direction*

In writing and reading letters, we are usually immersed in a language that is personal and revelatory: the words and sentences are used to address a named person with a street or post office address, and the subject matter is immediate and particular. Letters can be impersonal, but mostly they are not. Letters can be cluttered with abstractions, but mostly they are not. When the letters are between persons who care deeply about God and the soul, people who are honest and trust one another, the chances are high that we will find ourselves party to a conversation that gives dignity to language, a conversation that is congruent with the Lord of language. In the Counter-Reformation years in France, Francis de Sales, a bishop, and Jane de Chantal, a widow who became the superior of a women's community, wrote just such letters. (New York: Paulist Press, 1988)

Flannery O'Connor, *The Habit of Being*

Here are letters by a writer in Georgia who wrote parable-like short stories and novels that gained a reputation for shocking spiritually complacent imaginations into recognizing the presence and ways of God in their own alleys and backyards. These letters, collected and published after her early death in 1964, provide us with sharply articulated insights regarding why she wrote the way she did, her convictions on the nature of language and its specifically Christian rootage and orientation. She is one of the American masters at using "slant" language to penetrate blasé defenses with God's truth. (New York: Farrar, Straus & Giroux, 1979)

Walker Percy, *The Message in the Bottle: How Queer Man Is, How Queer Language Is, and What One Has to Do with the Other*

Percy started out as a physician, but he quit that and spent the best part of his working life writing six novels. Written over a period of twenty-six years across the last half of the last century, the novels diagnose the desperate spiritual poverty of life in America. He also erected some modest signposts along the way for anyone who might be interested in what Christians say about it. He is America's Kierkegaard, using the language of parable and indirection to penetrate cultural stereotypes with Truth.

This book is a collection of essays on the language that he uses in the novels: the ways language works and the ways it doesn't work; the way language involves us in living truth and the way language seduces us to live lies. We learn that there is a lot more to language than meets the eye. As we grapple with his grappling with language, we understand why he decided to leave the healing of bodies to the physicians and give himself to healing souls with his pen. He made a good choice. (New York: The Noonday Press, Farrar, Straus & Giroux, 1995)

Reynolds Price, A *Palpable God*

Reynolds Price is a writer who studied his craft of writing novels by immersing himself in the language of the Bible. He became convinced that the human need to tell and hear stories is second in necessity only to nourishment, even before love and shelter. "The sound of story is the dominant sound of our lives" (p. 3). He anchors this basic need of our lives in the forms that the biblical stories take as they come to us. Through repeated rereadings of his reflections (and his novels), I have acquired a strong sense of both the uniqueness and the inevitability of story. I have come to realize that all attempts to reduce story to explanation or definition or summary dilute the language in which God reveals himself to us and the language by which we can reveal ourselves to God and to one another. "Trust the story," Price seems to say. "Let the story have its way with you." Especially the story that Jesus tells. (San Francisco: North Point Press, 1985)

Index of Names and Subjects

Index of Scripture References